This is the remarkable account of a lone female cyclist's hazardous and often hair-raising 5000 mile journey from Karachi to Kathmandu. Although Bettina Selby, mother of three grown-up children, enjoyed much kindness and hospitality during her five month journey, the reaction of some local men to an unaccompanied Western woman on their roads was intensely curious, at times brusque, sometimes escalating to dangerous violence. Surmounting many difficult encounters with courage and great resourcefulness, she also had to face the heavy physical stresses of keeping going in broiling heat on dust-blown and treacherous roads shared with ancient buses, speeding trucks driven by maniacs, farm carts, herds of quadrupeds and hordes of usually unsympathetic local cyclists. In the mountains, the ride became even more dangerous – avalanches, floods, dacoits, amorous Moslems, bad curry and stone-throwing children.

Bettina Selby presents an unusual view of India and Pakistan and records some vivid, memorable scenes among many different people met on the road.

Riding the Mountains Down

Riding the Mountains Down

A Journey by Bicycle to Kathmandu

Bettina Selby

London
UNWIN PAPERBACKS
Boston   Sydney

First published in Great Britain by Victor Gollancz Ltd 1984
First published by Unwin Paperbacks 1985
This book is copyright under the Berne Convention. No reproduction
without permission. All rights reserved.

UNWIN® PAPERBACKS
40 Museum Street, London WC1A 1LU, UK

Unwin Paperbacks
Park Lane, Hemel Hempstead, Herts HP2 4TE, UK

George Allen & Unwin Australia Pty Ltd.,
8 Napier Street, North Sydney, NSW 2060, Australia

Unwin Paperbacks with the Port Nicholson Press
PO Box 11–838 Wellington, New Zealand

ISBN 0-04-910082-3

Printed and bound in Great Britain by
Hazell Watson & Viney Limited,
Aylesbury, Bucks

For Peter

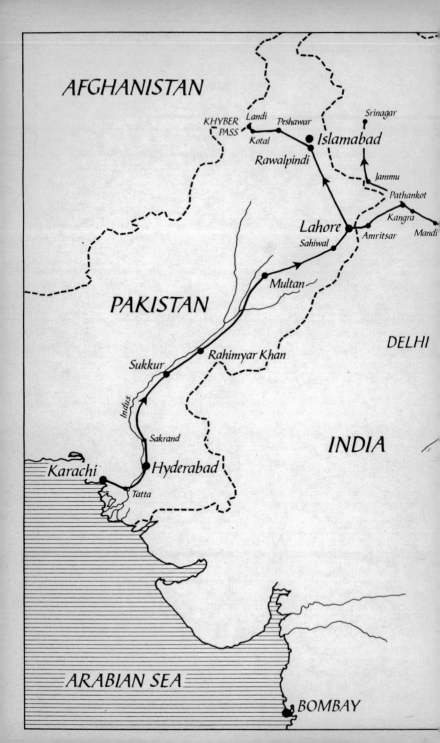

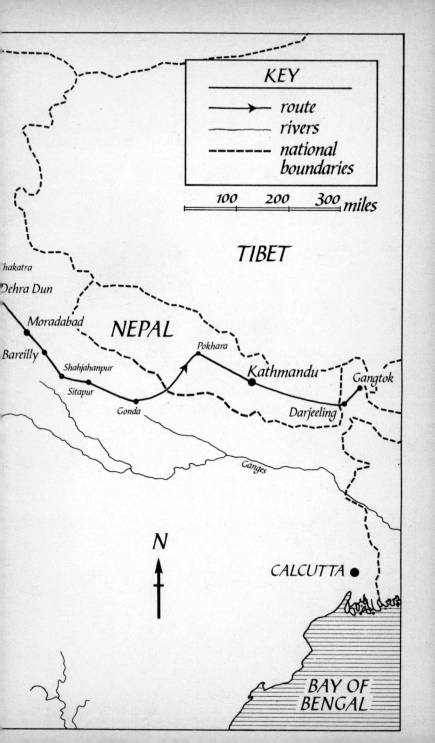

Contents

Illustrations

Pakistani girl spinning
Bus halt, North-West frontier
Kulu Valley woman
Spirit-burning ceremony, Tamang village

MAPS

'If the bandits don't get you the lorries will.'

'They have a particularly nasty line in leaping snakes, too,' confided one imaginative friend.

'The dust storms in the desert can kill you even in a car,' said another.

'And as for Moslem men!' said an anonymous caller. 'Well.'

No one though had thought to warn me about the arrivals hall at Karachi Airport, and this I thought at four o'clock on a hot February morning, with all my belongings lost or stolen, had the other horrors beaten hands down.

The hall was a large, low, grimy place, almost totally deserted, my fellow passengers having long since departed with their luggage. The empty baggage conveyor trundled around depressingly. A few bored-looking officials sat at high desks inspecting their nails or staring gloomily into space. Some baggage-handlers clad in dirty white pyjamas were curled up among the debris on the floor—obviously, no more business was expected that night. I had already approached the uniformed officials for help in finding my missing baggage, but either they didn't speak English, or they were deaf, or perhaps I was invisible to them, for not by the flicker of an eyelid did these men acknowledge my presence. It was all very unnerving.

My missing luggage was a large cardboard carton in which were a bicycle and four well-filled pannier bags. On this bicycle I proposed to spend the next five months travelling through some of the more rugged parts of the sub-continent. Only now it looked as if I shouldn't get further than the airport and I didn't even have a return ticket to London. Was my bicycle even now winging its way to Sri Lanka?

Spotting another official who looked a little more energetic and was carrying a walkie-talkie I decided to have one more try. 'Please,' I said, 'my bicycle hasn't come through and I fear it might have gone on to Sri Lanka.' The official regarded me with contempt and answered not a word. It was too much. I began to wave my arms about in a rather theatrical and self-indulgent sort of way. This afforded me some relief and I wondered if it was perhaps the beginnings of hysteria. It had an effect too upon the official who now said something into his walkie-talkie and went over to where the sleeping baggage-handlers lay. He roused two of these and they stumbled off out of the hall and into the darkness. I began to feel the first faint stirrings of hope.

After a tense 10 minutes alternating between hope and despair, I caught sight of the baggage-handlers standing on the tarmac yelling something unintelligible. Through the dirty windows I could see them grinning delightedly and holding aloft a battered cardboard box from which bits of my bicycle were protruding. I felt a great surge of relief but as I watched the box slowly collapsed in the middle and fell with a resounding crash to the ground. Joy quickly changed to consternation. The men dragged the box to the little hatch hung with rubber strips through which suitcases are fed onto the conveyor. The box was about twice the height of the hatch but the men were all keyed up and obviously determined to get it through somehow. My arm-waving was by now getting perilously close to the real thing and I closed my eyes to shut out the sight of the final destruction of my cycle. But again my performance had its effect and when I opened my eyes it was to see the two baggage-handlers, joined now by two uniformed officials carefully carrying the limp bundle through a conventional pair of doors. They laid it reverently at my feet.

I started to tear away the cardboard, the officials and the baggage-handlers joining in. It was a little like 'pass-the-parcel' at a party, only we were all tearing away together. I decided that Pakistani men were not so bad after all. Miraculously, nothing was broken or missing, although the box had obviously been tampered with. The men watched with a look of amazement on their faces as I reassembled the cycle, replacing pedals and realigning the handlebars and so forth. They clearly had never before seen a woman using a spanner. The bicycle seemed to intrigue them, too, and they kept stroking it and patting it while they held it for me to pump up the tyres. One of the men went off and came back with a cup of tea. The tea was very welcome for I was by now quite tired with the lateness of the hour, the emotion and the heat.

The first taste of tea on the sub-continent tends to come as rather a shock for it is made by boiling together milk, water, sugar and fine tea dust until it reaches the required consistency. Fortunately I had been warned of this and so did not immediately assume that someone was trying to poison me in order to steal my possessions. Courtesy demanded that I drink it with some degree of enthusiasm and I feel sure that any nanny would have been proud of my performance.

Now that I was reunited with my bicycle, everyone at the airport seemed determined to be as friendly as possible. The previously bored officials who hadn't been able to see or hear me now found that they spoke English after all and I was seen through customs and passport control like an honoured guest.

As they escorted me through the exit I was approached by a fat gentleman who bowed politely and said:

'You are Memsahib on a cycle?'

I hadn't thought of myself as such but it seemed to fit and there were no other women around, either on or off cycles, so I agreed cautiously that I probably was.

'You have photo for me?'

I wondered if he might be confusing me with some celebrity who was expected but I was given no chance to argue as he was a very forceful character. In no time I found myself seated with another unwelcome cup of 'mixed tea' in my hand, undergoing a sort of third degree.

'What is your good name?'

I told him and he wrote it down carefully.

'You are how old?'

I admitted to 47.

'You have husband?'

I said I had.

'He give you permission to come here alone?' he asked in a tone of great incredulity.

I explained that in England we don't think in these terms because of equal rights, and that anyway my husband was quite happy for me to do something I wanted to do for so long. I was all set to continue for some time on the subject of women's rights and equal opportunities, but this seemed not to be a subject that he cared for. He cut me short with a disapproving frown and asked:

'You have children also?'

I said I had three and added quickly, seeing the frown deepen, that they were all grown up now and out in the world and not needing me any more—I wasn't deserting them or anything. With the air of a man who is only doing his duty, he then asked:

'Why you come to Pakistan?'

I thought I had better not say that primarily it was because it was a good way to approach the Himalayas, the real objective of the trip, and that 1000 miles of flat country would get me nicely acclimatized to Asia before the rigours of the mountains. Instead I told him some of the subsidiary reasons. I wanted to see his beautiful country and the sites of the ancient Indus civilization. Also since I had studied the major world religions at university, I thought it would be interesting to see Islam in action. He seemed reasonably satisfied with this. I left him with one of my passport photographs. I had quite a stock of these for obtaining visas along the way. In due course the photograph appeared in a national newspaper at the head of a short article in Urdu and when it was translated for me I found that it was much more accurate than is normal for newspapers. I kept the piece which was to prove most useful later on.

It was still dark when the interview was over, so I waited a while for dawn to break and tried to convince myself that after all the difficulties and the months of preparation I was at last in Asia. As I told the journalist, I had wanted to make this trip for a long time. For years I had been planning to make a really long bicycle journey, but without quite knowing where I wanted to go. Having married young and been busy raising a family and earning a living, I hadn't had the time or the money for much travel, and except for a brief business trip to the United States, I had never been further afield than Western Europe. When at last I had both the freedom and the funds to make a long trip possible I couldn't decide which part of the world I most wanted to ride through. I started to study the atlas for inspiration.

What a lot of places beckoned. I toyed with thoughts of Africa, South America, the West Coast of the United States of America from Alaska down to Mexico, Indonesia, Malaysia; I almost plumped for China. But then one day, in a flash I realized that of all the wonders so enticingly displayed in the atlas, the Himalayas were what I most wanted to see, and I thought I should get to them first while I still had the health and (I hoped) the strength to pedal around them. After that the trip quickly took shape. It did seem logical to start at Karachi and cycle up the Indus Valley; through the great desert of Sind and the rich flat lands of the Punjab. The very names began to take on a magical potency. From Lahore I could cross the border into India and visit the Golden Temple of the Sikhs at Amritsar. By that time with more than 1000 miles behind me I should be well acclimatized and fit enough for the long climb through the Himalayas into Kashmir—the summer playground of the great Mogul rulers.

From there my plans would be fluid. I would be dodging in and out of various Himalayan valleys and I hoped to go through the ancient Tibetan Kingdom of Ladakh and Zanskar too, but that would depend on snow and road conditions. Eventually I would reach Kathmandu in Nepal and if there was any time left I might also be able to see something of Sikkim and Bhutan.

Altogether, I was contemplating a five-months journey of between 4,000 and 5,000 miles which should give me, among other things, marvellous views of the major peaks of the Himalayas. An exciting prospect but just a little frightening too, for I would have to be for the most part entirely reliant upon my own resources.

The bicycle I proposed to ride had been custom built for me two years previously. It was a very fine ten-speed machine, with a crossbar, for this is the strongest and most responsive type of frame. No expense had been spared in its building, because at the time I had a lot of money from the sale of my car which I no longer needed, as I cycled everywhere. So all its fittings were of the best quality. It was still as new and all that was needed to prepare it for the rigours of the journey was an overhaul of all the moving parts. My son had sent me a new saddle from America, the latest thing in 'anatomical' design. This proved a very welcome change from what I had sat upon before. Until I tried this one I had thought that a sore bottom was indigenous to cycling. The local shop who had built the cycle entered with enthusiasm into my plans. Not having a high regard for my mechanical competency they took over the preparation. If I didn't make it, it was not going to be because of any mechanical failure on the part of 'their bike'.

I was left free to concentrate on all the other aspects incumbent upon world travel by cycle. Life became a feverish whirl of shopping, telephone calls and visits to embassies. After exhaustive enquiries and much conflicting information I found that visas were not necessary for Pakistan and India; they were for Nepal, as were permits for Sikkim and Bhutan, but these could not be obtained in London as they would be out of date when I reached those countries. Inoculations were vital and took a lot of organizing as typhoid, paratyphoid, hepatitis, cholera, tetanus and other horrors I have forgotten, all had to be kept at bay by jabs at different times. Medicines, too, were necessary for all the nasty possibilities I could not be protected against and I accumulated pills and unguents in alarming quantities.

Clothes for five months. What sort of clothes could I take for cycling through hot Moslem lands where even an inch of exposed female skin is an incitement to violence? Fortunately a daughter was home for a while and she patiently helped me buy a suitable wardrobe. It consisted of a light green, cotton safari suit for formal wear which we found in the January sales, together with four fine cotton shirts—three of them long-sleeved to cover the arms. A dark green, corduroy hat with a brim from Harrod's men's department, cheaper there than in the women's department. A pair of tough cotton trousers, also green; these had elasticated ankles so they could be hitched up like 'plus fours' for cycling and quickly let down again when off the bike. A pair of very long, dark green, corduroy shorts, which fortuitously exactly matched the hat and were for wearing in Hindu countries where female flesh is not such an incitement. Three pairs of pants; a rat was later to eat one pair in Nepal so I was glad I had taken three. I reasoned that I could wash my bra out overnight so I didn't take a spare. No swimsuit as I didn't think I'd get a chance to swim-I was wrong but it didn't matter as someone lent me one when I needed it. I took three pairs of socks, one long woollen pair for cold mountain passes, one longish cotton pair for wearing with the 'plus fours' and short tennis socks for the shorts. For rainwear I had a green goretex anorak which I could also wear over my other clothes when it was very cold. In fact all my clothes 'mixed and matched' and could all be worn at the same time if necessary as they were all fairly loose fitting. I didn't take nightwear or shoes because of the weight.

Maps and guide books were a great problem. I could only find one very small scale map of the areas I wanted and all the guide books were out of date or impossibly heavy. In the end I cut out the relevant sections of some up to date guides and just hoped that I would find larger scale maps en route.

Tools and spare parts for the bicycle had also to be considered. There was unlikely to be anywhere, even in the towns I was to pass through, where the cycle could be repaired should anything go seriously wrong, for my type of bicycle is virtually unknown in those parts. Also I had heard that the most usual way of repairing anything mechanical out there was with a hammer.

Under these circumstances I thought it better that I rely entirely on my own rather basic skills. I packed enough lightweight spanners to fit every nut on the cycle, a puncture repair kit, tyre levers, a spare link for the chain and a little gadget for opening chain rivets, two spare cables, two spare inner tubes, and after much searching in tool shops, I added a pair of miniature pliers for holding the ends of cables should I have to replace them. I hoped fervently that I should have no need ever to use any of these things.

I took the dynamo lighting off the bike to save weight. I should not be needing it as I had made a firm resolve never to ride at night. I took a small torch with spare batteries and a slow-burning candle to see me through the electricity cuts which were said to be frequent on the sub-continent. Tyres were a headache for a long while: I could carry one spare but I would need at least two more and possibly three or four before the end of the tour. Poste Restante was far too risky for these necessities so I tried to enlist the help of other agencies, like the Diplomatic and various missionary bodies. No one seemed too keen to help until American Express said that their offices would gladly accept them and hold them for me until I came; so tyres were despatched at great expense to Lahore, Kashmir, Delhi and Kathmandu.

Although camping was said to be far too dangerous to contemplate on my chosen route, I did pack a sleeping bag and a goretex 'bivvy' bag in case I should find myself with no shelter in remote places. Washing things, sunglasses, notebook and pen, a few plastic bags and my tiny camera with ten rolls of film completed my trappings. Packed into pannier bags at the front and rear of the cycle, the whole lot weighed a horrifying 65 pounds but as there was nothing of it that I felt I could do without, I could only hope that they would not weigh it at the airport, which they did not.

2

As I left the airport dawn broke with a suddenness unknown in Europe.

The road into Karachi was bumpy and dusty and there were large deep holes in it where the drains had no covers on them. I was glad I had waited for daylight, for a tumble into one of these holes would at the very least have broken a wheel and ended the trip before it had begun. Lots of traffic and people were about at this early hour; few cars, many cycles but mainly hordes of buses. These last swerved into the kerb with no warning other than great blasts upon their horns. At once crowds of men jostled and pushed their way into them, while others hung on all around the outsides. The buses were garishly painted all over. Some of the men were in European dress but most were wearing baggy pyjamas. The cyclists were as rash and dashing as those in London so I thought that once I had adjusted to the habits of the buses I would feel quite at home and relaxed: for the moment it felt safer to concentrate on the road and the traffic and not try and take in the views too much.

On the outskirts of Karachi I stopped alongside another cyclist at a red light. I asked him if he knew where the hotel was to which I had been recommended. He seemed to know the name and indicated that I should follow him. After turning a bewildering number of corners my guide pulled up at an imposingly grand hotel, the sort to be found in any large city; not at all what I had in mind and definitely outside my financial limits. I waited until my guide was out of sight then set off again in search of something more modest. There followed a fruitless half hour trying to search and avoid the murderous traffic at the same time. The trouble was that I was tired by now, worn down by the incidents at the airport and the lack of a night's sleep. It was difficult to think rationally, too, in all the noise and bustle. There seemed to be no cafes either where I could consult my guide book over a cup of coffee.

Then I remembered that the guide book had mentioned that there was a Y.W.C.A. hostel in Karachi. These are normally good places to stay at, clean and comfortable and moderately priced. I found my way to this one after being misdirected countless times. In Pakistan, it seems, people don't like to admit that they don't know where somewhere is and would rather hazard a guess. The hostel had a room available but when I was shown it my heart sank for it was very dirty and the bed had obviously been slept in by at least one person without the sheets being changed. Still I felt I could look no further and it would have to do. I had my sleeping bag so I need not sleep in the dirty bedding. Tomorrow when I was rested I could look for something better.

Before I could collapse into my sleeping bag I had to pay for the room and as yet I had not acquired any Pakistani currency. The girl receptionist pointed out a bank within sight, about 200 yards away. Leaving my cycle locked at the hostel I walked. The bank had no exchange facilities but they sent a boy to show me the way to one which had. The boy appeared not to be pleased with this task for he stalked ahead of me walking very fast and when we reached the bank he jerked his head towards the entrance and stalked off again.

It took 40 minutes to change 50 pounds into rupees and when I emerged again I stupidly turned in the wrong direction and quickly became lost. All around me were men; I couldn't see a single woman. The men stared openly at me trying to make me meet their gaze. No wonder I keep getting lost, I thought angrily; it was impossible to look around and get my bearings because of all the eyes. There were beggars everywhere, too, holding up their begging bowls and clamouring to be noticed. Then I saw seated on a blanket, the most miserable bundle of humanity it was possible to imagine—a tiny, wizened, deformed little creature, all skin and bone and looking no more than a few months old. It was quite naked and sat unnaturally still with a begging bowl beside it. Horror stricken, I didn't know which I wanted to do most, pick it up and hold it or run away. Nothing I had read or seen prepared me for the actual horror of these baby beggars and they remained for me the single most disturbing feature of the trip. I walked away from this one feeling sick and angry.

Back finally at the Y.W.C.A., I found that another woman had taken over the reception desk. As I started to sign in she stopped me and asked if I really wanted to stay in such a dirty place. Rather surprised, I said I didn't but was too tired to look for something better. She said I was welcome to come and stay with her but that as she lived rather a long way out in a very tiny flat, I might be more comfortable at the cathedral where they had a guest house. She would take me there if I liked. Her kindness made me feel quite tearful but I jumped at the idea of the guest house and in a short while I was happily settling in to a large, old-fashioned room in an apartment in the cathedral compound—a haven of peace in that noisy, bewildering city. I was not in the guest house because there wasn't one as such, but was the personal guest of the English vicar and his wife, Robin and Jean Lankester, a retired couple who were doing a two-year stint there. They often had people to stay, they said; they lived very simply and I could take my meals with them and contribute towards the expenses. My room was shabby but clean and furnished with mosquito-netted iron bedsteads. After the poverty I had witnessed that morning it was as much luxury as I felt was decent.

Apart from lunch which I had when I arrived and supper which Jean woke me up for, I saw no more of Karachi until Jean woke me again for breakfast at eight the following morning. Fully recovered after my long sleep I felt eager to begin preparations to get the trip under way. Being in a city always makes me eager to leave it.

The first thing I had to do was to deliver letters of introduction which had been given me by the Pakistan Embassy in London; these were to various ministers and officials in

Karachi who were supposedly going to be helpful over different aspects of the trip. The Minister at the London Embassy whom I had met while doing my researches had at first tried to dissuade me from the idea altogether, but seeing that I was determined upon it he was giving me all the help he could. If I did not reach India in one piece he did not wish it to be his fault.

The most important thing was to find accommodation along the way. Hotels were very few and far between and even where available were not always suitable for unaccompanied women. My best course apparently was to get official written permission to use rest houses. These are places built to house visiting officials such as tax assessors, engineers, surveyors, rat-catchers and so forth. When not being used by these officials they were supposed to be available for tourists. In practice though the 'chowkidars' in charge of the rest houses cared very little for tourists and were reluctant to let them have rooms, but an official letter could, I was told, work wonders. How to obtain such a letter was a closely guarded secret not known even to my minister at the Embassy, but it was hoped that one of the letters of introduction would bear fruit.

I had also to visit the British Consulate to leave a copy of my passport and give them an outline of my proposed route—a practice advised in countries where people are prone to disappear.

Today though was Friday, the Moslem holiday, and all the ministries were closed so no letters could be delivered. Instead I went to church. In Karachi there are church services in Urdu and English on Fridays and Sundays in order to cater for the different weekly holidays. After the service in English, Jean and Robin introduced me to the congregation over coffee in the cathedral grounds. Most of them made the same gloomy predictions about my prospects as I had been given before leaving England. Tales were told of drug-crazed lorry drivers leaving death and destruction in their wake; of the latest attacks by the fearsome dacoits (bandits): and of course the ever-present threat of Moslem men, not to mention dysentery, sand storms and awful food.

Could you not go by train? they asked.

Plainly they thought I was mad. The British Vice-Consul who was also present was of more help; he arranged for me to visit the Consul on Sunday morning.

Since there was nothing further to be done that day, I thought I would do some sight-seeing. Just outside the cathedral compound was a stand for four-wheeled, horse-drawn vehicles called victorias, reminiscent of more elegant, leisured times except, that is, for the horses themselves; these poor creatures were definitely past their best. The driver of one of them hailed me in passable English asking me if I would like to go for a tour of the city and naming a modest price. Acting upon instructions from my hostess I offered a lower amount. The driver agreed to it immediately so I realized that I had not gone low enough as there should have followed more lengthy bargaining.

The victoria bowled along, at first through streets thronged with men and boys of all ages playing cricket. Some of the boys jumped up beside me and had to be threatened by the driver's whip to make them get off. Men strolled along hand in hand, taking their ease. Nowhere could I see a single woman, just occasionally a small girl appeared, scuttling along intent upon some errand. Obviously the holiday only applied to boys and men. Most of the men stared openly at me, some of them called out things in a jeering kind of way, but others seemed more friendly and said 'Hallo' and smiled.

Away from the centre, the streets were full of animals; camels were pulling great carts or just standing ruminating with that peculiar movement of the lower jaw, looking to my western eyes excitingly exotic. Pathetic little donkeys trotted meekly along under enormous loads. By most doorways goats and chickens were tethered—the chickens by a string around one leg. In this poorer part of town vast extended families appeared to be living in one-roomed shacks or in tenements of one-roomed apartments, together with their fowls and animals. To the casual observer though the people did not look noticeably ill-nourished or depressed.

On the northern outskirts of the city was a vast open air laundry, acres of it, with hundreds of 'dhobi wallahs' doing the city's wash which was spread out on miles of clothes lines to bleach in the sun. Beyond that was Karachi's shanty town— a lesson in human squalor and degradation. Here people existed with no more shelter than a rush mat on four sticks. An open sewer ran through their encampment and seemed to provide their only source of water as well as being a playground for their children. The stench of the place was awful and the sheer numbers of these dispossessed people was truly daunting, but seen in the context of the luxury hotels it was an outrage and made me feel as angry and impotent as had the baby beggars.

I arrived back at the cathedral in a state of depression, wondering if I was tough enough for Asia. Robin and Jean were sympathetic to how I felt, they had lived most of their lives among the poorer people of the world and had come to terms with poverty.

'You'll be all right, you just need a few days to acclimatize,' said Jean, and she was right. The shock of coming face to face with profound poverty and suffering occurred many times throughout the trip but it never again quite tied me up in such a knot of horror and frustration as it did in Karachi.

The afternoon I spent exploring the bazaars. Again there were no women to be seen, only men and boys buying and selling. Men squatting on the ground mending shoes or cleaning them; men with typewriters writing letters for other men; men perched on high stools being shaved or having their hair cut; men cooking all sorts of food unknown to me, on charcoal braziers. As the only woman about I felt most conspicuous especially as I was eyed with such open curiosity and often with what I took for hostility. I passed many cinemas with hordes of milling men around them, they were all showing trashy American films, depicting sex or violence—no sign of any women here either, except on the hoardings.

Feeling like the only representative of my sex left in a male world, I decided to go back to the cathedral in a rickshaw. These rickshaws are three-wheeled motor scooters with a canopy over them, very noisy and manoeuverable. My driver set off at a furious pace only to screech to a halt within seconds to ask someone how to get to the cathedral. He stopped at least a dozen times to ask the way and the half mile journey took 45 minutes, all spent going around in circles at breakneck speed. Nothing it seemed could be done in Karachi without the maximum of drama.

Jean and Robin offered to help me the following day and full of energy we set out to deliver my letters of introduction to the various ministers. It was a total wash-out. Supercilious underlings seized my letters and told us contemptuously to come back in a couple of hours, and when we did go back we were told just as contemptuously that the minister was too busy to see me and to come again tomorrow. After a couple of such incidents I decided not to waste any more time on officialdom but to depart on Monday whatever the odds.

A visit to the tourist office secured the promise of a room in a special rest house for the first night, and with the second night also catered for I was all right for the first 150 miles.

There was one letter that I was still keen to deliver; this was to a lady who had been instrumental in forming a Pakistan women's association after Partition. This organization had been started to help with the terrible social problems that Pakistan faced and also, I gathered, to establish the position of women in the newly formed country. The minister in London had been particularly keen that I should meet this lady so that I should gain some idea of how Moslem women saw their role in a changing world. At his instigation I had written to her about a month previously but had received no answer. The minister had then written and given me the letter of introduction, assuring me that the 'Begum' would be delighted to receive me. I had tried to telephone her on arrival to make an appointment but as the Karachi telephone system was notoriously eccentric, I had not yet succeeded.

Jean suggested visiting the cottage industry shop which was run by the Begum's organization. The ladies at the shop seemed to know all about me and my cycle tour and agreed that I must meet the Begum. They dialled her number, but before I could speak to her the phone went dead. The ladies urged me to cycle over to her house at exactly four o'clock, for this they said was the hour when, after her afternoon nap, it was most convenient for her to receive visitors.

Duly clad in my 'formal' safari suit and wearing my Harrods hat, feeling smart but a little warm, I set out at 3.15 in the hot sun to cycle the five or six miles to the Begum's house. Promptly at 4 p.m. (I had allowed plenty of time for getting lost), very hot and thirsty I entered the gates of an imposing residence. Definitely on the grand scale for that city of sharp material contrasts. A soldier armed with a rifle was on guard at the entrance. He at least was not expecting me for he brandished his rifle at me as though I was an intruder to be seen off. Never before had I had a gun pointed at me and I wasn't sure that I liked it. Quickly I took my letter of introduction out of my pocket and waved it at him before he should get too enthusiastic with the rifle. Without taking his eyes off me he called out something and a servant came out of the house. I told the servant who I was and that I had come to visit the Begum. He took my letter and went back into the house without speaking a word. I was left in the forecourt with the soldier, both of us perspiring in the hot sun.

I was left there for at least 10 minutes during which time the soldier must have decided that I did not constitute a threat, for he laid aside his rifle and squatted by the bicycle examining its various parts. He kept looking at me enquiringly and pointing to things on it which obviously puzzled him. I wished I knew some Urdu so as to satisfy his curiosity, but we managed tolerably well with gestures and mime. The servant re-appeared.

'You can go now,' he said.

'Go?' I queried with amazement. 'But I've come to visit the Begum. I had an appointment.' My thoughts were running longingly on a seat out of the sun and a cool drink. The servant went off and came back in a shorter time.

'The Begum is in a meeting and can't see you,' he said.

And that was it, no apologies, no regrets and no cool drink. I felt very angry and humiliated. At the time I thought hard things about Pakistan and the lack of courtesy of its people and vowed that I wouldn't again visit a Pakistani home. But this was a vow that I was to break innumerable times, and never again was I treated with anything other than courtesy and warm hospitality. There was a sequel to this incident but no satisfactory reason for it ever emerged.

I set off on Sunday morning to visit the Consul with very little time to spare, and had cycled about a mile when an ominous bumping from the front wheel announced that I had a flat tyre. Panic! there wasn't time to fix it and anyway all my repair things were back at the cathedral. Fortunately there was a garage near by and someone there who spoke English. I explained my predicament and in no time this helpful man had found a rickshaw and had told the driver to take the 'Mem-sahib' and the cycle to the cathedral and then to take the 'Memsahib' to the consulate.

'I tell him to take you double-quick,' he said as somehow I and the bike were squeezed into the confined space. The wheels stuck out on either side of the rickshaw like misplaced paddlewheels on a steamer and sharp bits of bike stuck into me. I tried not to think of what the oily parts might be doing to my formal wear. True to his instructions, the rickshaw driver took me back 'double-quick'. I kept my eyes closed as we zoomed suicidally through the busy traffic.

I dumped the cycle at the cathedral and remembering the geographical ignorance of rickshaw drivers I seized my map. With my navigation and the driver's 'double-quick' driving we made the consulate exactly on time. The Consul viewed my prospective ride with as much gloomy foreboding as everyone else had, but he didn't waste time on discussion— perhaps the Vice-Consul had warned him that it would be useless. Instead he had two letters written for me, one in Urdu and one in English, requesting all District Commissioners and Assistant District Commissioners to afford me assistance in booking rest houses along my route. These he had stamped with impressive seals. He also gave me a condensed lesson in useful Urdu phrases, such as 'Please not to touch this cycle' and 'Where can I make very important telephone call?'

I left the copy of my passport and my proposed route and

promised to telephone when I had reached Lahore. If they had not heard from me in four weeks, they would begin to make enquiries. The Consul's parting advice was to be under cover before nightfall and, If I did have to seek shelter in a village, I must make sure to get in amongst the women.

Feeling much more confident now that I was armed with official letters (though as the Consul warned me, they didn't actually guarantee anything), I took the waiting rickshaw back to town. There was just time before lunch to go with Robin to the government shop he had heard of which sold maps. I bought a map of reasonable scale which had rest houses marked on it. After lunch I tackled the flat front tyre. It proved not to be a puncture after all, but a loose valve-seating; a nuisance, as it would probably work loose again.

I wanted to find time to visit the museum which housed some of the oldest artefacts in the world, from the Indus Civilization of Mohenjodaro, but I had first to keep an appointment with the priest in the downstairs flat. This priest was responsible for all the Urdu services in the cathedral, and Jean and Robin had been anxious for me to meet him for not only was he a most delightful and interesting person, but being a much travelled Pakistani they thought that his advice would be valuable to me. It was to prove in fact the best advice I received from anyone in Karachi, though I didn't know it at the time. It was to the effect that should I reach Hyderabad safely—a possibility he seemed to hope for rather than to expect—I must consult the Bishop there about my best way of continuing to Sukkur, the area between Hyderabad and Sukkur being apparently the most dacoit-infested. I promised that I would consult the Bishop and hurried off to get to the museum before it closed. There was half an hour left before closing time, well worth the rush just to see the lively little pottery figures and the jewellery from the Mohenjodaro site, which was one of the earliest cities of the ancient world, and which I would be visiting in a week or so.

We were just finishing supper that night when a gleaming, chauffeur-driven Mercedes drew up outside the door, looking distinctly incongruous in the crumbling Victorian surroundings of the cathedral compound. The lady who emerged was an emissary from the inhospitable Begum of yesterday's abortive visit. She came bearing gifts of toffees and biscuits for my journey and was eager to 'make amends for the bad impression' she feared I had received the day before. There followed lengthy explanations about lost letters and different people mistaking their responsibilities. I couldn't quite unravel it but I gathered that an hotel room had been booked for me—she named an hotel notorious for giving its guests food poisoning. They had been waiting for me to telephone the office of the organization. I wondered how I was supposed to know this. The London Embassy should have told me, she said. It sounded all a little far-fetched to me but I thought it would be churlish to say so. I felt sorry for her having to try to cover up someone else's mistakes, so we talked about other things instead and I never did discover why the Begum hadn't received me.

That night I slept fitfully as always seems to happen when planning an early start for the following day. Warnings and worries chased each other around in my head so that it was a relief to finally awake at six. I wanted to be out of Karachi before the traffic got too thick and the heat too oppressive.

3

As soon as I was on the cycle and heading away from Karachi, the sense of excitement about the journey ahead came flooding back. The frustrations and worries dropped away and I began to enjoy the ride as I bowled along the flat road. The route I was travelling was the long way round to Hyderabad, going first eastwards to Tatta before turning north. I hoped that most of the traffic would be on the newly built highway which went direct to Hyderabad.

Alas for my hopes. After the first traffic-free hour, it was lorries all the way. Enormous, high-sided lorries which were painted all over in many colours. Not an inch of them was left unembellished, and on the tailgate were huge pictorial scenes of the chocolate box type; lions peering through jungles, luscious, simpering damsels; a smiling General Zia; heraldic beasts and so forth. Rows of miniature cow bells or metal shapes on the ends of long chains dangled almost to the ground all around the cab and at the rear; so I heard them coming from afar. In case I might not have heard them, they also had very loud horns which they started blaring from the distance and continued to blare until they were well past. So it was all very noisy, and dangerous, too, because amid such a cacophony the horn could no longer serve as a warning device. An additional hazard were the clouds of nauseous black exhaust fumes.

As they passed me someone would always lean out of the passenger side, often with the door held open, and leer at me. If the person knew any English he would call 'Hey Baby, Hallo Baby' or some such inanity. The ones who knew no English would wiggle their eyebrows up and down or stick their tongues out. Little boys, on the other hand, riding in the sort of palanquin that all the lorries had on their cab roofs, regarded me with loathing. They gesticulated angrily, indicating that I should have my face covered as their women do. I was very tempted to be rude to these little boys, realizing how they must lord it at home over their mothers and sisters. I dared not retaliate to the men's rudeness, for fear of consequences.

In between lorries I tried to take in something of the surroundings. The road ran in a straight line through a flat and arid landscape. There was very little vegetation apart from some scrub growth. Dust and sand covered everything. There were people with brooms sweeping the road clear of the encroaching sand, so the air, too, was full of dust. Nevertheless, there was beauty in the scene, once past the outskirts of Karachi with its raw industrial complexes and a huge petrochemical works. The sky seemed much wider than normal and was of a peerless blue. Occasional strings of camels could be seen, like silhouettes moving slowly over the sand. Hawks hung motionless in the still air.

It was hard to realize in such a desert landscape that I was in fact riding through the delta lands of the Indus River. Many of the creeks were dry now, but long ago the first Moslem invaders had sailed up them bringing Islam to the subcontinent with the Koran and the sword.

In those days it must have been a greener and more fertile place, with more people about. Even now it was not uninhabited and whenever I stopped to look at anything one or two figures would immediately appear. I saw that it was going to be very difficult to answer any call of nature in these circumstances. All along the road I had noticed squatting figures, backs to the road, staring stonily into the desert. With their baggy garments they managed with great propriety. I did not think I could do this, especially as people found me such a source of interest. The thought of attempting it and finding myself surrounded by curious natives was enough to dispel any desire I had to try.

I had travelled about 40 miles and my thoughts were turning

more and more to food and drink (a frequent preoccupation of cyclists) when I was suddenly aware of a motorcyclist riding alongside, regarding me intently.

'You are English, yes?' he asked.

'Yes, I'm English,' I replied with caution.

'I like English woman,' he said with great enthusiasm. I said nothing but proceeded with warning bells sounding loudly.

'English woman very sexy,' he confided.

'No,' I said. 'English women are not sexy.'

'You are not being sexy?' he queried incredulously. 'Not being sexy?'

'No,' I said with even greater firmness. 'No, I am not being sexy.'

'Me, I am very sexy man, so then please I am saying goodbye and thankyou,' and on this splendid note he revved up the engine of his 90 c.c. motorcycle and zoomed off.

So I understood from all this that here on the road, as in the city, I was a tantalizing sex-object; a sort of unholy temptation with my face exposed and unaverted; a woman who could be looked at! My 47 years were no protection at all. I might add that every inch of me apart from my hands and face was covered in loose fitting, utilitarian garments.

The hopeful, sexy motorcyclist decided to make another attempt and was waiting for me further along the road.

'You will be my guest. It is decided,' he said. 'We will eat in Maliki. I go now. I get there two o'clock. I prepare. You get there half past two o'clock. I meet.'

Maliki was where there was a famous necropolis, acres and acres of splendid tombs, from the time when Tatta had been the capital of Sind and famous over many centuries. I had planned to spend some time there. Fortunately, though, tombs are not my favourite tourist attraction. By pedalling hard I got to Maliki at 2.15 and rode straight through, seeing nothing of the necropolis nor of my amorous pursuer. I stopped two miles further on at Tatta, desperately hungry having cycled the whole 60-odd miles on nothing but a small breakfast and a few of the Begum's toffees. I could see nowhere to eat. There were a few tea houses, but the Consul had warned me that these were not places where women could go; even for men they seemed not really inviting, being very grimy and fly-infested. All I could do was to buy something from the bazaar stalls, a practice not recommended because of health hazards. I found a stall where a young boy was frying some green and yellow balls in bubbling fat. I pointed to them and in the interest of hygiene passed him a plastic container. Ignoring my container, the boy scooped up some already cooked and cooling balls with his grubby hands and placed them in a piece of newspaper. Handing me the greasy package, he snatched my one-rupee note (about 6p.) and put it into a cigar box, closing the lid with a flourish. My entourage laughed in appreciation, so even at such a low price, I think he might have swindled me.

I must explain about the entourage. It was something that was to accompany me throughout my time in Pakistan and India. Whenever I stopped, whether in desert, country or town, the entourage appeared. The only difference being that the town one was larger and less inhibited than the desert or country one. It was always composed of boys of varying ages from six or so upwards, with a youth or two and the odd adult thrown in for good measure. The hard core was aged about 14. These male persons would collect around me the moment I got off the bicycle, and follow me about wherever I went. They would stare and point, talking and giggling excitedly. They seemed to feel perfectly free to poke and prod the cycle and this annoyed me very much. By and large though I suppose they were harmless, but they inevitably wore me down until I would give up trying to see anything and just go away. This day I tried to ignore them while I ate the green and yellow balls which turned out to be spinach in a semolina batter—quite nice and chewy. Then abruptly my patience with these staring gesticulating boys was exhausted. I rounded on them and yelled at them to go away. It had not the slightest effect of course, they enjoyed seeing me get cross. So still hungry I rode off without seeing anything of the ancient splendours of Tatta either, thinking hard thoughts about Pakistani males.

The place where I was to spend the night was a rest house on a lake about 15 miles from Tatta. I found it easily enough for it was signposted in English, the first signpost I had seen that day which was not in the Urdu script. I tried out my Urdu phrases on the chowkidar and he showed me to a room which seemed quite adequate, though the water was not working. This was rather a bore since what I needed most after the use of a toilet, was a nice hot shower to wash off all the dust of the road. As previously advised, I gave the chowkidar 10 rupees 'sweetening money' and after some more attempts at communication with my Urdu phrases and with his equally sparse English he brought me some tea and food. The food was chapattis and some very highly spiced curried meat balls. Hungry as I was I could eat very little of the meat. After my meal I thought I would go to my room to rest and write in my journal but unaccountably the chowkidar blocked my path, trying it seemed to tell me something important, but what it was I could not discover. He went away, returning in a few minutes with a friend who knew slightly more English. Both of them now were trying to tell me something urgent, but I still could not understand. Both men kept pointing towards the distance saying 'Mr Abro, Mr Abro.' It seemed that they wanted me to go in search of the Mr Abro to whom I had an introduction from the Pakistan Tourist Board. He was in charge of the rest house and I thought that perhaps the chowkidar had decided that I needed to square it with him first. I couldn't see that it was necessary since all the arrangements had been made in Karachi and I had been assured that it was in order.

Seeing that I was not about to go in search of this Mr Abro, the chowkidar then beckoned me to follow him down the garden to a semi-underground shed—a sort of storeroom. He made signs of dusting down an ancient sagging string bed, and he appeared to be suggesting that I should spend the night there. Becoming more bemused by the minute, I shook my head and backed out. It was certainly not the sort of place I would consider spending the night in except in a dire emergency.

The chowkidar appeared to be getting more and more

34

worried. He and his friend had a lengthy discussion while I waited uneasily. Eventually the friend persuaded me to accompany him. We took a short cut to the road across a desert track. It was showing signs of getting dark (which happens suddenly in those parts) and I felt nervous. What were this man's intentions? I asked myself. I told him firmly that many people knew I was staying there that night—meaning him to understand that I was not without friends to enquire after me should I go missing, but he seemed not to take a lot of notice of this. We reached the main road right by the side of a small mosque. An old man dressed in dazzling white stared over the parapet wall at me, very stern and disapproving. It was the local mullah, who a moment later burst into song, calling the faithful to prayer. As the faithful came, men only of course, because only men in Islam are called, they too looked disapprovingly at me. Perhaps I was setting up the wrong vibrations for their prayers.

Still we stood at the side of the road waiting for I knew not what, nor whether I would wish to go with it when it came. I therefore told the man that I had promised not to be out after dark, and look, it was almost dark now. I think he understood the gestures with which I was learning to accompany my words, rather than the words themselves. He waved me back to the rest house and I reached it again just as darkness fell.

Half an hour later the man returned in a jeep with someone else who spoke good English and I at last learnt what all the fuss had been about. It transpired that there were two rest houses. The one that I had found (by far the nicer of the two) was for high-ranking military personnel. The chowkidar, in spite of accepting my 10 rupees, had become worried that an officer might turn up and make trouble about me being there. So the bike and I went off in the jeep to the right rest house, where I was shown into a large twin-bedded room with a washing room attached. Everywhere the paint was flaking off the walls, and even the concrete was disintegrating, although it had only been built six months before.

I decided not to take a shower because the floor of the wash room was covered with large brown cockroaches, and more of them were pouring out of great cracks in the walls. Instead I closed the washroom door and sprayed all around it with a cat and dog flea spray that I had with me, in the hope that the creatures would remain in there and keep off my person during the night. The noise of the faulty lavatory cistern continuously syphoning kept me awake for a long time, until I plucked up the courage to brave the cockroaches and go in to tie up the ballcock. By that time the cockroaches were everywhere, all over the walls and ceilings. Strangely, or perhaps it was because of the flea spray, they didn't come into the bedroom, and when I awoke to the daylight at about seven, they had all disappeared and I was able at last to wash in peace.

After a breakfast of chapattis and fried eggs—swimming in grease but very welcome, I set off towards Hyderabad into a strong headwind. The backs of my hands and my forehead were quite badly burnt. The sun the day before must have been much stronger than it had seemed. I pulled my hat down low over my eyes to protect my face and utilised my elastic knee bandages to cover my hands.

The country I was now riding through was almost total desert, with here and there a cultivated strip. By these were primitive walled villages, with ochre-coloured, mud-plastered houses. In the true desert there were occasional wretched little encampments where people were living with as great an appearance of poverty as in the shanty town outside Karachi. Perhaps these were nomadic people since there was no visible means of supporting life in such places.

The sun, noticeably hotter than yesterday, and the headwind made it an uncomfortable ride. Thirst was the biggest problem, aggravated by the amount of dust I was swallowing. Within a couple of hours I had drunk the contents of both water bottles. I began to look forward to reaching Kotri where I was to spend the night (I hoped) at the barrage rest house. A parishioner at the cathedral had given me an introduction to a friend of his there who was an engineer working on the hydro-electric scheme. As I neared Kotri at around lunch time, I began to be harassed by men in rickshaws. There would be as many as six people in these rickshaws—designed to hold two.

They kept overtaking and falling back and overtaking again, while their occupants leaned out leering and shouting. One rickshaw load in particular was so persistent that they had me practically snarling in fury. As I reached the centre of Kotri, a youth stood right in my path with his arms outspread and held his ground so that I was forced to stop. I recognized him as one of the most importunate of the leerers. Before I could move around him to get away, he thrust out his hand politely and said:

'Madam, I was waiting for you and I saw you coming so I was looking and now I am come waiting for you.'

So, thinking that perhaps he had read about my trip in the newspapers, I agreed to accompany him to a cafe for a cool drink. He turned out to be a pleasant though rather bossy young man. He had not in fact read about me in the news-papers; he had stopped me because he stopped all Westerners, in order to practise his English. After two fizzy drinks which he insisted on paying for (I could have done with a third if I had been allowed to pay for my own) I started off to look for the barrage rest house. My new young friend thought that he would come too, so did about 20 other youths and boys, totally uninvited of course. This entourage hadn't any idea of where the rest house was; I don't think they had even heard of a rest house, but they all had definite views about where we should go. After a lot of false starts they led me eventually to what turned out to be a nunnery. Before entering the grounds of what I hoped was the rest house, I got my bossy young friend to make the entourage stay outside, but by the time I got to the entrance and realized that it was a nunnery, the whole crowd was right behind me again. A sister appeared and I was told off (in Portuguese I think) for bringing them. I shooed the boys out and decided to abandon my efforts to find the rest house for the time being. Instead I thought I would go in search of the Bishop of Hyderabad to seek his advice as I had promised.

Hyderabad was just across the Indus from Kotri and as I cycled with difficulty over a temporary bridge solid with traffic I caught my first glimpse of the great river. I would not see it again until Sukkur, another 250 miles further on. I found the Bishop's house by going first to a church and from there being escorted by a kindly verger, who led me by bicycle through a maze of bazaars and narrow streets. It was three o'clock when I arrived there and the Bishop was having his afternoon nap. His daughter, a young girl of about 18, welcomed me with great warmth and hospitality, as though receiving middle-aged female cyclists was an everyday occurrence. She cooked me lunch in spite of my protests. It was the first proper meal I had had since leaving Karachi and it tasted wonderful. After lunch I was shown to a room to wash and rest until the Bishop woke.

The Bishop was a local man of about 55. He had previously been a parish priest in Hyderabad for 20 years. He lived very simply by British standards in an unassuming little house with a small garden. When he awoke and I had introduced myself, he insisted that I should spend the night at his house. Over supper we discussed plans for my journey. He thought that the route I had planned, along the smaller roads on the west bank of the Indus, was far too dangerous. Apparently most of the dacoit hideouts were on that side. Instead he advised me to travel on the main highway to the east. As for accommodation, he thought the only possible, safe thing to do was to spend each night with a Christian family. He would arrange for the first stop and send instructions that I was to be passed on with a letter to Christians in the next town. The Bishop was a man who inspired confidence. I readily agreed to his proposals and went to sleep that night feeling that I had strayed into something like a wartime escape story and was being 'passed up the line' from 'safe house' to 'safe house', practising 'enemy avoidance' techniques on the way. I wondered how I was ever going to do any detailed sight-seeing, already I had come 130 miles without seeing anything except the road and what lay within view on either side of it.

I left the following morning after promising to take great care and to write as soon as I was safely in Lahore. The family gathered at the door to wave me off. So preoccupied was I with all the solemn warnings of the night before, that I missed my turning to the highway and became inextricably lost in the maze of the bazaar streets. I was rescued by a small Moslem boy on a large, rusty old bicycle who, although he spoke no English, cleverly guided me through the thick crowds to the highway. He didn't seem to expect any reward for his help, but I gave him a handful of the Begum's toffees, with which he seemed delighted.

4

Whatever I had imagined Pakistan's A.1 to be, it was not like that. A single track ran in each direction, full of craters and potholes. There was a fairly continuous stream of the horn-blaring trucks and buses, wreathed in their clouds of noxious exhaust gases, and appearing in their colourful and highly decorated state as if they had strayed from some giant fair-ground. But far more numerous was the animal traffic: camel carts, oxen carts, donkey carts, horses and carts, pack camels, pack donkeys, flocks of sheep and flocks of goats; all wonder-fully bedecked in bright coloured woollen jewellery and hung about with tinkling bells. Sandy strips edged the road on either side and these were for the animals and cyclists to travel on. No one used them though until forced to do so because it was much easier going on the tarmac, in spite of the holes. Occasionally, a couple of trucks or buses, locked side by side in a life and death struggle for the lead, and taking up the whole width of the road, would cause a general stampede onto the sandy tracks. These were dangerous moments for me, for if I made too sudden a plunge into the soft sand, I was liable to be precipitated straight over the handlebars.

During a lull in the traffic, while I was enjoying the sights of vast green fields with iridescent green parrots flying low over them, two dogs launched an attack upon me. They appeared suddenly from nowhere—big dogs coming up fast, one on each side, silently, as they do when they mean business. There is something about cyclists which turns even quite decent dogs into potential killers. Some people say it is the high frequency noise which the spokes make. Whatever it is, I have learnt to fear dogs greatly when I'm cycling, and for this trip I had provided myself with a dog-deterring spray such as Californian postmen carry on their rounds. It doesn't cause a dog any permanent damage but is guaranteed to stop it for 10 minutes if aimed between its eyes from a distance of no more than 10 feet. This spray had given me tremendous confidence when I had fitted it carefully to hand on the cycle, but now that the time had come to use it, I realized that aiming it from a fixed point, feet firmly planted on the ground, was not at all the same thing as spraying from the saddle when every ounce of energy and concentration was engaged in keeping ahead of the brutes. Besides, I thought despairingly, if I did manage to hit one, the necessary slowing down would undoubtedly give the other one his chance to spring. So the spray stayed where it was as with lungs bursting and calf muscles shrieking I hurtled on. Fear must have lent me wings that day for though I am not normally a fast cyclist, I think I might have set a record for the kilometre dash and my reward was to see the dogs finally give up and slink away.

The 60 miles to the small town where the Bishop had arranged for me to stay were quite hard work after the affair with the dogs. The wind was against me and the sun was very hot, so I was not sorry to reach my destination and locate the home of the local midwife who was to be my hostess for the night. Her house was in the centre of the town down an unmade street. It was entered through a narrow door in a high wall. Once inside, I found myself in a small paved courtyard surrounded on all sides by high walls, but open to the sky. At one end was a little two-storeyed house, the upper part reached by an outside staircase. On the right-hand wall was a low rectangular kitchen, equipped with three Calor gas burners at floor level, a couple of shelves for the simple, handleless cooking pots, and a fly-proof meat safe. Just inside the entrance door were two tiny rooms; one was the hole-in-the-floor type lavatory with a bucket of water supplied for flushing. Low down within reach of the left hand was a cold water tap for washing one's bottom, toilet paper being almost unknown on the sub-continent. The other was a simple washroom with a drain in the centre of the floor and a bucket from which jugs of water are taken to pour over the body—an economical but effective method of taking a bath. The downstairs living quarters consisted of three connecting rooms, filled mainly with charpoys—the string beds which serve as sofas by day and beds at night, the bedding being stored in a separate place.

The family was small by Pakistani standards, just five persons; my widowed hostess, her aged mother, her son and his wife—shortly expecting her first child; and one remaining daughter who had just finished high school. Only the young people spoke any English, but everyone did their best to make me feel welcome. Water was heated for my bucket bath, tea was made and an egg cooked. The egg was important, a symbol of respect and friendship, though I did not know this at the time. My clothes were washed for me in a modern washing machine. This was part of the young wife's dowry and she was very proud of it and glad of an opportunity to show it off. While we drank tea, neighbours kept popping in—Moslem women mainly whom I was told had come to see 'the brave English Memsahib' travelling alone by bicycle. Apparently they had read the article which the journalist at Karachi airport had written about my trip and were pleased that I had visited their town. The young people had a copy of the newspaper and they cut out the article and wrapped it in cellophane for me to keep.

When all the visitors had finally departed, the two young women cooked the simple evening meal of rice, vegetables and *dal*—a kind of thick lentil soup. They squatted at their floor-level burners, their bottoms supported on very low stools. There was no dining table, and we all ate in separate corners, using bits of chapatti to pick up the food. I was not very good at this and was given a spoon. We spent the rest of the evening talking about life in Pakistan. Paul, the son, tried to explain just how frustrating life could be there, particularly for Christians in a small town. A dreadful sense of incarceration is unavoidable for the women, for they cannot go out alone even to shop without fear of harassment. Paul, as the only male in the household, has to escort them wherever they need to go, and this of course places quite a burden on him and his work suffers in consequence. My hostess goes out when her services as a midwife are required, but then some sort of conveyance and an escort are always sent to fetch her. Paul had wanted to do further studies after school but says that Christians always come at the bottom of the list for university places. I asked how the authorities know if a person is a Christian. This I was told was obvious because of the names. Most of the conversions to Christianity occurred in the last century amongst Hindus of the untouchable caste. The converts adopted new surnames along with the new faith—the names were mostly those of the missionaries who converted them. So a Christian is immediately known, even on a form. Paul now fears that his sister will not obtain a place at medical school even though her high school grades are very good. Everywhere I went I heard similar stories. I had no way of knowing of course whether they were true or were engendered by feelings of insecurity commonly experienced by minority groups. What did seem apparent though was the greater degree of freedom enjoyed by Christian women in the home, compared with Moslem women. I was impressed also by the way they stuck to their faith and practised it; for often they were as much as 50 miles from the nearest church and saw fellow Christians very seldom, sometimes receiving only a yearly visit from a priest.

We talked about my travels and they confirmed what the Bishop had said about dacoit activity in those parts. They said that because many of the dacoits have relations in the police force they are rarely caught. Also raids mainly occur at nights and the police will not investigate until the following morning, by which time the bandits are well away. The general feeling was that I would not make a likely target, especially if I did not travel at night, for the dacoits would wish to avoid the extra fuss which a disappearing European would generate.

I was allowed to choose where I would sleep. Pakistanis are companionable and Granny, my hostess and her daughter all slept together in the innermost room with the door firmly shut against the night air and the mosquitoes. They kindly invited me to share with them. The alternative, which I accepted with alacrity, was the outer room with just a metal grille to keep out intruders and otherwise open to the stars and the soft night air.

The following morning dawned fresh and cool. I was away early after a comfortable night on a charpoy disturbed only by the mosquitoes and the mullahs' calls to early morning prayer. These calls are alas relayed, not by romantic figures on tall minarets, but by badly aligned loudspeakers which blast one rudely awake while it is still dark. The policy is to leave no area of habitation undisturbed. The resulting cacophony of distorted, overlapping sound is quite the most awful noise I have heard in my life, and not at all conducive to a religious frame of mind.

There were only 45 miles to cover to the next 'safe house', and I had ridden about 20 of them when my back tyre punctured. Before I had time to more than register the fact, the driver of a donkey cart drew up and made motions of loading my bicycle onto his cart. I suppose he meant to take me to a place where it could be mended. I shook my head and did a little mime to show him that I would do it myself. He then beckoned for me to follow him and led me to a canal which ran parallel to the road, a little way off. Together we hauled the cycle up the sandy slope to the top of the embankment. It was an ideal spot for a puncture repair, water at hand, shady trees overhead and well away from curious truck drivers. I hoped that the donkey cart driver would now go away and leave me in peace. He did, but first asked for a cigarette. Since I had none to give him, I offered him a rupee instead. He seemed quite delighted with that.

Having mended the puncture, I spent a pleasant half hour writing in my journal. Lovely iridescent green parrots with enormously long tail feathers were flying to and fro between the trees overhead, and well tended fields stretched away to the horizon. Fifty years ago most of this part was nearly all desert. That was before the British built the barrage across the Indus River, at Sukkur, beginning the biggest irrigation scheme in

44

the world. Since then Pakistan has enlarged and developed the system, gradually reclaiming more and more desert land. The other bank of the canal was a well-maintained road for local traffic. Along it bowled a procession of ox carts looking exactly like the pottery ones I had seen in the museum from the Mohenjodaro site. The carts had great solid wooden wheels and looked immensely heavy. They were pulled by two magnificent brahmin oxen with wide-spread horns and great swinging dewlaps. One of the carts stopped just opposite me. The driver alighted, salaamed politely and then squatted down, staring. He stared at me, without moving, for 10 minutes, after which, quite unnerved, I pushed the bike back to the road.

I had not ridden far when I was hailed in English from a wayside cafe:

'Come in here and rest.'

Intrigued, I rode in to be greeted by three brothers who owned the cafe. The one who had hailed me had worked for some years in the hotel trade in England and was, he said, happy to welcome an English traveller to his 'hotel'. I was ushered with much ceremony onto a charpoy—the man who had been sitting there being peremptorily removed. A meal of potatoes, peas and chapattis was brought and I was even given a spoon to eat with. While I ate, the English-speaking brother plied me with questions about myself and my journey. I produced my Urdu press cutting which he read aloud to his brothers and to the village males who had by now assembled in great numbers. The other brothers sat on the charpoy with me, pressing me to more peas and potatoes while the English-speaking one thought of more questions to ask and pass on to the audience.

When I could eat no more, I was taken on a tour of the cafe and given a demonstration of chapatti-making. The boy who made them was very proud to have such a large audience, for of course all the village males had joined in the tour. He produced two fine chapattis which were formally presented to me for eating later. I always did enjoy watching chapattis being made; the dough is already worked, a small piece of it is taken, rolled quickly into a ball and then slapped rapidly from hand to hand until it becomes a thin perfect circle. It is then stuck onto the inside of a pre-heated, cylindrical clay oven, or in the home is cooked on an iron griddle. The result is delicious eaten hot, but rather leathery when cold. The whole process looks effortless but is not, as I found when invited to try.

When the tour was over, I was asked if I would care to rest now, out of the sun. But I declined and said that I must go, because anything less restful than being watched by the solid phalanx of village males I could not imagine. Also in spite of my much repeated Urdu phrase about not touching the bicycle, these men were unable to resist the temptation to fiddle with it. Already the foam handlebar padding had holes in it where it had been scratched away to see what was underneath. The brothers refused to accept any payment for the meal and warmed by their kindness I rode on.

The last part of the ride was not so good. The sun grew very hot and the continuous horn-blaring of the trucks gave me a headache. Importunate cyclists kept trying to ride alongside to ask silly questions, like was it beer or whisky that I carried in my water bottles—accompanying their questions with suggestive leers. I raced away from them, one after another, until one of them proved too able. He played the game of overtaking, dropping back and overtaking again until my patience was quite exhausted and I was snarling at him. Quite useless, of course, it made no difference and he kept it up until I reached the town where I was to spend the night.

A male nurse was my host here. He lived with his extended family in a house similar to that of the previous evening, but much larger and built around three courtyards. I counted 28 members of the household, from a new little baby of a few weeks, to an aged great-grandmother. Kingpin of the household was my host's mother. To be a mother-in-law in this part of the world is to be in a position of power, often the only power a woman can enjoy—though this is more particularly true for Moslem women. For when a son marries he brings his wife to live in the parental home and she becomes subject to his mother (to his brothers, too, if it is a Moslem household). In

46

arranged marriages, the nature of the mother-in-law is therefore of great importance to the bride for if she is not kind, she
can make the poor girl's life a misery. A wife's main aim is to
have sons so that she too will one day be a mother-in-law.
There was no doubt about who ruled this household. A bevy
of young women and teenage girls were kept continuously
busy, washing clothes, cooking, and cleaning, while my
host's mother sat in state directing the operations like a
general. The most adored member of the household was the
little baby who was the first child of my host. His name meant
moon; he had rings on his fingers, bracelets on his wrists and
ankles and his eyes were outlined in kohl. Not for a second was
he allowed to cry, the merest whimper and he was picked up
and played with by Grandma.

After being shown where to bathe, my clothes were taken
away for washing and Grandma directed that I should be given
a shalwar and kamise to wear. This is Pakistani dress consisting of very baggy trousers and a long close-fitting tunic top. A
long scarf is worn with it, draped to conceal the line of the
bosom, with the ends thrown back over the shoulders. In
practice the scarf falls off all the time as one leans forward,
which one is always doing because tables, including dining
tables, are always lower than seats. There is a constant flow of
provocative gestures as scarf ends are thrown back over
shoulders. The scarf can also be worn over the head and across
the face at need, as when men are present. I can't say I enjoyed
wearing this costume which seemed so baggy and at the same
time so constricting, but the neighbours who came in to view
during the evening were delighted to find me dressed in their
national costume.

I was given a large bedroom to myself, in which there was a
double bed with European springing rather than the usual
string. I hoped I was not putting too many people out. It was a
disturbed night full of the noise of crying babies, wailing
mullahs and buzzing mosquitoes.

In the morning I could not get away until quite late as the
family slept in, it being the Moslem sabbath and I could not
find my clothes. When I did track them down they were still

47

wet. I asked if I could iron them dry but my host wouldn't hear of it.

'It is their work,' he said, meaning the young girls.

Nor was I allowed to leave before being served breakfast. A boy had been sent out to buy a loaf of European style sliced bread. The whole loaf was fried and set before me, together with two fried eggs and a huge pewter pot of 'mixed tea'. I felt incapable of eating anything that morning having been pressed to so much more food than I normally eat, the night before. Fortunately I was served alone in the bedroom and so was able to secrete some away to dispose of later. When I was packed and ready to go, the whole family lined up to shake my hand and wave goodbye. A neighbour's boy was summoned to escort me on his bike through the town.

5

Having not been able to get away until 10 o'clock, the sun was already high and it was very hot. As the day wore on it became hotter and hotter. In spite of it being the Moslem sabbath, there was no noticeable lessening in the traffic flow. To make matters worse, the road in many places was under repair. This meant long detours along dirt tracks, where the amount of dust thrown up was truly frightful and made breathing a conscious effort.

My next objective was a remote farm about 50 miles away and difficult to find. My instructions were to make for a certain village, then go half a mile beyond it to a bus stop and then ask the way. So far, I had found the best method of 'asking' was simply to show the address on my letter to the first kindly looking man I saw when I got to the town or village. Failing that, petrol stations were always a good place to go for help because there was always someone there who spoke English. The only trouble about filling stations, if it could be called a trouble, was that they were so hospitable that they would not let me continue on my way until I had accepted a cup of tea. This, together with the accompanying conversation, could take up a considerable amount of time, so if I was in a hurry I had to avoid petrol stations.

The particular hurry today was for this stage simply to come to an end. There was no pleasure in riding through the continuous dust and fumes, having to watch the road surface the whole time to avoid the innumerable potholes and other hazards. In addition, I was harassed by two rude cyclists who caught up with me and rode alongside giggling and staring.

After about half an hour of this I could bear it no longer and tried to wave them away. This had no effect at all. I finished up screaming at them and threatening them with the police. I don't think the screaming bothered them but the threat about police appeared to have an effect and they moved off reluctantly.

I was beginning to feel like a dancing bear or a performing monkey with all this unwanted attention. It was difficult to equate the rudeness with the natural kindliness of the people. They didn't set out to be nasty, and apart from a few incidents which were to happen later, I never felt that there was any malice in their behaviour. It was just that they lacked the imagination to appreciate other people's feelings, or to respect their privacy. Anyway, the result of all the aggravation, the heat, dust and potholes, was that by the time I reached the place where I had to enquire for the farm of 'Bardur the Christian Man', I was already in a fairly fraught state.

I had found the village and then the bus stop beyond with its little wayside cafe and started to show my letter to ask where Bardur might be found; but it just didn't go well. There were lots of men there of a rather rough type who seemed to understand neither my English nor my Urdu. They crowded around me pushing and prodding me until I could stand it no longer, and pushed my way out of the crowd. I stood some way off shaking with tears of anger and frustration. I no longer cared whether I found the house or not. I just wanted to get away from men. To do them credit, I think they realized that they had upset me and were sorry, because they didn't attempt to come after me. I was pulling myself together and deciding to ride on to Sukkur, when a man on a motorcycle stopped beside me. Quite a different sort of man, gentle and kindly looking. He spoke the name of my intended host and courteously beckoned for me to follow him. So I realized that the other men had found someone who knew the house I was looking for and that he was going to take me there. We went a long way down unrideable sandy tracks, across drains, irrigation canals and fields until my over-stimulated imagination began to wonder if I was after all quite safe. We stopped before

I could become really worried. I couldn't see any sign of a house. My guide began to call, a long musical call with a rising note at its ending. There was no answer but after a short wait a man appeared hurrying towards us. 'Bardur, Christian man,' said my guide, the first words he had spoken to me since leaving the road.

The two men spoke together and I handed Bardur the letter which my last night's host had written. Bardur turned it over a few times without opening it, and I realized he could not read. After a second he passed it to my guide who opened it and read it to him. The letter was then handed back to Bardur and my guide salaamed to us both and went back the way we had come. Bardur turned to me and shook my hand, then picking up the cycle he wheeled it off through the field while I followed behind.

We soon reached the place where Bardur lived and for the next 16 hours I could have imagined myself to have strayed back hundreds of years in time. Apart from my bicycle there was nothing of the 20th century in that place. We entered through a narrow gap in a mud brick wall plastered over with cow dung and painted a dull ochre colour. Inside, tethered close to the gap, was a fierce guard dog. Bardur placed himself between me and the snarling dog as we passed through. I now found myself in a large compound, full of animals. In the centre 10 oxen and 10 buffalo cows were tethered around a manger. In one corner were two camels, in another, several goats. Dogs and chickens ran about everywhere. Along one wall were open-sided animal shelters with thatched roofs. Opening off this compound was a smaller enclosure with a beaten-earth floor; around three sides were archways to the family's living quarters. In the courtyard were two clay-built cooking places, a pump and two enormous clay amphorae for storing grain.

There were a bewildering number of people around, looking as if they felt as shy of me as I did of them. No one seemed quite to know what to do with me. Then one woman came over and touched the small leather cross which I wore and said 'Sister'. I didn't know if she was greeting me as a fellow

Christian or deciding that I was some sort of travelling missionary. It didn't matter either way, for it broke the awkwardness and soon everybody was smiling and busily pulling up chairs, making tea and cooking the welcoming egg—chillied this time. The smaller children, of whom there were about a dozen, still stood around, wide-eyed and solemn, so I distributed the rest of the Begum's toffees among them and soon they too had lost their shyness and the smaller ones were clambering onto my lap to see if I had any more.

The family appeared to consist of four able-bodied men, their wives and their children; about two dozen people in all. What the various relationships of people to one another were I never did discover. No one spoke any English at all (apart from the one word 'Sister') so all communication had to be through mime. As everybody found everyone else's attempts at this hilariously funny, we spent most of the time laughing.

Soon people were back at the tasks that my arrival had interrupted and I was busy with my camera taking photographs of age-old pursuits. One beautiful teenage girl was spinning wool at a large rough spinning wheel, another was winnowing rice, tossing it up from a flat wicker basket for the wind to blow the husks away. One woman was scouring handleless cooking pots with ashes from one of the fireplaces. Two women were washing the small children under the pump, the children protesting loudly. The men wandered in and out smoking a huge hookah pipe. As one man finished a task, he would take up the pipe, puff away for a few minutes and then pass it to another while he wandered off to do something else. They found my interest in their pursuits very funny and kept indicating different things for me to photograph. After a while, I wanted badly to go to the lavatory and discovered to my consternation that there wasn't one. The children went into the outer courtyard to pee and for more serious matters they were escorted outside to the great outdoors which is the only form of sanitation for most of the sub-continent. I had no objection to using the great outdoors as long as I could be assured of privacy. So far on the trip, the necessary privacy had been entirely lacking, so I had got into

52

the habit of not going at all between leaving one house and arriving at the next. This was really no hardship because I was losing such a lot of fluid through perspiration in the hot, dry atmosphere. Up till now though, there had always been a lavatory available on arrival. I tried several times to slip away into the fields, but each time one or two of the women would come after me and courteously but firmly lead me back to the inner courtyard. Women obviously didn't go out on their own here either. I was beginning to get desperate; I didn't see how I could mime something so indelicate and my helpful Urdu phrases didn't include this need. Then to my great relief the women decided to go all together into the fields to gather vegetables and they took me with them. This was my opportunity. I tried to slip off unnoticed behind some tall sugarcane, but before I had gone more than a few yards, one of the women caught me up and took my hand. Necessity came to my aid at this point; I released my hand, and darted off at great speed into the sugarcane calling 'Wait there' over my shoulder as I went. From the shouted conversation and the laughter behind me, I gathered that they had understood what I was about. When I re-emerged the woman was still there waiting to take me back to the others.

Back in the compound, preparations began for the evening meal. One of the bigger boys caught a scrawny little chicken and brought it over to where I was sitting. He drew his finger across its neck in an unmistakable gesture. I thought for a moment that he was teasing me, but then realized that he was showing me that it was to be killed for a meal in my honour. I was very touched by this, for these were poor people, very poor by our standards. My presence even for so short a time put an extra burden on their slender resources. In no way could I repay their hospitality, to try to do so would insult them; yet they never let me feel that my visit was anything other than an honour and a pleasure.

As soon as it began to get dark, the boys became busy dragging in piles of thin branches for firewood. The men closed the gap in the wall of the outer enclosure with a mound of sharply spiked bushes. The animals were led off into their open-sided shelters and tethered with thick chains. By the time all these tasks were over it was quite dark. The boys had lit a big fire in the inner compound, more to supplement the dim light of the paraffin hurricane lamps than for warmth. The meal was now ready and everyone sat around in little groups on the ground eating. I was served at a little table on my own. The meal was mainly rice and chapattis with a small amount of vegetables, their identity almost disguised by chilli powder. The little chicken passed almost unnoticed among so many.

After the meal, preparations were made for a religious service. Firstly Bardur came out with a book which he brought over to me. He pointed several times to my cross and then to the book, I think to show me that the book was a bible. My chair and table were then carried into one of the rooms and I was made to sit there with the rest of the people sitting cross-legged in rows on the ground facing me. For some long worrying moments, I wondered what I was supposed to do in this elevated position. I needn't have worried, all I had to do was to watch, which was no hardship for it was quite riveting. The service was sung throughout, tunefully and with great conviction; the musical accompaniment being provided by a narrow-necked, broad-bellied clay pot (which made a low-pitched, resonant drum) and long, flat metal tongs on which a complementary rhythm was played in a higher key. During the service the dogs set up a tremendous din and camel bells sounded quite near. Everyone fell silent while the men went off to investigate. I was reminded that this was dacoit territory where people have to be on the alert. The disturbance proved to be a false alarm and the service continued.

After the service the children were put to bed. The fathers sat on the charpoys with them talking quietly, until one by one the children dropped off to sleep. Then the adults drifted off into various rooms. I was taken into a little room which had four charpoys head to tail around the walls, several children were asleep in three of them. The larger male children were hauled out and sent off to sleep elsewhere—perhaps with the men. The women climbed in beside the remaining children and I had a charpoy to myself. The solitary storm lantern was left burning all night. I fell asleep while I was still wondering how I could sleep in a room with so many people. I slept well and was only disturbed once or twice in the night by people throwing things at a cat which had got in through the blanket hung over the doorway and was exploring the shelves above my head. This was my first night in Pakistan that was free from the loudspeakers of the mullahs.

Everyone was up at first light and about the morning tasks: milking the buffalo cows, sweeping the compound, collecting dung and shaping it into flat cakes for fuel, kneading dough for chapattis, churning the milk.

When the time came for me to leave, there was a reluctance on both sides—they didn't want me to go and I would have liked to stay and learn more about their lives, but to do that I would have needed to speak their language. All the women came out into the fields to see me depart, there was a long embrace from each of them and then I went with Bardur down the sandy track, back to the highway and the 20th century.

Riding along with my head full of thoughts about the farm and its people, I wasn't at first aware of all the police activity going on around me. Then I began to notice the long lines of lorries and camel carts, all pulled into the side of the road, with their loads (mainly stacks of sugarcane) being examined by policemen. I wasn't even sure if it was policemen doing the inspecting at first since both the police and the army dress in khaki. I wondered vaguely what they were looking for. I began to be aware of one policeman in particular, who carried a wicked looking stick and kept passing and repassing in a little van full of civilians. Then the same policeman, still carrying his menacing stick, began passing on the back of a small motorcycle. Each time he passed he saluted me and smiled and I began to wonder if I had been given an escort, and if so, who had ordered it. Hour after hour the policeman stayed with me, riding ahead, waiting for me to pass and then overtaking. If I stopped for anything, back he would come, stopping a little way away, never actually approaching me; it was just a trifle unnerving. It was useful though, too, because none of the usual teasing cyclists or motorcyclists was allowed to bother me, but were waved off by my escort the moment they showed any interest in me. At midday I rode into a wayside cafe to get something to eat. The policeman followed me in and cleared away all the males from around me, so for once I ate in peace.

During the afternoon the guard was changed. The first I knew of it was when a young policeman came roaring up on a motorbike, calling 'Good noon, good noon, I am new guard.' I hoped I would now find out who it was who had decided to provide me with a police escort and I asked the young man, but his English could not cope with this question, so instead I asked more widely 'Why guard?'

'For safety of body,' he replied. 'Pakistan very bad country.'

I could get no further information from him, though he rode beside me, practising his English, all the way to the outskirts of Sukkur. Here he disappeared and I was picked up by two intelligent young boys riding on a bicycle so new that it still had the factory's brown paper wrapping on it. The boys rode with me asking me many questions which would be considered rude if asked by boys in England, such as:

'What you come Sukkur for?' 'How old are you?' 'What is your caste?' 'You have got husband?'

Such cross-examinations feel rude even in Pakistan, but I'm sure they are not intended that way; everyone has great curiosity, especially about Westerners. I'm not sure that many of them would consider that it was possible to be rude to a woman, anyway. My two young Moslems were really very sweet, and kindly led me to where I wished to go in spite of my irritation over the questioning. They could not resist one final question, though. When I told them it was St Saviour's Church I was looking for, they led me first to a mosque and said:

'Very fine mosque this, why for you want go Saviour's Church?'

6

If I had thought that Karachi was a difficult place for a woman to be on her own, that was because I hadn't yet been to Sukkur. For the lone female Sukkur was a total 'no go' area and marked one of the low points of the journey. It had started well enough; I had been lent a flat, through the good offices of the Bishop, in a splendid decaying mansion left over from the days of the British Raj. Built on the top of the only high ground there, so as to catch every breeze that might be blowing in the sweltering heat, it was a cool and pleasant place. From its flat roof the Indus River could be glimpsed, with the great barrage built by the British to divert the waters for irrigation, spanning its colossal width. Close to the mansion, where once had been lawns and gardens, mean little houses had sprung up and intimate glimpses into Moslem domestic life were not only possible, but difficult to avoid. Most of the work of these households took place in the open courtyards and the young women seemed to be kept on the go the whole day, spurred on with frequent blows from their menfolk and mothers-in-law. Such an astonishing number of people lived in each tiny house that any sort of privacy must have been impossible.

Privacy was what I was now delighting in. Although I had only been a week on the journey so far, I felt worn out with the constant effort of struggling with language difficulties, making polite conversation at night and attempting to rid myself of the male followers by day. Within a couple of hours I felt a new person. With unlimited hot water to hand, I luxuriated in feeling free of dust and sand for the first time in days. I washed everything I could, cycle, clothes, pannier bags, and shook the dust out of everything that couldn't be washed. Just to unpack and arrange my few possessions on a shelf gave me enormous pleasure and seemed the height of gracious living.

That evening I was invited to dinner with a couple from the adjoining apartment. They were Australian medical missionaries who were doing an intensive language course before taking up duties in remote villages. Like all the missionaries I met in Pakistan, they dressed in native costume and kept as low a profile as possible, the wife hardly ever going out alone and the husband doing all the shopping that they needed. They said that they found it a hard, claustrophobic existence and they seemed to be in a constant state of fear that they might be suddenly expelled from the country.

Very early the following morning, I set out by train in a first-class, ladies-only compartment, for the 80-mile journey to Mohenjodaro, the ancient city, discovered only in this century, but thought to be contemporary with the earliest civilizations of all. It was an interesting carriage that had seen better days. The seats were benches arranged lengthways around the sides and down the centre. The padding, which must once have rendered them tolerably comfortable, was of horsehair which had now assumed interesting contours of bumps and hollows. Where not filled by quantities of sand, the hollows contained pools of water. As it had not rained recently, I could only conclude that these pools were left by an altogether unsuccessful attempt to clean the carriage.

I had it entirely to myself, for no other woman appeared and each time a man tried to enter, I told him firmly (as previously instructed by the helpful guard) that this was 'Ladies Only Carriage'; at which the poor fellow would retire, visibly discomfited, as though caught in a shameful act. None of the windows bore much relation to their frames; many were missing altogether and there were great gaps between the planking, so that when the train moved off, more and more sand filtered into the carriage, covering everything and making great drifts upon the floor—it would have made a lovely playground for small children. The bright spot of the journey was the guard, who appeared at one of the windowless apertures each time the train stopped at a station, which was about every 10 minutes, to ask me if I was all right and if there was anything I wanted, such as a cup of tea. Once he presented me with a pear, grown, he said proudly, on that very platform. Each tiny station had at least two or three tea stalls, which also sold a variety of fly-blown sweetmeats. I couldn't think why there were so many stations, since the countryside was mainly desert and very sparsely inhabited. In about two hours, the 60-mile journey to Larkana was completed; not bad going, considering the number of stops and the condition of the rolling stock.

From Larkana I had to take a bus for the next stage: this was an awful journey, squashed into the tiniest of spaces between inquisitive men, who constantly trampled upon my feet and kept up a continuous assault of sly pokes and pinches. At one stage I counted more than 70 passengers in a space designed for 30. The heat and smell inside the bus were quite overpowering, never have I been so relieved to end a journey. The final few miles were travelled in a two-wheeled, horse-drawn gharry; equally compressed, but at least in the fresh air.

Mohenjodaro when reached at last was something of an anti-climax. It was certainly impressive, if only for the extent of what had been uncovered; and I gathered that at least as much again was awaiting excavation. Impressive too were the facts related to me by the guide, about the banking houses, drains, weights and measures and other modern amenities which this city had enjoyed so many thousand years ago. But what was actually to be seen was just a few courses of unremarkable, dusty bricks: mile after mile of neat, low walls, enclosing rectangles of sand. More sand stretched away for the half mile down to the Indus, and try as I might I could conjure up no picture in my mind of what this once prosperous city and its people might have been like. Feeling that I had learnt more about the place from looking at the artefacts and ornaments in the Karachi museum, I retraced my steps to Sukkur.

While I was shopping in the bazaar that afternoon, a young man rode close to me on his bicycle and struck me hard across the face with his hand. I was wearing my hat and had my eyes down, so there was no warning. He obviously didn't want to rob me, but was punishing me for being a woman out alone; fro.n the brief glimpse I had of him, he seemed little more than a boy. There were lots of men around when it happened, but no one reacted or appeared to notice. I hurried back to the flat very upset by the cowardliness and pointlessness of the attack. When I told the missionaries about it, one of them—a young Scottish mother, said that she had suffered a similar attack in much the same way, but that her assailant had straight afterwards crashed his bicycle into a barrow of fruit, and she had then belaboured him with her shopping bag. If it was the same young man, he had been practising his riding since.

After this I felt very reluctant to leave the flat, but the necessity of getting some more money from the bank forced me out the following afternoon. I took my Swiss army penknife with me, open in my pocket; not that I thought it would prove much use in the event of a determined attack—I wouldn't have known how to use it as a weapon anyway—but just having it gave me confidence and I think I had a vague idea that if I waved it about in a threatening sort of way, it might put off a would-be aggressor. It worked, too. Several times on the walk to the bank, groups of youths made threatening gestures towards me, but when I took the knife out of my pocket and just held it in my hand they backed away. It was not a pleasant feeling though to have to be so aggressive and on my guard the whole time.

The bank did little to dispel my growing antipathy to the men of Sukkur. I had to wait while they tried to book a call to their head office in Karachi, for they had lost their copy of my encashment order and could give me no money without it. The clerks seemed to find it a huge joke that a woman should be in the bank at all. They kept snatching up my passport and other documents from the manager's desk and shouting out details about me to one another across the room, amid hoots of laughter. Finally I was stung into making a protest to the effect that though they might treat their women how they liked, I was not a Moslem woman and as a customer of the bank, I was entitled to some courtesy. I also told them the sort of impression I had gained of their town and of how eager I was to leave it, in fact, I said, if they couldn't find the encashment order, it didn't matter in the least, I had travellers' cheques and could cash those anywhere. My flash of temper brought immediate results, all was now respect, to the point of obsequiousness—'Please have a chair, Memsahib', 'A cup of tea? No? A cold drink perhaps?' The atmosphere was tense with the desire to please. By the time I left we were all the best of friends. It did seem sad though that even in a bank a woman could not be treated with normal courtesy, without first showing fight.

As I was struggling to cover the 120 miles which separated me from the next safe house, I heard the most enormous report, like a lorry tyre blowing out. It took me several moments to realize that the noise had come from the back wheel of the bicycle and that the tyre had parted company with the rim. When it happened, I was on the outskirts of one of the many staging posts which occur along the highway, to cater to the needs of bus travellers. In Pakistan people travel by bus a great deal and as these buses can hardly be called comfortable (as I had discovered), frequent stops were necessary. Psychedelic buses, each vying with the next in richness of embellishments—the more opulent the effect, the better the custom— were parked in great numbers on the rutted, rubbish-strewn ground flanking the road. Among them wandered the bus touts and gangs of small boys hawking a variety of fruits and sweets, all shouting their wares at the tops of their voices. Behind the buses were a straggle of garages, cafes, shops and stalls. As there were never any toilets (at least I never discovered any), passengers used any convenient wall or squatted among the debris. Flies were everywhere and the heat produced a shimmering, mirage-like effect over the scene.

I looked around for some shade in which to make my repairs. Across the road was a garage where a friendly proprietor invited me to use a small storeroom in the forecourt. By the time I wheeled the bicycle inside and turned it upside down, a large crowd of men and boys had collected in the doorway to watch. From their rapt attention, I might have been giving a Punch and Judy show rather than doing a prosaic tyre change; they were a pleasant crowd though, and if any boy ventured to come too close, the others would haul him back so that I had enough space to work—how different from the louts I had encountered in Sukkur. When I had changed the tyre and tube, I gave the old ones to the small boys, for the inner tube had such an enormous hole in it that it was impossible to patch. The tyre had about six inches of wire ripped right out of its rim and was certainly beyond my powers to repair. I decided that the blow-out was probably caused by the anti-puncture plastic tape which I was using for the first time (subsequently, I heard that other cyclists who had used this tape had also experienced dramatic blow-outs) so I gave this to the small boys also and they found that it made rather a good skipping rope, which was some consolation. The loss of the inner tube didn't worry me as I had another spare one, but the loss of the tyre was serious; there were 700 miles to go to Lahore, where the first of the tyres had been sent. With such rough roads tyres wore out quickly.

As soon as the cycle was together again and the tools packed away, someone brought water in a basin for me to wash my hands. After this I was borne off to the adjacent café for a glass of tea. The whole crowd seemed bent on doing anything they could for me. 'You have only to ask, Memsahib. It is good that you are come.' I didn't understand the reason for their friendliness, any more than I had understood the hostility in Sukkur, I just accepted it gratefully. While I was drinking tea and answering questions about the journey, the broken tyre was brought back, the wire stitched into place and covered with a canvas patch. I was amazed by such care and kindness and everyone was delighted by my evident pleasure. The old man who had made the repair was brought over to shake my hand, but he refused to accept any payment for his work. I rode off with my ideas about Pakistani men turned inside out again.

I had further need of assistance before the day was out, for my map was not accurate and the turnoff to the town I was heading for was not where it should have been. I was very tired too, having come over 100 miles in temperatures approaching 90°F and there was only about another hour of daylight left. I looked around for someone to consult about the route, but there were no filling stations or villages around as I was on a particularly lonely stretch of road. I began to feel worried about getting to shelter before darkness fell: all the dire warnings had made me extremely nervous about being out after dark. Then I saw a tractor turn onto the road from the fields ahead. I raced to overtake it and see what I thought of the men who were riding in it. There were two of them and they seemed decent, for at least they didn't catcall or leer at me, so I decided to risk it and shouted to them over the noise of the engine. The driver stopped the tractor and got down. By good fortune I had found someone who spoke English. When I showed him the address on my letter of introduction, he said that it was in the town where he lived, so I could follow him and he would take me there. He was a most courteous man, who told me that having approached him for help, it was now his duty to see me to safety. This seemed rather a novel attitude but it was nice to have someone so concerned for my safety and comfort—he kept stopping every mile or so to make sure that I was keeping up or to ask if I would change my mind and ride in the trailer. When we came to the hospital where I was to find the address of my hostess, a nursing sister called Zarina, and a relative of the first family I stayed with, he still did not consider his duty completed, but insisted that he accompany me to the house. Only when Sister Zarina had read the letter and welcomed me in, would he depart. I was very impressed.

Sister Zarina's house was minute, and consisted of just two tiny rooms, a small kitchen, washroom and toilet. She, her husband and two small sons slept in one room; two other nurses from the hospital shared the other. There was just space to squeeze an extra charpoy between the nurses' beds for me to sleep on. In such a congested household, I thought that they would be relieved that I proposed to stay only one night. Not at all, no sooner had the welcoming egg been served, than plans were being made about how I should be shown the town and whom I should be taken to visit. An itinerary was being worked out that would take at least a week. I tried to explain that my time was limited and that I had a very long way to go (in any case I was always reluctant to spend more than one night with people of such slender resources because of the added burden it placed upon them), but they just smiled and said, 'You must stay, Ilyas will insist.' Ilyas appeared while we were eating supper. He was Zarina's brother, a merchant seaman home on leave. Whether it was because of his comparatively greater earning capacity, or because he was the only brother to six sisters, something gave him the ability to get his own way. I found myself agreeing to spend the next day being escorted by him around the sights of the town, and from his air of determination I rather thought it might prove difficult to get away even after that.

A Lever Brothers factory producing soap and cooking oil is not what I would have chosen to visit anywhere, and certainly not in the Exotic East, but this is what Ilyas had arranged so I did my best to show an intelligent interest as we processed through the seemingly endless halls and galleries. The best thing was the fleet of camel carts but I saw these only incidentally and no one offered me a ride on one, which I'm sure I would have enjoyed. Straight from the factory, we went on to the hospital, a grim, insanitary place with patients and visitors spitting copiously all over the floors—no wonder they have so much T.B. After a mercifully brief tour of the hospital it was back to the house for lunch and photographs. For these I was dressed in my hostess's wedding clothes—shalwar and kamise made of a lovely diaphanous material in red and silver. I had to wear the waistband of the trousers around my thighs as I was so much taller than Zarina. Hardly a pause and we were off again visiting friends and acquaintances. In search of one of these, we motorcycled out of town to a farm, where the sugarcane harvest was in full swing. Two blindfolded oxen were walking around and around in a circle, driving a press. Great, flat metal dishes were filled with the resulting syrup and slowly boiled until it turned into raw sugar. We continued visiting until after dark and returned to Zarina's house with my head bursting from so many different impressions and so exhausted that I was unable to argue when Ilyas started planning the following day's programme.

I awoke the following day wondering how, if ever, I was going to get away. It seemed ungrateful, but I was longing not only to continue my journey but also to be on my own. Since my arrival about 40 hours previously, I had hardly spend a minute alone. In those cramped quarters and with Ilyas constantly in attendance, it just wasn't possible. Directly after breakfast another day of whirlwind meetings would begin, there was no way I could avoid it. Something intervened though. I don't know what it was, but at nine o'clock when we were due to set out, Ilyas appeared briefly to say that there was a delay, we would set out later. Good! that would at least give me some time to write letters and catch up with the journal. I wrote one letter, then another, and another. Ilyas appeared every so often to announce further delays; the little boys kept falling over my feet in their attempts to play in the tiny courtyard; my two sleeping companions, who were having the day off, had to squeeze past me every time they needed to go to another room. At 11.30 Ilyas came to announce what was for me the final delay. At that point I just had to get out and away. Calling out that I was just going to the post office and would not be long, I seized the bicycle (which was fortunately still packed, there having been no space or opportunity to unpack) and bolted. I had acted on the spur of the moment and knew that I should return and make my farewells properly. Instead I found myself cycling away as fast as I could, fearing that Ilyas would come after me on his motorcycle. Sadly, I realized I had met more than my match. Later I wrote making excuses for my precipitate departure, and I sent the little boys some good constructional toys, which wouldn't require too much space, but I didn't ever quite square the incident with my own conscience.

7

Perhaps it served me right for having bolted from male protection, for when I stopped at a small wayside halt to buy some things for lunch, I was mobbed by what appeared to be the entire population of a large boy's school. They were very intimidating and totally uninhibited boys. I fled with my goodies as fast as I could. Some of them, I could see, were preparing to give chase on their bicycles, so as soon as I had put some distance between myself and the village, I got off the road and, pushing the bicycle through scrub and thorn, I dropped down behind a bank, out of sight.

I now found that I had joined a mixed herd of sheep and goats which were grazing there. They took no notice of me, their whole attention being concentrated on the difficult task of getting enough to eat in that inhospitable terrain. The goats seemed to be browsing exclusively on the thorny trees, standing on their hind legs and stripping off leaves and branches as high as they could reach. The sheep had to make do with what they could find on the ground, which was precious little. They devoured with great gusto a banana skin which I offered them.

One after another, shepherds appeared and squatted on the ground in front of me. There were six of them ranging in age from two doe-eyed boys of 10 or 12, to some handsome 20-year-olds. Dressed for the most part in just a ragged pair of baggy trousers, they were nevertheless a graceful, good-looking lot. I was in no mood to appreciate their grace or physical charms though, as so often in Pakistan, I was on my guard, feeling pressured and rather scared. They started to address remarks to me in Punjabi, but I could only shake my head and say 'Angrezi'—English. They then tried Urdu, also to no avail; one of the smaller boys began to giggle but was frowned at by an older shepherd and quickly subsided. I got on with my lunch, offering pieces of orange all around; only the younger ones would accept, the older ones just went on sitting there, silently gazing. The only time they shifted their position was when the ebullient schoolboys, who must have seen me leave the road, came charging through the scrub to where we were. The shepherds rose to their feet, sticks in hand, and it was the turn of the schoolboys to run away. One of the shepherds caught up my plastic food container and made pulling gestures in the air, as though offering to milk an animal for me. I shook my head but he went off and brought it back brimming with milk—whether of sheep or goat I did not discover. In spite of my fear of contracting some dire disease, I could not offend such kind people by refusing to drink.

When I went back to the road to continue my journey, some of the schoolboys were still there with their bicycles. Only half a dozen or so now remained and such a small number was not at all intimidating, especially as they were riding two to a bicycle, which meant I could ride away easily from them at need. We all rode along together for a few miles, making simple conversation. They were interested in all things Western, as were most of the younger people in Pakistan. My bicycle particularly intrigued them, as gears and other modern refinements are almost never seen. Wherever I went, men would try to work out what the gears were for. Some decided that they were part of a motor and that the water bottles fixed to my down tube were the fuel tanks. Other men, whose interest in the West was more limited to the physical pleasures they were denied, were convinced that these same bottles contained forbidden delights, such as whisky or beer!

After my schoolboys had turned their bicycles back towards their village (and by that time I was fond enough of them to hope that they would not be in trouble for being late for their classes) I was free for the first time in days to spare some attention for my surroundings. Now that I was in the Punjab, I was passing through an entirely different landscape: miles of shallow pools linked by narrow strips of land on which palm trees grew. Long-legged wading birds walked slowly through the water, heads down, searching for food. Strings of oxen and water-buffalo wandered equally slowly across the ribbons of land. The pinks and blues of the sky reflected in the still water made it seem as if I was riding on the inside of an enormous delicate bubble.

As I had broken the chain of 'safe houses', I had now to decide where I should try to find shelter for the night. There was no possibility of an hotel in such remote parts, but the map indicated that there was a rest house in a small town ahead. Since I had not yet used the Consul's letter, requesting District Commissioners and their assistants to give me aid in booking rest houses, tonight seemed the ideal time to try it out. So arriving at the town, I made enquiries at the petrol station and was taken off with a bicycle escort, to the home of the Assistant District Commissioner. The Commissioner was out, but his wife, whose English was good, read my letter and assured me that there was plenty of room in the rest house and that her husband would take me there when he returned. In the meantime I must come in and have tea and a chat, as it was not often she had a chance to talk with an English woman. The tea did much to restore my dwindling frame. There were bananas, followed by rice pudding laced with carrot, rice sticks, English biscuits, and copious cups of tea. My hostess did not suffer from a dwindling frame—it was easy to see why. Feeling delightfully replete for the first time in a fortnight, I was taken for a tour of the house and grounds. I gathered that her husband had only just been given this position, and I think it must have been quite a step up for him because his wife was still radiant over their good fortune.

The house was a typical ex British Raj bungalow, built in a rambling style; high-ceilinged, to be as cool as possible in the terrible heat of summer, and depending upon an army of servants to keep it in good order. Even in labour-intensive Pakistan, armies of servants are no longer possible and the house looked as if even a major overhaul would come too late to save it. The grounds were extensive and traces of their former glory were still apparent here and there, in the careful landscaping, the almost obliterated tennis courts and overgrown flowerbeds. The stable block contained just one family of goats and a water-buffalo cow which provided milk and butter for the household. It was lucky that they had such a big garden, said my hostess, ideal for the animals to graze in.

The Commissioner returned while his wife and I were still strolling in the garden enjoying the cool of the evening. He wouldn't let me go to the rest house. I must stay with them, he said, though he added that he was very surprised to find a Western person fit to invite into his home. Rather taken aback, I asked him what he meant. They saw quite a lot of Western people travelling through, he said; young people mostly and they all behaved quite disgustingly. I gathered that this meant that they held hands in public—a practice totally abhorrent to Moslems who only hold hands with the same sex and consider any contact with women at all in public shocking in the extreme. I didn't attempt to tell him that Westerners find the constant hand holding and caressing that Moslem men do in public also rather odd, as I could see that he was a man of very definite opinions who would not take kindly to any implied criticism of his country's customs. Fortunately, he was called away after dinner which gave the rest of the family a chance to talk. The wife and her elder daughter, a young girl of 18 still at high school, were both very interested in politics, and wanted to know what people in England had thought about the hanging of Bhutto. Like many Pakistanis, they talked about Bhutto as though he was still there, in spite of acknowledging his death. Both women said they were 'passionate' for Bhutto and democracy. The husband being a government man had to like General Zia, but as they were not employed by the government, they could like whom they would. I asked if the daughter would go on to university after high school. That, I was told, would be for her future husband to decide. Very soon they would find a husband for her and she would then become his responsibility and he would consider whether he wanted her to go to university or not. I pointed out that this was hardly democracy. No, said the mother, maybe not, but it was their custom; the daughter's smile seemed to show that she happily concurred with this view.

When the Commissioner returned, preparations were made for bed. I was to have the daughter's room while she joined the two younger children in the parents' bedroom, which was also the living room. I demurred about putting them all out, but was told that Pakistani families prefer to sleep altogether and that the 12-year-old son always shared his mother's bed anyway, as he was nervous without her. 'We do not ever have sex in front of the children,' said the Commissioner. As it had not occurred to me that anyone should want to do this, I was not sure what response was expected. 'Never,' he repeated. 'It would be disgusting.' Perhaps he thought that we hand-holding English did do this and was attempting to educate me. I assured him that English people too would not wish to have sex in front of children, and that normally, children in England have their own bedrooms. But this he thought was cruel and bad for family life. I did wonder though how babies were conceived under the circumstances.

I was not sure whose guest I was the following night, as I was shared out among six families in a very poor part of a town, famous for its schools and colleges. I had been going to stay in the guest house of a nunnery and was looking forward to the peace and privacy that this promised, but when I arrived there I found that a service was in progress in the adjoining church. While waiting for the service to end and the sisters to emerge, several young Christians who had not attended the service struck up a conversation with me, and in their normal hospitable fashion, they hauled me off to meet their friends and relations. Once there it was not possible to move again without giving offence. Not that I wanted to anyway, for they were delightful people who had a lot to tell me about Pakistan; particularly about schools and teaching. They were all teachers, the women, too, which was unusual. Most of them were in their middle 20s and had two or three children, and each couple had a mother or elderly female relative to look after the children while they were at work. In spite of both parents working, their living standards were very low and their homes were poorer than any I had yet stayed in.

These dwellings were very small and opened off a narrow alley, down which ran an evil-smelling, open drain. Only one of the 20 houses in the alley had a lavatory and to get to that, one had to squeeze past a water-buffalo cow and her calf, whose tiny shelter was knee deep in droppings. Another house had a washroom. Whether all 20 homes shared these facilities, I did not discover. All the walls were built of unfired bricks which were fast crumbling away, so that everything was coated in a thick layer of dust. They were rented houses, which accounted for the general neglect and decay, I was told. Teachers could seldom hope to obtain posts near their homes because there were so few schools in Pakistan, so they had to find work where they could, and even then, wages were poor. They thought that standards of education were very low in Pakistan and that there was far too much rote-learning. The best schools were run by the missionaries, but few of these remained because some time ago they had been nationalized. Then the government, finding that this had not worked well, attempted to hand them back to the various missionary bodies, but many were reluctant to accept them because of their run-down condition. Most of the missionary schools now operating charged quite high fees and as a result contained more Moslem than Christian children. Some of my friends worked in missionary schools but most of them were in government ones.

During the course of the evening I must have met about 60 people, most of whom were teachers, all eager to exchange views about life in our respective countries. We talked far into the night and I left the following morning warmed by the good fellowship but very tired and permeated with the insidious dust of the place. Dust was everywhere on the road, too; it lay thickly on the bushes and trees at the verges and swirled up in choking clouds each time a vehicle passed. I longed to reach Multan and the good hotel I had been told of. The other attractions of Multan, famous shrines of Sufi saints and beautiful mosques, paled in comparison with thoughts of comfort, good food, privacy and lashings of hot water. Thinking about these delights sustained me as I ran the usual gauntlet of leers and cries of 'Hey baby, baby' from the passing trucks, and the inane remarks from the motorcyclists; one actually asked me what my bust size was!

I was to look back nostalgically to the heat and dust, as being almost ideal riding conditions compared with what was to come. For during the afternoon, within the space of half an hour, the sky filled with great towers of cloud; a violent wind suddenly lifted up the cycle with me on it and deposited us on the other side of the road—fortunately no truck was passing at that moment. Then the heavens opened and it rained and rained, in great blinding sheets. I had been told on the best authority, that whatever eventualities I needed to prepare for, rain was not among them. It never rained outside the monsoon period, my informant said, and that was four months off. In fact, in the area around Multan, it used not to rain even during monsoons. A Sufi saint in the 16th century while being slowly burnt to death there, had cursed the city, condemning it to perpetual scorching heat and drought. It appeared that the curse was losing its efficacy, although many local people claimed that the real reason was that the extensive irrigation and resulting increase in vegetation was changing the weather pattern.

Whatever the cause, it went on raining in the most un-restrained and excessive manner, making it difficult and even dangerous to cover the remaining 20 miles. Being formerly such an arid zone, there was little if anything in the way of drainage for surface water, so the rain lay where it fell, with the depth increasing all the time until the road was no longer visible. Traffic slowed down to my normal cycling pace, and even so created tidal waves. I slowed down even further, terrified that I would break a wheel by falling into some hole which I could not see.

I cannot think how I reached Multan without breaking anything. The City was in an even worse state, for the water here was over a foot deep, and deeper still in places. Men with their trousers rolled up above their knees and holding large, black umbrellas over their heads paddled barefoot through the murky water aswirl with dead rats and other horrors. At least I was not beset by the usual curious crowds; no one even noticed me in my rain-sodden anonymity. I cycled around looking for the hotel, wondering if they would let me in and choosing my route by going along whichever road seemed to contain the least depth of water. Even so my pedals kept disappearing below the surface. After an hour's fruitless wandering, I saw the spire of a church inside a walled garden; near it was a house and I went and knocked at the door, hoping to find someone to direct me. It turned out to be the Bishop of Multan's house, and when, after some initial expressions of horror from the servant who opened the door, the Bishop and his wife had ascertained that a perfectly normal person lurked under my by now very disreputable exterior, they welcomed me in and insisted that I stay. Soon I was wallowing in lovely hot, clean water, after which, too tired even to eat, I slept a sleep of total exhaustion until awoken in the early morning by the mullah's calls to prayer.

I had no heart to explore Multan that day, as where it was not still knee-deep in water, it was ankle-deep in evil-smelling mud. I pedalled off in my damp shoes, hoping that the weather would return to normal as quickly as possible. The ominous clouds of yesterday were still there and for the first time since I had left England, it felt quite chilly. Every village and town I passed through had been flooded and was either still awash or filled with a black, viscous mud which stuck to the bicycle wheels, clogging up the space between the tyre and the mudguard until the cycle ground to a halt and I had to get off and remove the nasty stuff.

At the Bishop of Multan's suggestion, I spent the night at a convent in what I believe is the only Christian village in Pakistan, Village 133 (the British numbered all villages for ease of administration and the system has remained). During the night, I dreamt that someone was emptying bucket after bucket of water just outside the cell window and awoke to find that it was no dream, torrential rain was indeed bucketing down with tremendous ferocity. When I awoke again it was to bright sunlight with all the clouds vanished and the air smelling fresh and cool.

The road was dry by the time I left and I bowled along it at a good pace with the wind for once behind me. Before long I was caught up by another cyclist; from the large metal containers on either side of his back wheel, I could see that he was a milk-seller. He must have sold all his milk because he had no difficulty in keeping up with me. Surprisingly, he didn't seem to want to engage in the usual 'chatting up', nor to play the annoying game of overtaking and falling back, but just to have a friendly race. I was quite happy to respond to this, so we tore along together, getting faster and faster, neither of us really wanting to outpace the other, but just enjoying the headlong progress. After a few miles of racing, we were both a little puffed and he made signs of inviting me for a cup of tea. I declined at first, but after he had repeated the gesture a few times, I nodded assent (it is not considered polite to accept the first time anyway). We stopped at the next roadside café, which was an isolated little place and when we had parked the bicycles, he did a very curious thing—he took hold of my hand and led me, ceremoniously, to a seat. I was really worried for a moment, because as I said earlier, Moslem men just do not hold hands with females or touch them at all in public, it is an absolute taboo. So either I was being mistaken for a man—a possibility I thought extremely unlikely, or else I was being treated as an honorary male, as the Saudis had to do for Mrs Thatcher when she made a visit to their country. I decided that it was the latter and felt most tremendously honoured. I was brought a cup of tea and a rather English-looking sticky cake. My companion had ordered nothing for himself, being probably too poor to afford even one cup of tea. I wasn't having that; if I was to be an honorary male, I might as well exercise my power and buy us both tea. He drank his when it came but would not let me pay for it. The impasse was resolved by the café proprietor treating both of us, after he had read my Urdu press cutting aloud to all the men in the café while I sat there trying to look modest.

My companion turned off the road soon after that and I

went on through waterlogged and muddy villages to Sahiwal, where I had been advised to seek shelter for the night at the American Mission Hospital. A traffic policeman who directed me there, invited me to spend the night at his home. I wished afterwards that I had accepted his offer, for my welcome from the women doctors at the mission was anything but eager. They were, I gathered, funded by the Fundamental Baptist Church of the American Deep South and tended to regard anyone not of a fervent, evangelical persuasion with a certain amount of suspicion. Over supper that night, one of them leaned across the table and asked me, 'When did the Lord enter your life?' As this was in the middle of a perfectly ordinary conversation and quite without any preamble, I was rather at a loss as to what I could reply, since I don't really think in those terms and consider it impertinent to foist my views on others. I muttered something non-commital, about being a Christian whose church didn't operate on quite those lines, hoping that we could change the subject. I had reckoned without the fervour of the true evangelist. This woman considered no one who was not 'Born Again' could be any kind of Christian at all and for the next half hour she attempted to show me the error of my ways. I couldn't help thinking what a waste it was when there were so many Moslems around for her to proselytise. Before I left she gave me a little booklet, called *Five Spiritual Truths* which read rather like a system for life insurance and was illustrated with simple diagrams of trains to explain how easy and obvious was this 'road to salvation'. I was having a look at it by a canal where I was eating my lunch when the shock wave from a passing train blew it into the water.

My last stop before Lahore was spent at the home of a Rural Dean, a charming man who made no effort at all to convert me to anything. He had quite enough to occupy his energies, as he told me during the evening, in trying to protect his little flock from religious persecution. This persecution seemed fairly trivial at first hearing, but it did in fact bite deeply into the fabric of people's lives. Men, for example, were not allowed to drink tea in the cafés—a real deprivation this, since the men's social life revolved largely around the cafés. Food couldn't be sold or prepared by Christians and, in some cases, Moslems were not prepared to sell to Christians either. The Dean's main asset in his war against prejudice was education. The best school in the district was the one run by his wife and had as many Moslem children as Christian. In order to obtain a good education for their children, Moslem parents were having to allow their children to mix with the Christian children and so the Dean felt that attitudes were slowly changing. With the local mullah, or rather his loudspeaker system, he was in more direct conflict and before I went to bed that night, I was warned of what would happen the following morning. Nonetheless, it was a shock to awake, soon after five o'clock, to two distorted loudspeakers, one chanting Moslem prayers and the other expounding the Christian reading for the day, which was from the Book of Daniel. As both were in Urdu, I couldn't tell which was which.

8

Lahore was a city of delights, marred only by the indifferent, unseasonable weather. Even the rain though could not dampen my sense of elation at having completed the first thousand miles of the journey without serious mishap, especially as so many people had considered that part of the trip far the most dangerous. I celebrated by filling in some of the hollows I had developed on the way. In fact, for the first three days, I feared that I had developed an insatiable appetite, for even after four huge meals a day, I was still hungry. As soon as I had finished one meal, I would find myself looking forward to the next. Between meals and showers I explored the city, finding great pleasure in just strolling about without everyone staring at me, for Lahore is a very cosmopolitan city, well used to seeing Europeans. The food bazaars interested me the most, with their wonderful displays of vegetables, all beautifully polished and arranged in great colourful pyramids. Most of the usual English vegetables were available, all very much larger than our own. In addition, there were all sorts of strange varieties which I did not know but longed to try. Just as inviting and even more colourful were the fruit stalls. I found it impossible to pass them without trying something new, such as guavas, papaya, mangoes, and at least five different sorts of bananas. Best of all though were the shops selling dried fruits and nuts; these were like Aladdin's cave, filled with opened sacks and baskets, containing every variety of nuts—in shells, shelled, dried, flaked, powdered and pressed. Figs were threaded onto string and sold by the yard. I bought so much from these shops for the journey ahead that I could not carry it all.

For the serious sightseeing I was invited to join an energetic elderly American couple who, like me, were staying at the cathedral guest house. They hired a mini bus with a driver and guide from the tourist board and we set off one wet morning to visit the architectural splendours of the Mogul city. The driver and guide turned out to be one and the same person. He didn't speak any English and his idea of guiding was to drop us outside each place on the itinerary with the entrance tickets and then dive back into the car, or into the nearest tea house, to await our re-emergence. Our first stop was at the celebrated Shalimar Gardens. I think the charm of this place probably lies in the thousands of little fountains, but as none of these was actually working and what water there was, was coming down as cold steady rain, we didn't really warm to it. The Red Fort was much better as here at least we were under cover most of the time. It had been the main palace of the Mogul Emperors and all of them had added buildings to it over the centuries of their rule, so that now it was like 12 Hampton Courts adjoining one another and would have taken a week just to walk through all its rooms and courts. An hour and a half gave us no more than the briefest idea of its decayed magnificence. The Badshai Mosque was next on our whirlwind tour. This was on an adjoining site so the fortunate driver was able to continue resting. Actually, he didn't have that long, because in order to enter even into the courtyard of a mosque, you have first to remove your shoes. As the courtyard was the largest in Islam (about the size of St Mark's Square in Venice), and it was very wet, we didn't really fancy it. There were several more visits scheduled, but after our faint-heartedness at the mosque, we all decided that we had had enough for one day and returned to the comparative comfort of the guest house.

There were few of us at the Cathedral Guest House which was not surprising because, like so many institutions left over from the British Empire, it had fallen on hard times. Built as a Diocesan House at the end of the last century for all the visiting clergy who came to attend conferences or to have their teeth fixed, it had to be very large and was consequently proving difficult for the impoverished Church of the present day to maintain. Personally, I liked the dark bedrooms, named after

78

those virtues so beloved of the Victorians—Tranquillity, Humility, Charity, Fortitude and so forth—with their iron bedsteads and sagging springs; at least there was room to move around and a desk to write at. The washrooms were rather grim, though a good clean would have done a lot to make them more bearable. The hot water situation got most people down. There was one hot water point situated on the verandah which went right around the outside of the first floor. In theory this was no problem as servants would bring you hot water whenever you needed it; in practice it meant going without or staggering 50 yards or more with your precious water slopping around your ankles. People are very adaptable, though, and most were prepared to put up with all such minor inconveniences, even the cooking, for the place had a charm all its own.

The falling ceilings, however, were more than flesh and blood could bear for long—even those in the room aptly named Fortitude. A hundred years of accumulated whitewash and plaster was detaching itself in large flakes. One would leave a room freshly swept and cleaned and return to it an hour later to find every surface covered again with a thick layer of debris. Sometimes the falling pieces were of quite a weight and could inflict a nasty wound. Nights were awful, for one fell asleep wondering if asphyxiation or severe concussion would prevent an awakening. The American couple fled to the Hilton. 'Hang the expense, life is more important'. I made plans to move on, for there was nothing further to keep me in Lahore. I had made contact with home, and checked that my husband was managing and that all our scattered children were well and happy. The British Consul in Karachi had been informed of my safe arrival and all the thankyou letters to my kind hosts along the route had been sent off. There was, however, a serious hitch to my plans: the unseasonable weather showed no sign of changing. Here it was only raining, further north snow was falling and the road to Kashmir was blocked. I would have to wait at least a week. Rather than hang about in Lahore with the falling ceilings, I thought I would make a bus trip to the North West Frontier.

Armed with a borrowed rucksack and a sheaf of introductions, I left the cycle locked in someone's garage and boarded the 'Flying Coach' for Rawalpindi. The coach was unbelievably luxurious, with only one person to a seat; it even had its own café at the half-way point with toilets and tables and chairs, commodities which I didn't think existed outside the towns. I shared a table with a man from Peshawar, his niece and her baby. The man was now living in Belgium, running a shop which sold Pakistan and Afghan carpets. He had come home for a holiday and was gathering all the scattered members of his family together for a reunion—about 50 of them. He invited me to join them when I reached Peshawar, suggesting that I should see how Moslems lived.

At one point, the road crossed over the Salt Ridge, a strange narrow belt of hills running diagonally across the Northern Plains. It was a bare, eroded landscape of gullies and cliffs. Many trucks and buses had left the road on this stretch; their twisted remains lay at the foot of the precipices. Fortunately we had a comparatively good driver who seemed in no particular hurry, in spite of driving a 'Flying Coach'.

As it was late afternoon when we reached Rawalpindi, there was not time to go on to Taxilla which was my first intended stop. Instead I took up one of the introductions and stayed the night with the vicar of a church and his wife. I was very glad I had done so because although I did not see much of my host who was busy on parish work, I spent a delightful evening with his wife and her sister-in-law. The sister-in-law was shortly to be married and was busy assembling the trousseau. They spread out all the clothes on the bed for me to see. There were 30 costumes, mostly the traditional Pakistani dress of shalwar and kamise, but saris, too, and pyjamas—which are day wear, very like shalwar and kamise, but not so baggy. Most of the clothes were heavily embroidered, work done by small boys. In addition I was shown the ornate, heavy jewellery which is probably just worn once, for the wedding. My hostess was outspoken about the waste and stupidity of the dowry system which she said ruins families and means that many girls can never hope to be married. Most of the garments are never worn. She herself still had 20 outfits packed away in boxes from her own wedding 10 years before. It isn't just the clothes which are a burden, furniture and electrical goods also have to be provided, even if the in-laws' home, in which the bride will normally live, is stuffed full of such things already. In many cases the in-laws have to build sheds to store the dowry which can take up too much house-room.

I was beginning to get some insight into the frustrations of life for a Pakistani girl with a lively mind like my charming and attractive hostess. She had had four brothers and the whole family had united in making sure she conformed, so that nothing would get in the way of her eventual marriage. As a little girl she had longed to learn to swim. Near her home was a swimming pool with one day a week reserved for women only. She hadn't been allowed to go though because her brothers had thought that if people had seen her there, they might have considered she was immodest! There had been no question of allowing her to have further education, either; that would also get in the way of marriage. She hadn't wanted to marry, having had more than enough of male domination by that time. Several matches had been arranged and she had held out against them all, but in the end she was worn down by the constant pressure her family exerted on her and she had just agreed to whatever they wanted. On the whole the marriage had worked out well, she thought, and being a vicar's wife gave her quite a lot of scope for her energies, since great demands are made upon the clergy in Pakistan.

It had been raining most of the night and when the bus pulled up in Taxilla the following morning in the middle of a huge puddle, it was really pouring. I looked around for some shelter and saw that someone was beckoning me from an open-fronted shop. It was a chemist's, the interior of which was filled by a doctor's couch and a large desk with a stetho-scope prominently displayed upon it. Pharmacists in Pakistan call themselves medical practitioners and have a much more exciting time than their British counterparts, diagnosing and prescribing, instead of just making up medicines to other

people's orders. Pakistan is a great place for unqualified practising of all kinds, including dentistry and driving. There is, for
instance, a street in Lahore where the pavement is jam-packed
with men whose speciality it is to clean out ears for people who
require this service. They employ fearsome looking instruments of astounding length, which they ply with great gusto.
From the expressions on their clients' faces, one expects to see
the instrument emerging through the other ear. But although I
had watched the procedure for a long time I had not actually
seen this happening.

My medical benefactor supplied me with tea as well as
shelter and I was very grateful for both. I was now only three
kilometres from the ruins of ancient Taxilla and when the rain
had eased off, a friend of the practitioner took me off to the
tonga stand. The fare should have been one rupee, so when the
driver demanded eight and we compromised at five, I natur-
ally assumed that he would take me straight off on my own.
Not a bit of it; I and the horse were left waiting in the drizzle for
the tonga to fill up with one-rupee fares. The injustice was too
much and in spite of passionate pleas, I got down and stalked
off. I next tried a Suzuki van which I was assured would be
moving off immediately, but after 15 minutes of being soul-
fully stared at through the windows by half a dozen schoolboys, and realizing that the empty Suzuki would also not
move off until it too was packed full, I climbed down from this
also. The various helpers who had involved themselves in my
journey were nearly in despair by this time, for they felt they
had to get me on my way or lose face. They stood in a line
across the road and forced a passing bus to stop. After a fierce
impassioned speech to the driver and conductor, I was
bundled on board. It stopped every 10 yards or so to load
passengers, livestock, sacks of rice, flour and vegetables and
during the journey we were passed by both the tonga and the
Suzuki, but eventually I was deposited, without payment, at
the gate to the museum.

Where to stay was the next consideration. There were two
choices: the Tourist Hotel just across the road from the
museum which also housed the Tourist Office, or the Youth

Hostel, which the guide books described as 'reasonably clean'. As I was getting no answer to my knocking at the hotel and as the rain was again bucketing down, I thought that I would go over to the Youth Hostel and see what 'reasonably clean' meant. I had forgotten that you can't just look in Pakistan. Before I had had time to take in my surroundings, a charming old man and three lively youngsters, whom I took to be his great-grandchildren, had booked me in, committed me to lunch and dinner and shown me my room. It was the dirtiest place that I had been in so far. Everything was encrusted with an ancient, ingrained, grey greasiness. I thought I might just be able to survive for one night and escaped as quickly as I could to the museum.

This was 'A treasure trove of priceless Gandhara Busts of Buddha' said the guide book. 'A fascinating marriage between Greek and Buddhist art following Alexander the Great's conquest of these parts'. There were certainly a lot of these stucco busts; to my untutored eyes they looked very alike. There were also some very jolly artefacts and some fine barbaric jewellery which I enjoyed very much.

After lunch at the hostel—chapattis and a dreadful soup made from chilli with a few bits of potato floating in it—I thought I had better see something of the ancient ruins for which Taxila is famous. They are of various cultures which flourished between 500 B.C. and A.D. 500 and they include cities, monasteries, palaces, universities and stupas. So in my already sodden cycling shoes and with a large hostel umbrella I set off. I knew that it was hardly the right conditions for this type of sightseeing, but I also knew that nothing could persuade me to stay in that awful hostel for another night. It had to be today or never.

To reach the first city site I had first to go through a village where men were busy constructing ancient works of art in preparation for the tourist season (there had been a notice at the museum warning about the many fakes for sale). Several characters paddled over to offer me a Buddha 'Very reasonable price' and when this was not happening, boys were hectoring and jostling me. Rounding on them with my umbrella had no effect at all so I resorted to carrying my penknife open in my hand and had no further trouble.

I had left the road and was headed for the site of the first city when I noticed four youths looming up fast behind me. For some reason I felt nervous of them and opened my penknife again. It amazed me that this was taken seriously, for it served only as a threat and would have been quite useless as a weapon, even to someone who knew how to use it. Halfway up the main street of the site the youths were suddenly opposite me, and one of them started to talk to me in quite fluent English. He said that he came from Shepherds Bush in London and was here on holiday with his cousins, but he was dressed in shalwar and kamise like the others and had a shawl over his head like them. The others had backed right off when he was talking to me which was very unusual, and they also kept beckoning him to come away. I thought at the time it was because they were getting so wet, but they showed no sign of seeking shelter, and when I next saw them, they were going up the long flight of steps beyond the city, which lead to the palace of Asoka. I was halfway up these steps, when another man trotted up behind me. This man had an umbrella too and was rather out of breath, as though he had been hurrying. He seemed determined to accompany me, and as he was nice and polite, I didn't try to freeze him off. We looked around the ruined palace and the stupa and he seemed to know a great deal about it. He offered to show me the best of the other sites via shortcuts which would avoid going back to the road. In retrospect, I think it was foolhardy of me to accept, since it was very lonely out there, especially on such a wet day, but having been used for so many years to taking people as I found them, I had forgotten the need to be wary. As we moved off across country, I saw the four youths looking down at us from the palace walls. I hadn't seen them at all while we were there. Abdul, my guide, led me across fields and river and obviously knew the area well.

I began to enjoy the day in spite of the rain. It was all rather like Scotland except for the Buddhist bits. We visited lots of different sites, all very interesting, with plenty above ground to see—much more pleasant, I thought, than Mohenjodaro. One of the best preserved was a Buddhist university of the third century A.D. Abdul said I could look over this by myself while he went off to see about something. The man in charge of this site, who lived in a little hut inside the walls, had heard about my cycle trip on the radio and was pleased to meet me. After holding forth at length and in quite extraordinary English about the Gandhara statuary in his charge, he led me off outside the walls and asked if I would care to have tea. Without waiting for an answer, he scrambled ahead of me down the steep hillside until we stood in front of one of a group of what looked like haystacks, but with a little door in the side about two feet six high. When we had squeezed through this narrow door we were in a spacious hut made of tree boughs, plastered and thatched on the outside, so that the boughs were exposed on the inside and made useful fixings to hang things on. It was an enchanting place, snug and warm and as neat and clean as a Victorian parlour.

There were a dozen people there apart from ourselves, and they were of all ages, from a very old man to a tiny baby. They all had the most beautiful features and the women and girls seemed to enjoy an untypical equality. They were tribal people, I was told, nomads who spent eight months of the year travelling with their flocks in the high lands of the Northern Territory. They made tea for us over the open fire in the centre of the hut and with the museum official as interpreter, we talked. They lived a good life, they said, travelling was a fine thing. They would have been on their way now but the old man was sick. The interpreter told them about my travels and they said that I should be staying with them; I did not belong in a hotel, being like them, a 'free person'. I only wished I could stay, it was so very much more appealing than the awful youth hostel. If I had stayed, I think I would have found it difficult not to join them on their trek, for I have never met any people that I found so fascinating. I was worried though about Abdul, who had been waiting all this time, thinking that I was going to be 15 minutes and an hour and a half had already gone. He was still waiting, although he looked rather fed up. I asked him why he had spent his afternoon showing me around, wondering if he was expecting a tip. I was very happy to pay him, since he had been an excellent guide and I should not have seen anything like as much without his help. He wouldn't accept any money, though, saying that he sometimes acted as a guide but today he had stayed with me because of the bad men and for that there was no payment, 'It was his duty.' The 'bad men' were the four youths. According to Abdul they were local robbers who preyed on any lone tourist visiting the antiquities. Only a week ago they had robbed a Japanese tourist while holding a revolver to his head. Abdul regarded my scepticism as Western naivety. 'Here,' he said, 'such things are common, the police know all about it and do nothing because they share in the spoils.' I didn't know what to believe. Certainly Abdul had nothing to gain by telling me lies, since he refused to accept any payment at all anyway. Oddly enough, after Abdul had told me about the robbers, I began to be nervous about his motives, for we were heading through increasingly remote country towards the last of the sites and it was not far off nightfall. My fears were baseless; I was delivered safe and sound to the Youth Hostel, in total darkness, just before seven.

The hostel looked even worse at night, and again I wished I could have stayed with the nomads in their winter quarters, or with Abdul's family as he had invited me to do. Still I was welcomed kindly enough into the noisome, freezing kitchen. A young woman was cooking, squatting on the high cooking shelf alongside her little stove, tossing any debris onto the floor below. This was the mother of the small children I had met earlier, who were now sitting around waiting hopefully, like me, for something to eat. The old man was also there, entertaining a friend, as old and as toothless as himself. The friend explained that the young woman was the wife of the old man, and that the little children were his. 'What do you think of that, huh?' he asked, a glint in his eye. I could see that the old rogue wanted me to be shocked, so I shrugged in a casual sort of way, as it was none of my business and the young woman looked quite contented with her lot. My supper of omelette, rice and tomatoes was not bad by local standards; there was just not enough of it after the long day. By 8.30 everyone was in bed, for it was the only way of keeping warm. I was glad that I had brought my sleeping bag and did not have to use the hostel's greasy blankets.

I awoke to another wet day, thinking crossly that I might as well be back in England where the rain would at least be anticipated. Breakfast was quite uneatable, being yesterday's chapattis fried in an evil-smelling grease. I left on one of the curved-sided, elaborately decorated buses, which had miniature silver minarets on top and rows of swinging chains all around. I now realize why these buses are driven so dangerously; it is a frightfully cut-throat business running a private bus in Pakistan, and part of the reason for the elaborate decoration is to attract custom. They also post touts along the route to grab passengers in advance—I saw one man nearly pulled apart when the touts of two rival buses caught hold of an arm each and tried to haul him off in different directions. If the bus ahead is getting all the custom, the bus behind will try and overtake, but the front bus will strive to maintain its position and the two of them will race along abreast for miles before one of them gives way. Anything coming from the other direction must somehow get off the road for it is seldom that an overtaking bus will give way for oncoming traffic. The horn button is kept depressed the whole time and as the horns are amazingly loud, the only way to survive with hearing intact is to wear ear plugs. Our driver was very pushy indeed, and I was surprised and pleased to arrive in Peshawar without suffering any major disaster.

I had an introduction to an English woman, Peggy Shepherd, working for a mission in Peshawar, but due to the rains having flooded most of her little house I stayed in an hotel nearby—a comfortable place, serving the best food in Peshawar, including a delicious local bread. There is nothing like the sort of conditions I had unwillingly endured at Taxilla for making one grateful for comfort. I loved Peshawar. I think I would have liked it a lot anyway as it was a jolly, bustling, swashbuckling sort of place, full of big, fierce men bristling with weapons. As befits such an ancient frontier town, every sort of commodity was on sale in the bazaars, gun shops being particularly evident.

The next day dawned bright and clear, and after an early breakfast, I went to find the bus for the Khyber Pass. Although it was an hour before the bus was due to leave, it was already crowded. People were very kind though and rearranged things so that I had a window seat next to an English-speaking, chain-smoking Afghan. The bus was going all the way to Kabul, said my neighbour, which is where he lived. He was returning there now with his young nephew whom he had taken to a hospital in Pakistan to see if something could be done for the boy's failing eyesight. Little hope had been offered, and sadly it was thought that he would soon be quite blind. I asked what things were like for most people in Afghanistan now. 'Not good,' I was told, people did not get what they needed and life was very confused.

On the outskirts of Peshawar the bus passed the vast Afghan refugee camp. It is estimated that there are over 60,000 people living there in tents and this is only one of several such camps. It must present tremendous problems for the Pakistan government, although the voluntary agencies are much in evidence, too. The plight of refugees always seems to raise a good deal of international sympathy, whereas the terrible conditions I had seen among the indigenous poor tends to go unnoticed.

The road left the plains abruptly and began to wind through hills which were bleaker than any I had seen. There seemed to be little or no vegetation anywhere and yet there was no shortage of dwellings. Every house was a fortress and outside each one were men with rifles and ammunition belts. Herds of goats grazed the bare hillsides and it was clear that there were cattle, too, since the walls of the houses and some of the larger rocks were plastered with dung cakes. These dung cakes can be seen everywhere in towns and villages in Pakistan and are an essential element in the economy as they supply the fuel for most of the cooking. They burn and smell rather like peat but instead of being stacked like peat, they are made into flat cakes by being slapped from hand to hand like chapattis. When they are stuck onto a wall, the hand print is left on the surface. Many people who do not realize the function of these cakes think that they have been placed there purely for decoration.

Further up the pass, the dwellings were much poorer, often just caves. Lines of women could be seen carrying water up rugged paths to these caves, often from wells over a mile away. These were tribal people with their own territory. Only the road itself was Pakistan, and on either side tribal law applied. The ochre-coloured hills were crowned with forts and watch towers. Set into rocks along the roadside were memorial plaques to the British soldiers who fell here in their constant battle to keep the pass open. Things seem quieter now, but it is certainly not a settled area and it is almost impossible to obtain permission to travel here, or in any of the tribal areas.

The bus passed through Landi Kotal, the last frontier town, and went on to the actual border at Torkham. There was no question of my going on into Afghanistan, even if I had wanted to, for no sooner did the frontier guards realize that there was a Western person on the bus than I was hauled off and given to understand, helped by appropriate gestures with their rifles, that the border was closed to foreigners. I created quite a lot of interest as the only Westerner at the frontier, particularly with the money changers, of whom there were lots, all hoping for dollars. After the interest and the importuning had died down, I found a seat where I could sit and watch the bustle. Constant foot traffic was crossing the border in both directions. There appeared to be little or no check, and people staggered through carrying huge loads. They could have been smuggling anything. Even quite small children were bent double under their burdens. Many of the children could pass as British, and I did wonder if the soldiers had left more than their bones here. As I sat there watching the scene and writing in my journal, the owner of the café brought a table over to me and gestured that it was for me to write at. I thought this was very kind of him, especially as he didn't wait to see if I wanted to order anything.

After I had watched for a while, I went over to the guard

house to see if it would be in order to walk the six kilometres back down the road to Landi Kotal. 'No, very dangerous, men with guns, bang bang, all the time,' said the officer in charge. I said that I would not leave the road, I just wanted to take photographs of the forts and hills. 'No photographs, bang bang,' repeated the officer. So there was nothing for it but to ride down to Landi in one of the Suzuki trucks which served as taxis. I was offered a seat in the cab between the leery driver and his even leerier young companion, but chose to sit in the back with the other passengers, or rather we all perched on the sides; it wasn't possible to sit on the floor because of the spitting. The truck sped down through the hairpin bends at a fearsome pace, with the leery boy leaning out of his window to offer me hashish on the worst corners.

Landi Kotal was very much what one might expect of a frontier town in these parts. Knee-deep in mud and refuse, guns and drugs. In recent years this has become one of the main heroin-producing areas in the world and many of the local youths and children are now apparently addicted to this pernicious drug. I walked through the narrow, crowded, muddy streets, a little scared and rather intimidated by the constant shouts of 'Hallo mister'. A man sitting in his open-fronted shop cutting sheets of glass beckoned me over to take a glass of tea with him. We were not able to converse, but we smiled and nodded affably over our tea. Later this man passed me in another part of the town. He had a fearful gash in his hand and forearm, presumably from the glass. He stopped and showed me the wound. I mimed that it needed sewing up, he nodded agreement and went off, I hope to find a doctor.

Coming down the Khyber in the late afternoon was lovely with the forts and watch towers casting long shadows on the barren hills, and the distant snow-covered mountains, rosy in the light of the setting sun.

Peggy Shepherd was dining with me that evening at my hotel. Over a delicious meal of subtly spiced curries, quite the best I had eaten so far, she told me of how, like me, she had fallen in love with the North West Frontier when she had visited it some years previously. She had been lucky enough to return to work in a mission hospital in Peshawar and was very happy with her life there.

Wandering around the endlessly fascinating streets of Peshawar the following day, I stopped for tea at a little café. The man who brought my tea told me that he was a 'B.A. economics and was doing an M.A. by correspondence course,' but alas, he had to work in a tea house!

'The curse of my country, one must work for seven.'

Apparently, he had six sisters and a widowed mother, so he was the sole provider.

'I have sister M.Sc. gold medalist, what the good? I marry her off. Your country, mother and father work, make all fine for children. Here if you have daughters, sisters you weep. Where you find all fine things for the marriage? The clothes? The furnitures? The refrigerators? Many too much things.'

He shook his head sadly and then asked the so often repeated question of young Pakistanis:

'How I get to study in England?'

I answered, as I always did to this question, by telling him how difficult it was now in England for foreign students with all the cut-backs, and how, what with our cold climate and high cost of living, it was not nearly as desirable a place to be as he imagined. So we parted in mutual accord, both sad about the state of our respective countries.

The rain seemed to be at an end. There had been three days now of continuous sunshine and it was beginning to get hot. Time to return to Lahore and the bicycle and continue the journey.

9

Back at St Hilda's, still with its falling ceilings, I overhauled the bicycle as far as I was able with my limited set of tools. Ideally the bearings should have been cleaned out and re-greased because of all the flood water I had ridden through since Multan. Still, thanks to the excellent preparation it had received in London, nothing had actually seized up. Considering the nature of those first thousand miles I thought that both the bicycle and I were in surprisingly good shape and ready for the next stage of the journey. Tomorrow if I could cross the border controls at Wagah (not always possible, said the guide book) I would be in India.

Now that I was about to leave Pakistan I began to feel quite nostalgic about it. In spite of the constant hassles with importunate males, and all the staring, the spitting and the lack of privacy, I had received so much kindness and seen so much of interest. It was not, I thought, a country that was really suitable for tourism, but it was one to which I would want to return some time.

My last evening in Pakistan was spent in a gracious house in a model village in the suburbs of Lahore as the guest of Farida and her family. Farida was an attractive young woman employed in the American Express office who had helped me find my mail and spare tyre when I had first arrived in Lahore. She had also achieved the near miracle of getting me a phone call through to London. For a young girl of good family to be pursuing a career in Pakistan is quite unusual and costly, too, in loss of prestige and marriage prospects. Perhaps it was her own independence that had made her warm to me and my travels and had made her keen for me to meet her family. I was driven to her home in the car which daily took her to and from work; whatever the level of emancipation, I gathered that travelling alone or on public transport is just not done. Farida had visited both America and Britain and she told me later in the evening that her experiences of the English had not at all endeared them to her; she had found them unfriendly and stand-offish. With this in mind she had made sure when inviting me that I should arrive in time for tea, after which I could decently be taken back to Lahore if I proved to be uncongenial. Patently I must not have seemed so, because I was pressed to stay to dinner, which I gladly did, for I found her large family and the many friends who dropped in very good company indeed. As usual, the conversation kept coming back to Pakistan itself, and in particular to General Zia's latest ruling about people being made to wear national dress to work and what nonsense this was. Nearly all the Pakistani people I met seemed to have a great pride in their country no matter how much they criticized it, and to care very much that visitors should gain good impressions of it, too. This I found a very endearing characteristic which I looked back to with nostalgia when in India, where people rather expected one to be unfavourably impressed.

When I was taken back to St Hilda's at about 11 o'clock, I found the high, wrought iron gates of the Cathedral Close were closed and locked, although the watchman whose job it was to do the locking-up had been instructed to wait until I returned. There was nothing for it but to climb in over the spikes, an incongruous means of entry at my age, I thought, especially when being watched by the two young men who had driven me back.

After a last gritty night under the falling ceiling of Tranquillity, it was good to be on the bicycle again, pedalling through the early morning unadulterated air, heading for the border and India. Without the distractions of traffic and the necessity of being constantly on my guard, I was conscious of a sense of elation and excitement, I was really here in Asia, having come through one great country and about to enter another; countries that until now had been only names on a map.

My sense of contentment lasted as far as the border, some two hours' ride. There all was bustle and confusion, crowds of people and vehicles milling around in a haphazard manner—another side of the magic of Asia. I had been warned about the very long delays that can occur at this, the only open frontier post between the two countries. Such is the great antipathy that each has for the other that the greatest difficulties are placed in the way of Indians or Pakistanis passing through. This is very hard for the many families who have been split by Partition. While I was in Lahore I met several Europeans who had waited at the border all day without success. I was lucky enough to experience no such difficulties. To the Pakistani customs I simply showed my Urdu press cutting and received first class service.

'Very nice photo,' they said. 'If we know you coming we line up for salute you,' and they waved me through, such is the advantage of being the only person travelling by bicycle.

Indian Passport Control was a much more intimidating affair with 12 large, fierce-looking Sikhs seated around an arrangement of tables as in Leonardo's 'Last Supper'. Here I was subjected to a stern battery of questions, the answers to which were all printed in my passport which my questioner was holding. I didn't think I'd better point that out though, as I didn't wish to offend him. Eventually I was allowed to pass on to custom control. This looked decidedly grim, being a bleak, comfortless, open-air waiting area separated from the inspection tables by a high chain-link fence. The gate in the fence was guarded by an armed Sikh in military uniform—all the officials seemed to be military and armed. The guard took my passport and put a cardboard number inside it, placing it at the bottom of a large pile of similarly numbered passports. 'Go away and wait,' he said. 'We will call you.'

The waiting area smelt like a latrine and was in fact bordered by flat, grassless fields whose sole purpose seemed to be to serve as a huge open-air loo. There were about 50 Pakistani families before me, all with mountains of luggage. I could see

94

through the fencing that the ones who were currently being inspected were having every item of their belongings subjected to the most searching scrutiny. This, I thought, was going to take at least a week until my turn came round. I had heard that it was possible to speed things along by carefully placing rupees inside your passport. Quite apart from the expense and the risk of being imprisoned for attempted bribery, this seemed a dubious moral course and I thought I would see what reason and sympathy could achieve. There were notices around such as 'Nothing To Declare Use The Speedy Channel' and 'We Are Here To Help You Please Ask' and 'See The Superintendent for Complaints'. I thought I'd start with the last one and asked the hatchet-faced Sikh who had numbered my passport if I might see the superintendent. When he came, he was all brass buttons and red tabs, and listened most courteously while I told him of how I had almost no luggage and that as my bicycle had no lights, I simply must get to Amritsar before dark. I would have clinched it with my press cutting which had served so well thus far, but now I was on the Indian side where Hindi is the lingua franca and Urdu no longer of any use. Sympathy and reason alone were enough though and within 10 minutes I was through customs and on the other side. I hadn't had to open anything, just tell them about my dollars and travellers' cheques. Since I still had quite a lot of these, the officials were most affable and friendly.

The other side of the border was very little different from the Pakistani side, the same flat fields of the Punjab stretched away as far as the eye could see with the same water-buffalo, oxen and even a few camels—though it was getting a little far north for this species. The roads seemed better surfaced, with less traffic and that appreciably slower. India has its own motor industry and produces the Ambassador, a car based on the old Morris Oxford, which has very little performance. This is a great boon to cyclists who share the road with them. Another difference was that there were women around; nearer to Amritsar, there were even women on bicycles—unheard of in Pakistan.

Amritsar is a town particularly sacred to the Sikhs. It houses their most holy and beautiful building, the Golden Temple. It is also a town which saw some of the worst abuses perpetrated by the British Raj, in particular the infamous massacre, an event made universally public in the recent film *Gandhi*. Whether there is a special antipathy towards the British because of this terrible incident, I don't know, but I found Amritsar a daunting, intimidating place.

At first everything went relatively smoothly. I found the railway station where I had been told that Pakistan rupees could be exchanged at favourable rates for Indian ones. I never did understand why people were so eager to acquire the currencies of other countries that they were prepared to pay way over the official rate to procure some. I changed my modest number of rupees, rather wishing that I had brought more since the rate was so good. I then started to look for an hotel but could not seem to get free of the area of the railway station. Whenever I stopped to try and get my bearings, a crowd gathered round me, and though I had found the crowds in Pakistan infinitely trying, these were even more so. For in addition to the staring there seemed to be a total absence of friendliness. No one smiled or said anything. Always in the Pakistan crowds someone would know a little English but this was not the case here. The reason for this was the decision of the Indian government after Partition to remove English from the curriculum of the state schools and make Hindi the national language. This has resulted not only in greater separation between North India and South India—for the South Indians refuse to adopt Hindi as their first or second language—it also means that state-educated North Indian children are at a great disadvantage when seeking employment, because English is a necessity for very many jobs, but is taught only in the private schools. Many poor Indian families beggar themselves in order to obtain private education for their children. For the hapless traveller it just creates difficulties. I felt the difficulties to be almost insurmountable on this occasion, surrounded as I was by silent hostile crowds, and was greatly relieved to spot a sign on a gate saying Christian School—surely someone in a Christian school would know enough English to help me find an hotel? Inside, I found a pleasant, elderly man who did speak English. He offered me tea but was unable to direct me either to a tourist office or to a suitable hotel.

'Amritsar not safe for European lady. Very bad place. Violent peoples. I send you with porter to Christian gentleman, he is very good man, arrange all things.'

I set out with the porter who was mounted on an enormous, ancient bicycle and in a short while found myself in a prosperous-looking suburb. We came to a square of two-storeyed, large, white houses surrounding an area of pretty, well-kept gardens. The address I had been sent to was the upper part of one of these houses. As we started to mount the steps, a Sikh emerged from the lower part of the house and hailed us. Most Sikhs are tall and well-built and with their impressive beards and turbans they are imposing figures. Without their turbans, their hair arranged in a top-knot—often covered by a tiny, lace doily, they have a faintly comical aspect, rather like bearded and trousered Victorian aunts. The effect was further heightened in this case by the decided chubbiness of the gentleman who appeared to be in his late 50s. He told us that the man we were seeking was out at present but please would I come into his apartment and wait; the man upstairs was a friend of his.

'Indeed we are as brothers, it is my duty to assist his friends.'

I explained that I was not a friend but had merely been sent to him for advice on finding a hotel or tourist office. Perhaps he knew of somewhere suitable?

'There are no good hotels here, very dangerous place, Amritsar, better you come inside and refresh yourself until my friend returns.'

After this second warning about the dangers of Amritsar, I thought I'd better comply, for nightfall was not far off now. The Sikh, whose name was Ginny, called his servant and ordered tea. I felt hot and sticky and would have welcomed the opportunity to wash; instead we drank tea and chatted, on and on and on. I began to find the situation irksome and my companion even more so. His conversation seemed extremely silly and filled with rather prurient innuendo, interspersed with fits of giggles.

'Always the European ladies are finding me fascinating,' he said at one point. 'Many stay with me, we have good times.'

I asked when he thought his friend would return.

'Oh,' he said evasively. 'Maybe later, maybe tomorrow, I think perhaps he make holiday, he is gone two weeks now.'

At this stage I began to have definite suspicions about Ginny's intentions and said that I really must go and find an hotel where I could bathe and rest and have a meal: also I wanted to visit the Golden Temple as I was leaving Amritsar early the following morning. Ginny would not hear of me leaving. His friend, he said, would never forgive him if I came to harm wandering the streets of Amritsar, also, it was his sacred duty as a Sikh to protect women and travellers.

'You stay,' he said. 'Wash here, later we eat, if my friend not return you sleep here, plenty room, come, I show you.'

I followed him to a large bedroom with a double bed in it, out of which led a washroom. Like the rest of the house, the bathroom had been built to a high standard; the fittings were expensive but badly cared for. Nothing worked properly and there was an unpleasant air of dirt and decay. I washed as best I could in the trickle of cold water which was all the shower would produce and I wondered what I should do. I did not wish to offend Ginny by misconstruing his motives—there were after all the problems of cultural differences—on the other hand I did not wish to find myself in an embarrassing situation.

When I came out into the bedroom though, there could no longer be any question of misunderstanding. There was Ginny lying on the bed, wrapped in a quilt, and nothing else as far as I could see. Fortunately I had dressed in the bathroom and had the moral supremacy of the fully clothed. I told him coldly that he had quite the wrong impression, amorous adventures were not what I had come to India for, and would he please remove himself so that I could gather up my things and go. Mustering up what dignity he could, he shuffled out, still wrapped in the quilt. He was back before I had finished packing the cycle, fully clothed and very much on his dignity. He was deeply hurt and shocked, he said, that I should so misunderstand him.

He had merely been resting on the bed while I was not using it, and now I was spurning his hospitality and where would I go to in the dark, in this dangerous town? There was certainly food for thought in this last remark. While not for a moment believing his excuses, I did not think that Ginny was a violent or dangerous character, and there was a lock on the bedroom door and enough heavy furniture around to make the room secure. Better perhaps to take a chance with what was at present merely an embarrassing situation than risk far greater dangers in the dark, forbidding streets.

We returned to the sitting room where Ginny chatted away as though nothing at all untoward had occurred. At about nine o'clock he suggested that we go to his club for a meal. This seemed a good plan as I had not eaten since breakfast, about 14 hours previously and was faint with hunger. Also, although not exactly frightened of him, I was apprehensive and thought it would not be a bad idea if a few other people saw us together, just in case. Before we left, I put the bicycle in my bedroom so as to have my things to hand when I returned. I would feel altogether more secure if the bicycle and I were on the same side of a locked door.

We set off in a cycle rickshaw; our combined weight, I was sure, being far too much for the poor, thin rickshaw boy. The club was set in the middle of extensive grounds and had probably once been quite grand; now it was definitely seedy and smelt unpleasant. I could see a large gaming table through one door but no people, the place had an empty, forlorn look. We went into a bar which was also empty except for a barman and two other men who appeared to have reached a sentimental stage of drunkenness, their arms around each others' necks and tears on their cheeks. Ginny ordered food and double whiskies, but I asked for beer instead. Food came, bread and highly seasoned meat and a plate of raw onions, all sloppily served on dirty, chipped crockery, but nonetheless very welcome. No one else ate anything; they were all too busy drinking and translating sentimental Indian poetry for my benefit. We only stayed there a little over half an hour but Ginny managed eight double whiskies in that time. I resisted all offers of drink, thinking it very important to remain quite sober.

One of the sentimental poets drove us back and I suppose he could not have been as drunk as he seemed because we arrived safely, though I would not care to repeat the journey. When we got out of the car, there was a silly scene when Ginny took the car keys and pretended to drop them down a drain, while the poet pleaded tearfully for them back. This game went on for quite a while. The servant meanwhile had the front door open and I took the opportunity to slip into my room and shoot the bolt. After a while Ginny knocked inviting me to come and have a drink. I said I was in bed and about to go to sleep, I wished him good night and said I would see him in the morning. There was a rather nasty pornographic poster glued to the wall which in no way added to my peace of mind. I kept the light on because I felt safer and was too nervous to sleep anyway. Every half hour or so there was a knocking at the bedroom door but I pretended to be asleep. I must have dozed off towards dawn but was awake and dressed by seven. There was no sign of Ginny so I had to leave without thanking him for his hospitality—I hoped I would not find myself in such ambiguous circumstances again.

Before leaving Amritsar I was to be taken up by yet another Sikh, a very different one from poor Ginny. I met him at the bookstall in the market, just outside the Golden Temple, which I had found only after the greatest difficulties—Amritsar really is a most confusing place. The bookstall distributed free Sikh literature and was run by the Pinkewara, a charitable organization which amongst other things cares for the sick and destitute. The nice old gentleman in charge of the stall offered to look after the bicycle while I visited the temple. As it happened, the temple was not open just then, so I only got tantalizing glimpses of lovely golden domes, marble colonnades, and splashing fountains.

'You are alone here, my daughter?' asked the old Sikh gentleman as I returned to collect the bicycle and go in search of breakfast. I said that I was and could he recommend somewhere near where I could get an omelette. He then invited me to accompany him to his home and eat there. I thanked him but said I was on my way to Kashmir and must reach Pathankot, 80 miles away, before nightfall. 'You will go by bicycle, my daughter?' he asked incredulously. I told him of how I had already come right through Pakistan and that after I had visited Kashmir I planned to cycle through as many of the Himalayan valleys as I could as far as Sikkim.

'I salute you with folded hands,' he said. 'You are very courageous person. Please to visit my humble home, which is on the Pathankot road and so not out of your way. We will cook you omelette and maybe I can help you.'

Just getting clear of Amritsar and on to the right road would be help enough and probably save a good hour, so I accepted his offer of breakfast as long as I was allowed to buy the eggs. Although he protested at this, I insisted and was glad that I had done so, because when we arrived at his home, a tiny village on the outskirts of the city, and I saw the extreme poverty in which he lived, I would have felt very guilty about eating his food. The stench of the place was terrible, because the only drainage was open channels in the narrow dirt alleys between the houses. The houses themselves were mostly just very small crude shacks.

While the women of the house made chapattis and omelette, my host told me that he was called Sampuran Singh—which means perfect lion—and that he had been in the British Army in his youth, and after that he had worked in the postal service. He was retired now and did voluntary work for the Pinkewara. He had a wife and two daughters, his pension and his good health. He was, he said, a fortunate man. I thought he was, too, for he radiated peace and contentment and his conversation was full of interest and humour. I was his daughter now, he said, and his family was my family. When I returned to Amritsar I would stay there with them, in the meantime he would pray for my safe journey.

I knew that I would not be returning to Amritsar, not on this trip anyway. It was a great pity that I had not met Sampuran yesterday and so avoided the uncomfortable night at Ginny's. Poverty and its attendant smells notwithstanding, I would have been far happier with my new family. Before I left, Sampuran said that if I met with any difficulties on the road, I was to look for the yellow flag of the nearest Sikh temple and ask for help there, since Sikhs, he said, were more to be trusted than most men. He presented me with half a dozen stamped, addressed postcards—'For news of our daughter'. We still correspond.

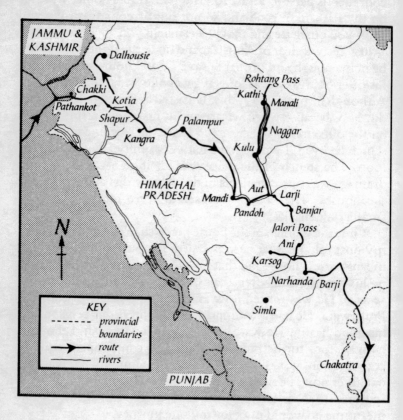

Himachal Pradesh and Kashmir

10

For a long time I had seen what I had taken to be a thin line of cloud stretching along the northern horizon. I hadn't paid it much attention for all around me was the bustle of heavy traffic and the reek of exhaust fumes. Endless lines of army trucks thundered past, filling the air with choking dust. Thirty miles on in an ugly little town called Batala, the traffic finally ground to a halt, having woven itself into a gruesome tangle of trucks, rickshaws, buses, flocks of sheep, cars, horses and carts and bicycles. All had tried to squeeze through somehow, mostly on the wrong side of the road. Several carts had overturned and one poor little donkey, who had been pulling a cart far too heavily laden, was now hanging in his harness from the upended shafts. Several policemen were shouting loudly and laying about them with their long wicked-looking sticks, adding to the general chaos. It was then that having somehow extricated myself from the mêlée—another advantage of travelling by bicycle—and now having a temporarily clear road, I saw that what I had taken for a line of cloud was in fact a great wall of snow-covered rock. Over 100 miles away still, dwarfed by distance, but unmistakably the Himalayas. They filled the horizon from east to west, sharply outlined against a blue sky, infinitely remote and yet totally dominating the landscape. I felt wonder, disbelief, awe and excitement by turn. If the trip ended now, I thought, it would have been worth it, just to have seen this.

All through the afternoon as I continued northwards the mountains grew clearer and higher and the flat fields of the Punjab began to give way to rougher, less fertile ground.

Villages were not so frequent and the air smelled sweeter with less traffic around; a lovely day to be cycling.

Ten miles south of Pathankot the road to Kashmir turned westward to follow the line of the Himalayas as far as Jammu, where I planned to spend the following night. From Jammu it again turned northwards to snake its way among the lesser ranges, until it reached the great Banihal Pass—the natural bastion of the Vale of Kashmir. I had thought that I would have to go out of my way to Pathankot to find shelter for the night, but several people had told me that there was a good rest house at Modanpur which was always empty at this time of year. As Modanpur was in the right direction I had decided to make my night's stop there. I reached it at about 5.30 p.m., very tired after the previous night's lack of sleep and hungry too, having eaten nothing since the omelette. There was a very good tourist café, where I satisfied my hunger with delicately spiced chicken and delicious saffron rice, after which, feeling happy and relaxed, I wheeled the bicycle across the road to the rest house.

The rest house was full! I stood there stupidly, failing to comprehend. It couldn't be full. There wasn't anywhere else to go; Pathankot was 30 miles back and I could not cycle that far, tired as I was. In half an hour it would be dark and on that road full of large potholes it would be suicide to attempt it. The chowkidar shrugged his shoulders.

'Sorry, Memsahib, all full with army men.'

A large, military Sikh who had been lounging in a basket chair on the verandah, rose to his feet and yelled at me.

'Did you not hear the man? Take yourself off, here is no place for you.'

I replied that I didn't really know where to take myself off to, as I had been assured of spending the night there. This unleashed a spate of anti-British sentiment from the officer, which included alleged abuse of Indian students by the British Government; rudeness of Mrs Thatcher when visiting India; and stupidity of Englishmen for allowing their women to roam about like vagrants. This last remark hit home; I was beginning to feel rather like a vagrant. I couldn't think why all these military types were not camping with their soldiers instead of filling up the rest house; it all seemed very unfair. I was not prepared however to let this bully see that he had upset me and hurried away.

I had stopped a few hundred yards further on and was shedding a few quiet tears while bent over the map, pretending to study it, which was the only sort of privacy I could find, when a voice from behind me asked kindly:

'Madam, why are you weeping?'

This shedding of tears was to become quite a feature of my journey. It worried me very much at first, but after I met other female travellers who had been in the sub-continent, I discovered that it was a very normal occurrence there; almost impossible to avoid, because of life being so difficult and frustrating for women in that male-dominated society.

On this occasion I was almost inclined to start crying all over again because the voice sounded so kind, but at the same time a certain ridiculousness in the situation made me want to laugh. So between gulps I told the kind enquirer of how I had been turned away from the rest house, and didn't know where to go. He was a military Sikh also, but quite the antithesis of the other. I was not to worry or upset myself, he told me; he lived in married quarters on an army camp close at hand. He would offer me the hospitality of his home, that is if his wife returned on the bus from Amritsar. If she did not return, it would of course not be suitable for him to entertain me, but I still must not worry, for in that event he would take me to a brother officer whose wife was at home. I was quite happy not to worry, for I felt that he was a man I could trust without reservation.

His wife did not in fact return on the Amritsar bus. However my rescuer remembered that his daughter was now 15, at which age a girl is counted as a woman, so if I did not object, he could still, with perfect propriety, offer me the hospitality of his home. Before we entered his house, he called out both his son and daughter and presented them to me, so that I could be assured that all was as it should be. It was a very small house, simply furnished, but comfortable and clean. After eating a meal cooked by the daughter and a young servant boy, the children spent several hours doing their homework while their father sang prayers, which gave me a very welcome time to myself to write in my journal. I did feel fortunate that I had the opportunity to visit so many homes and meet so many people of the country, but there were times when it was the greatest luxury just to be by myself, not having to make conversation and answer questions.

I awoke at 6 a.m. to a lovely day and to my host's singing of the morning prayers. The prayers continued for upwards of an hour, so by the time breakfast was over and everyone had had their turn in the tiny washroom, it was nine o'clock before I set out, the little family gathering round for a last farewell, and to wish me luck, and invite me to stay again on my return. I rode off warmed by so much kindness. I had to stop very soon though and spend a half-hour adjusting the bicycle gears. The cycle had spent the night in the servant's room, and I think he must have been unable to resist the temptation of trying to find out how it worked.

The road to Jammu was very up and down with an atrocious surface. It presented a tortured landscape of scrub, bisected by wide, dry water courses lined with huge boulders brought down by the monsoon rains sweeping down the Himalayas in the annual floods. I thought that it was probably these boulders which had scoured the concrete road blocks, creating large craters and removing the surface altogether in places. Everywhere there was evidence of attempts to control and contain the rivers but it didn't seem as if they were winning yet. There were plenty of people about working their small, rock-strewn fields; women and girls being much in evidence because the people here are mostly Sikhs and Hindus and so do not restrict their women to the same extent as Moslems do. I saw one group of young boys and girls watering their buffaloes in a muddy pond, swimming them out to the middle and then climbing out onto their backs and jumping from one to another, the animals appearing not to mind at all. On the bank another huge buffalo lay on its side in the mud with a tiny, naked child fast asleep on its dusty, sun-warmed flank.

I watched this delightful scene, reflecting on how the water-buffalo is probably the most important animal in the sub-continent, and that although the great brahmin oxen are far more beautiful, it is the humble buffalo that holds everyone's affection. It has a strange misshapen appearance, its huge, shapeless body somehow contriving to look immensely fat and yet bony at the same time. Over a very low, sloping forehead, its horns are plastered down to its skull, almost overhanging its pale blue, myopic eyes. Thick short legs like tree trunks support the huge body. The whole effect looks incongruous as though it had been put together from bits and pieces. Its many uses, from beast of burden to supplier of milk and of dung for fuel, were already known to me; but one I had not thought of was revealed later when I visited Delhi—that in a country where the cow is sacred and so beef cannot be eaten, the buffalo can fill the gap. Buff steaks, buffburgers and roast buff are a welcome part of the diet of those who can afford to eat meat.

Jammu was only a 50-mile journey, so I reached it early in spite of the bad roads. It stands at the very feet of the Himalayas and the railway terminates here. For travellers to Kashmir there is a choice of continuing by aeroplane, which takes about an hour, or going on the ancient Mogul highway, which takes all day by bus. I thought that I could probably do it in three days by bicycle.

I had planned on spending the night at Jammu in the tourist centre which had 128 bedrooms. Although it was only four o'clock however, all the rooms had been taken, the train having arrived before me. I was just beginning a preliminary tour of the other hotel accommodation when the usual, helpful male stopped to ask if he could assist, and while I was trying to persuade him that I really didn't need help as yet, a much younger man rushed up saying, 'I am a Christian, too, what is the trouble?' I assured him that there was no trouble. I was merely looking round the town, deciding on which hotel to stay at. The young Christian looked horrified—I was begin-ning to form the impression that Indian males consider hotels are not suitable places for unaccompanied females, though in retrospect I think it is just that they consider unaccompanied females need their protection in all situations. This is not an unreasonable assumption in the sub-continent.

'You must come with me to Bishop William,' said my self-appointed protector. 'He knows all things and will tell where it is best for you to go.'

Quite a crowd had gathered by this time, so I went off with the young man to meet Bishop William. As we walked, he told me that he was called William too.

'I am named for the Bishop, he is very good, very kind man; thanks to him I have very good job in bank. I think everybody loves him here. You will like him, I am sure.'

William was quite right, it seemed impossible not to like the Bishop. Later, when I returned from Kashmir, I spent several days with him and his wife and developed a respect and affection for him akin to that of young William's. On this first meeting I was merely aware of a large, rather elderly Indian gentleman, bubbling over with good humour and kindliness. When I tried to apologize for intruding upon them, he seemed genuinely surprised—how could a visit be an intrusion? he asked, laughing, wasn't it always good to meet new people?

Over supper I met someone else who was staying there, a Scot whose daughter had vanished a year ago in Kashmir. She had been travelling with another girl and they had been on their way to Ladakh. One morning she had gone out for a short walk on her own and had never returned. She was just 20 when she disappeared and in spite of extensive searches, nothing had since been heard of her. I thought of my own daughter, the same age, currently exploring South America. How could I bear it if such a thing happened to her? Not knowing if she was dead, or alive somewhere and hoping to be rescued. I could imagine few things worse than that. This poor man had spent most of his time since the incident travelling to and fro, placing advertisements in newspapers and following up any clues.

After we had eaten, young William returned to take me to visit his mother who, he said, was not very well and seldom went out but who enjoyed having visits. They lived in a

Pakistani girl spinning

Bus halt, North–West frontier at the foot
of the Khyber Pass

Kulu Valley woman

Spirit-burning ceremony, Tamang village,
on trek to Langtang, Nepal

noisome ghetto of open running sewers and narrow dirt alleyways with tiny houses crowded together. It was a Christian ghetto now of Roman Catholics who had originally been low caste Hindus. In this ghetto, Bishop William was revered, for when he first came here many years ago, he determined that he would so something for these downtrodden people, although as a Protestant Bishop they were not his flock. Finding that there was no Roman Catholic school, he threw open the Protestant school to them, so that the children at least would have some opportunity to improve their lot. I gather the opposition to this truly Christian act is still reverberating. William's house was desperately poor; his mother, who was about the same age as me, looked ancient and shrivelled. She had raised 10 children in those miserable surroundings, and now her sole support was this one son. She hobbled painfully to their tiny lean-to kitchen to make tea. I told William I didn't want any, as I couldn't bear to have her wait on me when it was clear she was ill and in pain; but as he pointed out, she would be deeply hurt if I refused; so I drank the tea and she smiled and thanked me graciously for coming.

As we walked back through the bazaars to Bishop William's house behind the town, the last of the light shone on the snow-covered slopes towards which I would be travelling in the morning; they looked remote and infinitely lovely, in sharp contrast to the poverty and squalor I had seen in the town.

I was up and away by eight o'clock on a quite glorious sunny morning. The road started climbing at once and at first it was all I could do to stay on it, for all around me was confusion. Scores and scores of buses and army trucks driven by grim-faced Sikhs all jockeying for position, engines revving, clouds of exhaust gases pouring out into the pristine air. It was more like the start of a Grand Prix. No one would give way, so there was nothing to do except to get right out of the way and let them fight it out. Many minor skirmishes left one or more victims blocking the road completely which gave an opportunity for me to slip through. As I climbed higher, precipices began to appear on the left and solid rock faces on the right, so now there was nowhere to get out of the way except over the edge and I could see that many solid objects had indeed broken through the parapet and plunged into the ravines below.

Between convoys the road was clear and I could enjoy the scenery with just an occasional eye for the potholes. At one point there were troupes of monkeys playing by the roadside, two distinct species, I thought, but they were wary and moved off quickly when I stopped. The brilliant green, long-tailed parrots were everywhere, as they had been since Karachi. The landscape was very varied, with forests, scrubland, terraced hillsides, and always ahead, drawing the eye, those lovely snow-topped peaks.

I crossed two ranges of foothills, each higher than any mountain in Britain, but mere hummocks here in relation to the giants ahead. It was fine riding, especially as now that I was out of Moslem territory I felt that I could wear shorts—albeit rather long ones—without giving offence. Shorts make an appreciable difference on a bicycle. They are not only cooler, but don't pull on the knees the way trousers do. The gradients too, although steep, were very regular, making for a pleasant rhythm. By one o'clock I had cycled 45 miles to the rest house at Udhampur where, for the first time at one of these establishments, I was able to negotiate for a room without incident. It wasn't the greatest room that the chowkidar led me to, being in need of a good clean; nevertheless I felt elated to have managed to get it without any kind male having to come to my aid. I was just attempting to stretch the chowkidar's English a little further and arrange for some food, when I was hailed by a man sitting on the rest house verandah, surrounded by small woolly dogs.

'Come and have a cold beer,' he said. Nothing could have been more inviting, for I was hot and thirsty after the climbs. He told me that his car had passed me on the road but had developed some fault, so now he was waiting here while his man fixed it. I could see a white Mercedes in the drive with a uniformed chauffeur at work on its engine.

'I think it is nearly fixed now,' said the man. 'I can take you on to Srinagar, there is room for your bicycle on the top.' I thanked him for his kind offer but explained that I was bicycling for pleasure and not out of necessity. I told him about my trip so far and of where I was intending to go. I could see that he found the whole notion incomprehensible, so I changed the subject and asked him about himself and his dogs. He was in fact a V.I.P., being in charge of prisons in Jammu and Kashmir. He was also a Christian and knew Bishop William and was, he said, doing his best to reform the prisons and rehabilitate the prisoners in his care. While we talked, men kept coming up to him, salaaming respectfully and listening with great respect while he gave them orders. Very soon plates of food and more beer arrived. It was all delicious and more like a holiday should be. I wondered why I couldn't make things appear like that. Then I remembered that I was not a V.I.P., and that probably that sort of life wouldn't suit me, certainly not being in charge of prisons.

All this while the five little woolly dogs, all of a special Tibetan breed, kept wandering off and being brought back and men approached to salaam and take orders. Also by this time I was feeling very sleepy after the beer and was finding it difficult to keep my eyes open. So it was with some relief that I saw the chauffeur come up to make his salaam and announce that the car was now ready. Everyone stood around in deferential attitudes while the official and his dogs were packed into the Mercedes. Before he left, I too received my orders. He was sorry that I would not travel with him, but he still considered me his guest; dinner had been ordered for me for seven o'clock, a whole chicken—I was please to make sure that it was a whole chicken, because these people could not always be trusted! He had also ordered hot water for me to bathe, a man to take my clothes for washing, breakfast, food for the following day's journey and more beer! All was paid for, I was not to give them anything. There was nothing I could say except 'Thank you'. After he left, I was moved to a much nicer room where all through the rest of the day various items of food kept arriving. Being the proxy guest of a V.I.P. certainly had its advantages.

The next range rose to over 7,000 feet, a climb of 30 miles with hairpin bends every few hundred yards. I had started early while it was still cool and I had the road to myself for the first hour and a half. It was sheer delight at that time of day to be cycling upwards on easy gradients, breathing in the pure mountain air, full of the scent of growing things and loud with bird song. Every steep hillside was terraced into innumerable small fields, some of them no bigger than a tablecloth. Dotted about the terraces were flat-topped mud houses. The people who worked this land looked very poor, prematurely aged and bent; they did not respond when I waved a greeting. I passed through groups of nomads driving their flocks up towards the high pastures, the children proudly carrying the smallest lambs; these people all looked better clothed and fed, and waved and smiled as I passed.

The higher I climbed the more euphoric I felt, that is until the convoys started passing. Then I had to concentrate on survival. The bus convoys were not too bad, as there were seldom more than five of them together and their Sikh drivers, though dashing, were very competent at leaving me just sufficient room to stay on the road. The army lorries were the real danger and there were literally thousands of these—one single convoy that passed me that day had 319 trucks, plus jeeps and other vehicles. I think many of these military drivers were asleep at the wheel, because they would suddenly veer out of the line for no reason at all and as there was barely room for two vehicles to pass on those roads, the smallest mistake could prove fatal. Fortunately for me that day the precipices were on the right hand side, so the worst I could suffer would be to be crushed against the rock face. These rock faces carried interesting exhortations, painted in huge lettering, such as:

'DON'T BE RASH AND HAVE A CRASH' and 'DRIVE WITH CARE REMAIN AWARE' and 'NO HURRY NO WORRY'. My favourite one asked with a zen-like simplicity 'WHY IS HURRY?'. From the number of breaches in the parapet wall it didn't seem that these sobering texts were having much effect.

The reason for the military presence was that this was still disputed territory. India holds it but Pakistan lays claim to it, and a small United Nations peace-keeping force maintains a permanent watch. Other vulnerable borders with the U.S.S.R. and China are also no great distance away through the passes. So it was quite clear why there had to be all this unwelcome traffic, but what wasn't clear, and never did become so, was why all motor vehicles in the sub-continent had to emit such appalling amounts of noxious exhaust fumes, great black clouds of the stuff, which turned my clothing black in a matter of minutes and did goodness knows what damage to my lungs. I reached the top of the climb gasping for air like a stranded fish. There was snow here at 7,000 feet and it felt very cold—I hadn't noticed while I was climbing—so I didn't stay to admire the view but pushed on over the other side, and was back down to 4,000 feet in a matter of minutes.

For the rest of the day my route was continuously blocked by landslides, brought down onto the road by the recent unseasonable rains. Many people were engaged in clearing away the debris, but often the road was completely blocked to all but a bicycle. It was my turn to pass many of the convoys which had earlier swept past me, including the very long military one. The precipices were on the left again and now a turbulent river followed the line of the same valley, flowing downwards, full of logs, as I pushed on upwards.

I reached the small cluster of dilapidated buildings which comprised the town of Ramban an hour before nightfall. One of the buildings was the rest house; a grimy place, but a welcome sight nonetheless, for I was pretty tired after 60 tough miles. I was given a suite of rooms—huge double bedroom, slightly smaller dressing room and a bathroom of palatial proportions—the whole lot lit by a single 15-watt bulb. All this cost the equivalent of one pound, five pence with an extra 25 pence for bedding, hardly a fortune, and I would gladly have paid more for a few more light bulbs. When I mentioned this to the chowkidar though he said, 'No problem, electricity is not very good working here. Later I bring candle.' He was a very friendly chowkidar and spoke English, which was an unusual accomplishment for chowkidars. He promised to return in a short while with 'Very extra special dinner'. True to his word, he was back in an amazingly short time, a bottle of beer under one arm, both hands clutching a large tray. His friendly smile was now an alarming leer, until I realized that, in the deep gloom shed by the 15-watt bulb, what I had taken for an enormous expanse of teeth was merely a half candle he was carrying between them. He set everything out with great style and flourish, while my mouth watered in anticipation. He was out of the door bowing politely before I had the cover off the first dish. It was awful. Truly, I think it was the worst meal I have ever been served and that includes some terrible memories of school dinners. The main items were rice, curried vegetables and dal, standard fare and although not exciting, nourishing and wholesome. After I had tasted this rice (which was stone-cold) I decided that it had probably been sitting in its present congealed state for several days and had collected quite a lot of foreign matter in that time, like ashes from the fire, the odd fly and so on. The dal was in an advanced state of decomposition and also deathly cold. The vegetables would probably have done me no lasting harm since they contained enough chilli to preserve them for ever, but I'm sure they would have removed my stomach lining, so I didn't care to risk them and turned my attention instead to the final dish. This was the 'extra special' item, a meat dish. I could tell that it was meat because it consisted mainly of large pieces of bone to which rock-hard fragments of sinew adhered. The 'gravy' with which it was dressed defies description.

I dined on oranges and beer and as it was very cold at this altitude, once the sun was down, I went to bed to write my journal by the light of the candle. By 8.30 I was drifting off to sleep with cheerful thoughts of an early start, so as to reach Srinagar the following night and enjoy the sybaritic pleasures of good food and comfort; to travel well one must remain an optimist.

It rained in the night. I knew in my sleep that it was raining but didn't want to recognize the fact. In the end I was forced to, because it rained with the total abandon that it had in Pakistan and the noise on the tin roof was like thunder. I knew, before dawn broke, that there could be no question of continuing that day; the roads would be rivers, and rock and mud would be pouring off the hillsides in fresh landslides. I felt deeply depressed at the thought of having to spend another day in these dark, dismal rooms and tried to sink back into oblivion.

Breakfast arrived at eight, I had ordered it the night before for seven, but as the chowkidar cheerfully observed, 'No need early breakfast, Memsahib not travel today, very much snow on mountain.' Breakfast was boiled eggs and tea, a great improvement on dinner. The chowkidar did not comment on the uneaten dinner, he merely suggested that I pay him what I owed so far. There was a list on the bedroom wall setting out the charge for each item of food and service. All the rest houses have such a list and it is a good idea—at least in theory. In practice it doesn't always work, as in this instance, because the chowkidar charged me just over double the correct amount and I didn't have the courage to argue.

It was a most depressing day, almost pitch dark inside because so little light could filter in through the dirty windows, in front of which was a deep verandah. I had nothing to read and after cleaning the bicycle—rather a waste of time considering the terrain ahead, I could think of nothing to do. There was a slight let-up in the rain at about four so I donned my waterproof and went out. It was just as depressing outside, the few little hovels were now awash in a sea of mud and the turbulent river had become a great torrent of yellow water rushing down at an alarming pace. I walked about for a little and got wet in spite of the cagoule.

When the chowkidar came to negotiate dinner, I tried to order a fire because I was so cold but the chowkidar said that was not possible, instead he would bring a 'Kashmiri Kangree'. Not knowing what this was, I asked cautiously 'How much?' 'Oh, not at all,' replied the chowkidar. 'Private Kangree, I bring.' When it came, it was a woven basket, snugly fitted around an earthernware pot containing live coals of charcoal. The chowkidar removed the blankets from the bed and made me sit on it with my knees drawn up; he placed the kangree beneath my bent knees and replaced the blankets; we then returned to the question of dinner. I had the printed list of prices by my bed, and pointed to the item that read 'Chicken, rice, dal, chapatti and salad, RS.10.' The chowkidar nodded doubtfully and went away. He was back immediately.

'No chicken, Memsahib, have lovely mutton.' A strong smell of scorching had him diving under my blankets (a good thing I was fully clothed). He piled ashes on the kangree and replaced it, and again we tackled our culinary problems. I said, 'I couldn't eat the meat last night.'

'No, no, not hard, soft, soft,' said the chowkidar. 'My responsibility.'

That means I'll pay double if I don't like it, I thought cynically. But, in the morally weaker position of being in bed with his private kangree I capitulated with 'No bones then'.

'Bones? What is bones?' asked the chowkidar, with the deepest suspicion. After a lengthy and exhausting explanation of bones, I thought he had the idea, and I wondered what would come. I felt hungry enough to eat anything. I might have guessed, it was yesterday's meat—'lovely mutton'—now off the bone and even more like shoe leather. The chapattis and the salad of raw onion were all that was edible. I was braver now though and challenged the chowkidar and the meal was reduced to RS.8. As I went to bed I thought I would leave in the morning, whatever the weather, lest I perish!

The rain had practically stopped when I set out at seven the following day. The chowkidar was nowhere to be found, so I left the money which I owed him, plus a little extra—for the use of the kangree—and went in search of an omelette in the horrid little bazaar. By the time I had finished the omelette the sky was a little less overcast and the rain had quite stopped. I started the climb. On my left the precipices grew steeper and the valley bottom ever further away. On my right the rock faces were loose and constantly shifting. I was just passing the scene of a previous rock fall where two men were on their hands and knees clearing away the last of the rubble, when I saw the rocks above start to move. Fortunately I did not freeze, which could have been fatal, but kept cycling, shouting at the men, who were unaware of their danger. We all three just got to safety as the rocks crashed onto the road behind us. That was the closest call, but throughout the day there were frequent landslips. Mostly I found I could work out if there would be time to pass—the need to maintain a steady rhythm when cycling all day up very steep slopes takes precedence, even over fear. The authorities are attempting to stabilize these friable slopes by planting trees on them, and where this has happened, they write self-congratulatory notices, such as 'THIS USED TO BE A LANDSLIP BUT WE HAVE FIXED IT—BATALE FORESTRY'. Other notices which cheered my way were 'DO NOT LOSE YOUR NERVES ON THE STEEP CURVES' and 'ONLY WITH NERVES CALM CAN YOU ENJOY THE VALLEY'S CHARM'. I was the only transport moving up the mountain, everything else having been halted by the landslides; vehicles were occasionally coming down though and on one of the 'steep curves' I met about 20 army trucks at full throttle, nose to bumper, with a jeep coming even faster on the outside of them. I don't know how I survived this; there was neither time to think nor room to manoeuvre anyway. Somehow I found I had just scraped through between the jeep and the trucks and had come to a halt shaking with shock and anger.

After three hours of steady climbing I was feeling hungry and spotted a sort of cave-like café built into the side of the hill. A very grimy small boy was making pancakes in a great iron dish of fat. They were sweet pancakes, greasy and satisfying. I could have eaten a dozen of them, but stopped after three, which was just as well because those three gave me considerable stomach pains later on.

I toiled on, the gradients becoming progressively steeper and the air noticeably thinner and harder to breathe. I didn't think it could be much further now, as my map showed the pass to be at 9,570 feet and I thought I must already have passed the 9,000 mark. I had had snow all around me for an hour or so and when I stopped to take a picture, it felt intensely cold. I had seen no living thing for several hours. Nothing I thought could exist in that bleak and desolate landscape, and I shuddered at the thought of maybe having to survive a night there if something went wrong. But still the road went on in a seemingly endless line of tight bends and false summits and I thought I would never reach the end of it. Then suddenly, as I crested yet another rise, there was the mouth of the tunnel. I was at the top!

11

The Mogul emperors who had made the Vale of Kashmir into
their summer playground would not have been able to come
here, as I had done, in late March. In their day there had been
no tunnel, and the last few hundred feet of the mountain does
not become passable until late May. So their first view of the
fabled valley, as they sat in their gorgeous palanquins, would
have been of crystal clear lakes and acres of almond trees
covered with clouds of pink blossom; the whole scene ringed
by snow-topped peaks, shimmering against a blue sky.
Thanks to modern engineering I was able to gaze on this same
scene when it was a waterlogged morass, seen dimly through
cold, driving mist. It was not an inviting prospect. However, I
was fortunate to see even this, because as I had approached the
tunnel entrance a soldier had come forward to bar my way.
'No lights,' he had shouted at me roughly, waving me towards a queue of waiting vehicles. I could see that there were
no lights in the tunnel, which was over two kilometres long,
but built in such a straight line that the pin-prick of daylight at
the further end was just visible. I told the soldier I would go
through carefully, walking when it became too dim to see. At
this he caught hold of my arm and started to haul me away.
Somewhat annoyed, I shook his hand off. This action for some
reason roused him to a fury and he raised his fist in a most
threatening manner. Fortunately, an officer rushed up and
pulled the soldier away, and while he was fiercely haranguing
the man, I took the opportunity to dart into the tunnel—
thinking only of getting clear from the unpleasant scene. I had
got about as far as the daylight reached, when I heard a vehicle

enter the tunnel behind me, the noise of its engine drumming against the tunnel walls. For a moment I panicked thinking that it was the army coming after me. But then I reasoned that they would hardly run me down in cold blood, so I continued pedalling as hard as I could down the middle of the road, the headlights of the pursuing vehicle illuminating my path. There were one or two nasty moments when the back wheel skidded on the uneven and broken slabs, but at last I was through and could see that the vehicle behind was not the army but just a private car whose driver had followed my example and defied the soldiery. After that they all came through, cars and buses, and everyone called 'Shabash' (well done) to me as they passed.

It was much colder on the Kashmiri side with a nasty, penetrating wind blowing. I didn't linger over the unlovely view but sped down the 10-mile descent as fast as the road surface would allow. There was a tourist café at the bottom, where I caused something of a sensation, as no one there had ever heard of a cyclist coming over Banihal Pass before. So it was 'Shabash' and handshakes all round and more offers of cups of tea than I could drink.

That was one of my only two pleasant memories of Kashmir. Having got to Srinagar, I couldn't wait to leave it. It wasn't just the unrelenting cold and the ceaseless rain, though they were enough to make me want to get south again fast. The place was one big tourist trap, for everywhere I tried to go, hordes of touts pressed around me, all shouting their wares at once, and all trying to take me somewhere I did not wish to go. It seemed impossible to negotiate anything, from a room for the night, to picking up my mail, without being cheated. The few European visitors I met there all shared similar experiences and were equally disenchanted.

There was no possibility of getting through to Ladakh for months, so after three days I decided to return to Jammu and travel the Himalayan valleys of Himachal Pradesh from the south.

Getting out proved more difficult than getting in. I was told that the road was now completely blocked by massive landslides and that when it was cleared only convoys would be allowed to go down under army escort. At the Tourist Office I was advised to try and join one of the buses in the first convoy which was due to leave in the morning. It was while I was at the huge bus depot attempting to arrange this that I met Lateef. At the time I was trying to shake off the crowd of importunate touts, keep a hand on my bicycle and pay the ticket clerk all at the same time. Someone in the crowd behind me asked, 'Why are you in such a hurry to leave?' 'Because,' I said over my shoulder, 'I hate it here, the cheating, the weather, the mud, the touts, everything.' Nobody said a word in reply, they just melted away until only the man who had asked the question remained, and this was Lateef, a neatly dressed, friendly looking man of about 35. He asked if he could buy me a cup of coffee, over which we could talk about 'the unfortunate feelings' I had about Kashmir. I agreed as long as he promised not to try to sell me anything; and as long as I could buy the coffee—being back in a Moslem country made me eager to preserve female equality. Actually it was a relief to tell someone about all the petty annoyances and frustrations of the past two days; of how I had been lured onto a houseboat, under the pretence of 'only look, Memsahib' and then being virtually held to ransom; of agreeing prices for meals and then being charged double, and so on. Lateef professed himself horrified by my adventures, though I couldn't believe that he was unaware that such things were the general rule here. He asked me if I would come back with him and meet his family, if I felt like it I could spend the night with them. He explained that I would be doing him the favour by being prepared to trust him after such 'unfortunate experiences'. I didn't see that I had anything to lose—if I didn't like it I could always leave—so I accepted.

Lateef lived on a houseboat and in fact his family owned three. Any lingering doubts I had about him were quickly dispelled when I met his charming family, particularly the three delightful children. All of them, two boys of 10 and five, and a girl of eight, spoke some English, for although they were Moslems they attended the R.C. mission school. The wife and mother spoke no English but nevertheless made me very welcome. The wife told Lateef that I looked as though I was 'frozen to my bones' and fetched blankets, a kangree, and a special Kashmiri garment to wrap me up in. The garment was rather like a fisherman's smock, only much longer and looser fitting and made of a thick blanket material. It had very narrow sleeves, but mostly the hands were left inside. Grown-ups and children wore this practical smock and underneath it they carried their Kashmiri fire pots—the kangree; giving everyone, little boys included, a distinctly pregnant appearance. It is a very satisfactory garment for keeping comfortable in a cold, damp climate as I can now witness.

Blissfully warm for the first time in days, I sat on a cushion on the rush-matted floor, the boat gently rocking to the motion of passing lake traffic. While the women prepared vegetables, the children did their homework. They all read to me in English and showed me their other textbooks. I found these poor, but their level of attainment was quite equal to that of English children, except perhaps in mathematics. In the case of little Lateef, who was only five, it was well in excess of most English boys of his age. Lateef was clearly proud of his children and had their futures already planned. The eldest boy was his sister's child and he would be married to Lateef's daughter, so that together they could manage the houseboat business. Little Lateef would have a few more years' schooling, and then start working with his father. There was no room in his plans for any personal choice by the children which I found a trifle chilling. I found it chilling, too, when he told me of how he approved of the maiming and blinding of persistent offenders in the Bombay gaols, as a warning to others. He could not understand why anyone should object to this practice when clearly it worked, Bombay's crime rate having fallen drastically, he claimed. He would have been just as shocked, of course, by many Western customs, particularly by the freedom of young people to choose their own marriage partners. None of this spoiled the pleasure I found in his company, though, and I listened with fascination to the account of his working year.

In the late summer, Lateef wandered the mountains in search of precious stones—sapphires, topazes, lapis lazuli and many others, sometimes trading for them with wandering Tibetans and nomads. The winters he spent in a hired workshop in Gujerat, cutting and working the gems, returning to Srinagar in the spring to sell the finished stones to the jewellery makers. He said that the mountain slopes where he went were very remote and unknown to tourists; if I returned with my husband one year, we could all go there together. While Lateef had been showing me his collection of gems, the women had prepared the evening meal, and I was led off to dine in state on their prize houseboat—normally hired out to rich tourists. I would have much preferred to stay and eat with the family; but Indians, who are normally so gregarious and have no time at all for our notions of privacy, regard eating as a solitary pursuit. After the meal Lateef brought out a treble recorder—a gift he told me from another traveller he had befriended. He played it very well in a purely Eastern manner, entirely by ear. I told him I played, too, and at his request, gave him a small sample of classical Western music. The rest of the evening was spent with paper and pencil explaining some of the rudiments of Western notation to a very apt pupil. I could see that the best way of repaying his hospitality would be to send him some recorder tutors on my return to England.

Lateef had promised to see me onto the bus in the morning. This proved to be an invaluable service, and I doubt I would have been able to cope with it unaided. About 50 buses were due out in the first convoy, and the muddy bus park was a seething mass of people and luggage. No one could board the buses, which stood waiting, for the numbers on the tickets which had been issued didn't correspond with the numbers on the vehicles. An announcement was made that all the tickets had to be changed. This was done with the maximum of difficulty as a massive rugger scrum descended on the booking clerk. I stayed aloof from this and cowardly let Lateef join the scrum for me. Thirty minutes later, it was found that the new numbers still didn't correspond, so back everyone had to go to find out which numbers went where. It was all rather fun, I found, when I could just stand back and let someone else do the worrying. Eventually the chaos was sorted out and everyone found the right bus and started to pile their bedding rolls and cases onto the roofracks. Cunningly, we waited, and having shamelessly bribed the conductor, the bicycle was placed on the very top, where it would be less likely to sustain damage.

Suddenly, almost without warning, and with no time for last goodbyes, the convoy was off, only two hours behind schedule. All was noise and confusion again as 50 buses and an equal number of trucks fought for position in the line. We started well down, but driven by a determined elderly Sikh in a pretty, pink turban, we forced our way up to five from the front. I think we might have made it to the number one position if after an hour the whole convoy had not come to an abrupt halt. We had stopped in a tiny and very muddy village, consisting of two squalid cafés and two shops selling walnuts. I thought at first that it must be a stop for refreshment, for although only an hour on our way, considerable energy had been expended before the start; and I did wonder vaguely how two cafés could deal with the needs of so many passengers. I need not have worried; six hours later we were still there.

It was 24 hours before we got going again, and during that time the only people who seemed at all interested in finding out what was happening or when we would get under way again, were myself and three black ladies from Zimbabwe. Everyone else simply accepted the delay with Asiatic fatalism. There were, at a conservative estimate, about 2,000 people in that convoy and all their bodily needs had to be met by those two cafés and the muddy area adjoining the road. The cafés had no lavatories. When I knew that I would have to relieve my bodily needs also, or sustain an injured bladder, I nearly despaired, for I simply could not function in those circumstances—I did try, but my body refused to co-operate. The trouble really was clothing; in voluminous Indian dress, one can squat with almost perfect decorum. In Western trousers, it means indecent exposure. I made a mental note to provide myself with a wide skirt for future emergencies and started to walk back towards Srinagar, looking without success for somewhere private. There was nowhere until I came to the tourist café I had visited on the way down. Here there was a lavatory actually labelled 'Ladies'. It was only a hole in the ground, but it did have a door.

As night fell, the temperature dropped dramatically. The ladies from Zimbabwe became convinced that they would not survive the freezing night and I shared their doubts, for it was indeed deathly cold. We went over to one of the cafés to see if it was warmer there. Both of them, with commendable opportunism, remained open the whole time and must have made quite a killing—even though most of the Indians carried their own food. Their biggest killing, though, they made by hiring us a room which would have been expensive even by big city standards. We haggled fiercely over the price, particularly the African ladies, for they had been travelling around India for several weeks and were in an advanced state of disenchantment. 'Just one long rip-off,' they said, when I asked them how they had enjoyed their holiday. They tried to elaborate on this but words failed them, they could only repeat sadly, 'Just one long, long rip-off.' The 'room' we were shown to, after our lengthy negotiations, was underneath the café. It was about nine foot square and two greasy charpoys had somehow been squeezed into it. A few pathetic items of clothing hung from nails on the stained walls and one of the charpoys was provided with a few verminous-looking blankets. We were to have a stove, too—an old oil drum with holes punched in it, burning some sort of coal which gave off noxious fumes and which probably would have suffocated us during the night had it not gone out after an hour or so. The stove was rather a mistake really, apart from the fumes, because after the boy had managed to get it alight (it took him ages and quantities of petrol) several of the bus drivers squeezed into the room to enjoy the warmth and we had the utmost difficulty in ejecting them. After the last of them had been persuaded to leave, we set one of the charpoys against the door to save us from further intrusion and arranged ourselves for sleep. The three black ladies chose to squash together on one charpoy for warmth and protection, they said. I had my sleeping bag so I left them the verminous blankets; in spite of the terrible cold, they could not bring themselves to use them.

We were called at 6.30 by our conductor and staggered out of our little cell with stiff, aching limbs. Everywhere people were performing their morning ablutions, gargling and spitting with great noise and gusto. Spitting is one of those Indian customs which Westerners find particularly difficult to adapt to and often become quite neurotic about. Indians regard it as a social and religious duty, a cleansing of the body of harmful matter, and they perform this duty frequently, particularly in the morning. Mud and garbage squelched underfoot and it was difficult to weave a way to the bus without treading in piles of excrement. In total contrast to this squalid scene, the morning had burst in a glory of pink and gold on the surrounding peaks.

By 8.30 the convoy was on its way, grinding up towards the pass. It was not to get very far down the other side before avalanches again halted its progress. I left it at that stage, the army escort turning a blind eye as I rode off. The exhilaration of swooping effortlessly down through the seemingly endless 'steep curves', air rushing past me, was quite wonderful. Only the occasional rock falls and places where parts of the road had disappeared altogether temporarily halted my headlong progress. Before nightfall I was back in Jammu with Bishop William, in temperatures well up into the 80s. Mrs William thought that I was looking thin and tired and suggested that I should stay for a while before I continued my travels. I thought this a good idea, too, especially considering the still unsettled weather conditions in the Himalayas. It was difficult to accept her kind offer though, because Bishop William was now retired and they were clearly living in fairly straitened circumstances. However, after some persuasion, she agreed to let me contribute towards the housekeeping. I grew very fond of Mrs William and her many quiet kindnesses. A stream of small children and women from the poor quarters of the town were constantly at the door and none went away empty-handed. Many people came just to pour out their troubles and for these, too, she always had time. Yet she spent long hours shopping and preparing delicious meals which, much to the Bishop's annoyance, contained very little chilli, in deference to the weakness of the English stomach.

They had both suffered many misfortunes, having lost two of their three sons; one—their youngest and possibly their dearest—being destined like his father for the priesthood, had died of a mysterious illness in his early teens. The eldest, a boy of 20, had been found lying outside the gate one night, stabbed to death. No one had ever been charged with the crime, though it was generally assumed to have been the work of fanatical Moslems. They were cut off from the rest of their families too by Partition, having come originally from what is now Pakistan. It is difficult for many British people to appreciate the importance of the extended family in the lives of Asiatics, living as we do in 'nuclear families'; there, a child grows up in a close, involved interaction with as many as 100 related persons. I thought it a measure of their Christianity that they seemed in no way embittered by their experiences.

In the Bishop's company, I found Jammu an interesting town. Everywhere we went, old boys from his school came up to see if they could do anything for him. One day we both had business in the bank and went there together a little before closing time. I had to leave the Bishop and go upstairs to have my travellers' cheques dealt with. Here I found the clerks very rude and unco-operative, for they said it was far too late for them to bother about travellers' cheques and I must come back the following morning. Since I had planned to go to Delhi the next day, I was not pleased about this and went to find the manager. I needn't have troubled: Bishop William, scenting problems, had already straightened it all out, and the clerks being some of his old boys, could now not have been more helpful. My money was changed in minutes and when it was handed over the Bishop, not quite satisfied because the notes were rather grubby, got them exchanged for crisp, clean ones.

I was taken to see the local law courts. These were housed in what had once been the Maharajah's harem. Here all the business was conducted in the large enclosed gardens at the centre of the buildings where in former times the harem ladies would have taken their exercise. Little pens were set up all around the edge where the advocates discussed cases with their clients, separated from the next pen only by a fence of chicken-wire. Prisoners, attached to jailers by manacles and long chains, sauntered about greeting friends and having discussions with their advocates. They were there to bribe judges, too, one man told me; he said that hardly any cases actually came before the courts, being invariably settled by bribery and that this saved the courts a great deal of time and money.

When I decided to take the train to Delhi in order to obtain the necessary visas for visiting Nepal and Sikkim, even getting my ticket for the journey involved the old boy network, Bishop William and I being entertained to tea in the station master's office while the business was being arranged. I thought at the time that this was a rather long-winded way of obtaining a ticket, but this was before I had tried to buy one for the return journey without his help. Travel is so cheap and tiring in India that I thought it well worth going first class. Bishop William wouldn't hear of this. Poor people, he insisted, were much friendlier and kinder, so I travelled third class. The Jhellum express takes 20 hours to cover the 200 miles to Delhi; not exactly express speed, but not too uncomfortable a journey, either, by local standards. Travelling by night, the hours of darkness were spent stretching out on thinly covered planking, arranged in tiers; small children sleeping in the luggage racks. The only real discomfort was during the last two hours when local people travelling into town fought their way into the carriage, elbowing and boring for a space for themselves and their possessions—very trying in that heat, considerably worse than the rush hour on the London tube.

I didn't expect to like Delhi, since I seldom like any towns very much. I was here purely on business anyway, eager to complete it as quickly as possible so as to get back to the mountains. Still there were compensations, not the least of which was the curious place at which I stayed—Ringo's, a sort of flop house, left over from flower power days; not very high in the comfort scale but redolent of the gentler values of the

'6os. This place was still a mecca for young European world travellers, I being the oldest person there by a couple of decades. Not that I felt at all out of place, the other guests were very friendly and only too happy to take me in hand and help me to get the most out of Delhi, telling me where to find really good ice cream, how to cope with Delhi Belly, and a host of other useful tips which held me in good stead throughout my stay. Less attractive were the few pale remnants of the Hippie cult—confirmed junkies, ghost-grey and closed to normal human contact.

Many of the younger guests were travelling for a specific time, between or after their studies. These would probably then return to their countries and settle down. There were others, though, for whom world travel had become a way of life, an addiction from which they could not break free. Some of them had been wandering around for years, staying a while here and there to earn a little money to continue their wanderings. Most of them were poised on the edge of flight to cooler climes now that the hot season was about to break upon India. I had little time to sample all the delights to which my young guides pointed me, for I was determined to obtain my visas, arrange for my eventual passage home and get the train back to Jammu within 48 hours. They said such a schedule was impossible, given the nature of Indian bureaucracy.

The second compensation I met as I emerged from Ringo's the following morning, and I did not at first recognize him as such. He was a tall, upright Sikh of about 60, with dark flashing eyes and an impressive waxed moustache—a figure who could have come straight from the pages of a Victorian novel. He was in charge of a motor rickshaw which he was determined that I should hire. I was equally determined to walk.

'Madam, I am knowing Delhi very well. I will take you to all the good places, double quick.'

I told him that I was not sightseeing but when I had explained what I had to do, he was even more eager for me to hire his services.

'Madam, I am thinking you are really needing me. I am

ex-British Army and know all these places. I think you hire me for whole day, maybe we get all done.'

I thanked him for his offer but said that I couldn't possibly afford to hire him for a whole day.

'No problem, money not important. You pay me what you want.'

So we settled on what seemed a very low price and away we went. I began to appreciate my good fortune almost immediately, for unlike other rickshaw drivers I had encountered, this one did not stop every few yards to ask directions. In spite of the snarled-up traffic, we raced along in fine style, taking to the pavement where necessary and finding shortcuts through narrow, winding alleys. In a commendably short time, we were drawing up with a flourish outside the first of the government departments. Here too my Sikh proved his worth, for he accompanied me inside and smoothed my path through the minefields of petty officialdom. One of the problems in a labour-intensive country like India is that the person you have come to see is protected by a host of lesser men, in a descending scale of importance. The further down the pecking order these men come, the more determined they are to exercise their importance and prevent you from reaching your objective. My Sikh was wonderful with them; by some magic he had them transformed into helpful, smiling beings, eager to facilitate my passage to the appropriate official. Having reached this exalted personage, all difficulties were behind me and it was 'No problem', cups of tea, compliments and courtesy. The same pattern was repeated at all the various departments and at the Nepalese Embassy—though this last was a trifle more arrogant and there were no cups of tea. We shuttled to and fro between them, the rickshaw buzzing along like an angry bee.

At the end of four hours, I had acquired a permit to visit Darjeeling and Sikkim, a promise of a visa for Nepal and airplane tickets—both of these to be called for later. I thought it was high time we had some lunch, so my Sikh took me to the place where he usually ate. This was a sort of open-sided shack, with a long communal table down the centre and benches on either side. Each person was given a steel dish, divided into compartments, into which was placed rice, dal, two sorts of curried vegetables, two sorts of soup and chapattis. For about 20 pence a head you could eat as much as you liked. Small boys, clad in sarongs, rushed around, refilling plates as fast as the food was consumed. It was tremendous value, though difficult to eat without a fork or spoon; later I realized I had acquired Delhi Belly.

There was now time to kill before picking up the visa and tickets, so my Sikh suggested that he show me some of the sights. Perhaps there wasn't a lot to be seen in New Delhi, or more probably my Sikh had other ideas, because where he took us was to a large dusty park, and once there he seemed determined to seek out the least frequented corners. I was not unprepared for this because there had been quite a few leers and twirling of moustaches at me through the driving mirror, and our long waits had been enlivened by such remarks as 'Madam, I have admiration for you—you are together with your body.' So now I took the initiative and led the way to where there were more people and to where the charming sight of a huge Brahmin ox pulling a lawn-mower across the grass had me clicking away with my camera until it was time to go and pick up the various documents. My Sikh was visibly displeased by my lack of co-operation; back in the rickshaw he tried a more direct approach, inviting me to spend the evening with him 'For massage and lying relaxing in the grass'. Heady stuff! I tried to explain, as kindly as I could—for I really liked him very much—that tempting though his offer was, for a married woman such activities were really not on. He thought this only showed that I 'was of no heart' and had never loved.

Back at Ringo's I tried the cure for Delhi Belly and reflected sadly on how difficult it was for any unaccompanied Western woman, whatever her age, to travel the sub-continent without eliciting amorous advances.

In the morning I felt much better, the cure having worked, and I set out, full of energy, to get a railway ticket for the Jhellum express back to Jammu. My friends at Ringo's had warned me of the difficulties of obtaining railway tickets and had advised me to hire the services of a professional queue-stander. They said that of all Indian bureaucracy, station booking offices were the worst, and that the clerks had a policy of selling a maximum of 10 tickets an hour, which resulted in hundreds of people fainting after standing waiting for 10 hours or more. Queue-standers did the waiting for a modest fee, the only problem being that they required several days' notice and I didn't have the time. A further inconvenience was that Europeans had first to obtain a form from another part of the city before they could even begin to queue. I was en route for the form when I saw my Sikh rickshaw driver again, all smiles and eager to convince me that there were no hard feelings. He drove me to where I had to go, refused to let me pay and so we parted in friendship.

There were about 50 young Europeans waiting for their forms. Two of these were anthropologists who had been doing post-graduate studies in a remote village in Sind. They also knew Jean and Robin Lankester, with whom I had stayed in Karachi, and had been told to look out for me in Kashmir. So it was an interesting wait spent comparing Pakistani experiences. We went to the station together and I found that the confusion and difficulties forecast by the Ringo guests had been in no way exaggerated. It was like a scene from Dante's *Inferno*, with thousands of people rushing frantically hither and thither, long queues of the desperate or sadly resigned, interspersed with the fallen bodies of those who had fainted or perhaps expired. It seemed impossible to find out where to go as there were several floors containing endless booking offices, each one of which dealt with only one specific train on one specific day. My companions spoke Hindi but this was no help, since there was no one of whom to ask directions. Eventually by sheer luck we found the correct window for my train; the queue here was truly daunting and we could see that what I had been told about only selling 10 tickets an hour was quite true. Never had the bicycle seemed more the ideal way of travel than at this moment. Then it occurred to us that at other kiosks we had seen signs saying 'Officers and Ladies Only'. We thought it worth a try and took up a position parallel to the head of the queue, saying firmly 'Ladies Only queue' when challenged. It worked. I was issued with my ticket, the only obstacle placed in my way being that the exact money to the smallest coin had to be ready; the giving of change was not the booking clerk's job. As there was no way of finding out what the fare was before the booking clerk told one, we found this rather fiendish. The same procedure was then repeated to obtain tickets for my companions. Before we left the station, we were delighted to see that our parallel queues of 'Ladies Only' were still there, with Indian and European women standing in them. It seemed only fair that it should be so.

12

I was hoping now for a more gentle time, riding through peaceful mountain scenery on my way to the Kulu Valley. India, though, for all its philosophy, is seldom a peaceful place. The first incident of the day occurred within a few hours of bidding farewell to Bishop and Mrs William. It was about 10.30 and the sun already high and very hot. I had drunk the contents of both water bottles and was on the look-out for somewhere to refill them, when I spotted a standpipe in a small village along the way. Several young girls were there filling their water jars and splashing each other, giggling and generally enjoying themselves. When I appeared, they fell silent and moved back. No amount of smiling on my part reassured them or elicited any response, so I washed the sweat and dirt off my face and filled my water bottles. In the meantime the girls were screaming for help. I think they didn't dare run away in case I stole their huge brass water jars. Their shouts brought several women, but they didn't respond to my smiles either. Before I could move off a man came running up, brandishing a mattock, obviously prepared to do battle with some desperate character. Fortunately he did respond to my smile, which by this time must have become a trifle fixed. He dropped the mattock and came over and shook my hand—an unusual gesture for a Hindu, since by their caste laws the touch of someone of a lower caste makes them ritually unclean. All non Hindus are outside the caste system, so Hindus cannot with impunity shake hands, even with the Queen. In the days of the Raj, the British were tacitly assumed to be of the 'padre caste' but this was purely for convenience, it did not make them any less 'unclean'. The mattock-brandishing Hindu was probably an untouchable. He wasn't at all keen to let me get on my way, but seemed to be inviting me to come into the village to partake of refreshment—all this was conveyed by mime. The smallest girls had recovered enough to give me charming shy smiles, but the women were still regarding me with the deepest suspicion so I thought I'd better get on.

An hour later I found that I had lost my map. It wasn't a very good map, but it was the only one available and impossible to replace outside of Delhi. Without it I would be lost, since my accurate but very small-scale British map did not show such details as rest houses, or roads built since Partition. So back I went, searching carefully on both sides of the road. Half an hour later, a lorry screeched to a halt in front of me, several men leapt out and ran towards me, one of them waving my map. They seemed delighted to restore my property and wouldn't accept a reward; but how they had come by it, or how they knew it belonged to me, I could not find out.

By lunchtime I was back at the village where two weeks earlier the fierce Sikh had harangued me about my country's iniquities. It seemed to have been considerably longer than that because of so much happening. I had another good meal at the tourist café and pushed on towards Chakki where my map indicated there was a rest house. It was not a good afternoon for cycling, being hot and sticky. A strong headwind had blown up, too—always more of a curse than any hill. With a hill you know you will eventually reach the top, and if your gears are low enough it can even be pleasant. But a headwind is unrelenting and takes all the pleasure out of the day, making progress a matter of grim endurance. So when I reached the Chakki rest house after 30 miles of this wind, I was more than ready for a rest and several gallons of tea.

It was an isolated, pretty place, set amongst wooded fields, with a little stream running past—ideal I thought for a peaceful night. The chowkidar turned out to be one of the sort who considered it his job to repel tourists. There didn't appear to be anyone else staying there, so it couldn't be that there was no room, but no way would he let me through the door, he just kept flapping his arms at me and saying something like 'shoo shoo'. I was quite determined not to move. I hadn't much energy left anyway; so I just sat in the garden, thinking longingly of hot tea, with the sweat slowly drying on my skin. I must have sat there for about half an hour, trying to look unconcerned, but finding it difficult. It paid off, though, for the chowkidar tired of the situation before I did and came out looking most annoyed. He gestured crossly for me to follow him, and guessing that he intended to take me to see someone with more authority than he had, I went with him willingly enough. He led me to a wooden hut about half a mile away which had 'Office of the Sub-Divisional Engineer (Construction)' written over the door. Once here things went better, except that everyone who was remotely connected with construction squashed themselves into the office to have a look at this strange British woman who was riding a bicycle around the Himalayas. They were kind, courteous men, quite unlike the usual Indian crowds, and they quickly organized tea and brought cakes and sweets, 'tut-tutting' and saying that I looked hot and tired and shouldn't have been made to walk to the office. The poor chowkidar got roundly told off by everyone and I felt quite sorry for him. After all the men had had a go at pressing me to more food and tea, the sub-divisional engineer made them leave so that he could talk to me. He started by telling me that he was a Christian and that I could trust him; then he asked gently if I had any money. I assured him that I had lots, but I could see that he did not believe me—like many people, he found it hard to credit that anyone will travel around on a bicycle if they can afford some other means of transport. I showed him some of my travellers' cheques to convince him that I was well provided for, but I was very moved by his evident intention of helping me had I proved to be destitute.

After this everyone was allowed back in, and we all drank more tea and ate cakes and talked. They told me I was to be their guest for the night and would listen to no objections. The chowkidar was sent for and given his instructions about how I was to be housed and fed—everything being translated for my benefit. I was then escorted back to the rest house by half a dozen of the men, one of them wheeling the bicycle. It felt curious but very pleasant to be so cosseted. I don't think the chowkidar was half so pleased though, because supper when it came was not meat, vegetables and rice as instructed by the engineers, but a boiled egg floating in a pool of curried water.

'Dalhousie', I had read somewhere, 'is a poor man's Simla, a Southend amongst hill stations, not a Brighton.' This rather pejorative description had so intrigued me, I thought I would go and see it, since my map showed it to be only about half a day's ride off my route. Maps, however, being flat, can be very deceptive about distances in hilly country, and it took eight hours' very hard riding to reach Dalhousie, perched as it was above 45 miles of very steep gradients. It was worth the effort for the quite stunning views of the great Himalayan peaks to the north, but as a place for enjoyment, I much preferred Southend. When Lord Dalhousie, at that time Viceroy of India, funded its beginnings as a hill station, the British Raj was flourishing and bank clerks and their wives and other people lower down the social scale than those who graced the slopes of Simla, came here to escape the terrible heat of the plains. Little remained to remind one of those days, save old enamelled tin advertisements in some of the shops for long vanished brands of whisky and chocolate. It had a decidedly scruffy appearance now and army camps were very much in evidence. Of Indian bank clerks and their wives, I saw no sign. Perhaps they came here later in the season. I stayed in the large, beautifully sited youth hostel where there were only two other guests, both European. We ate together in the recommended restaurant; it was the only one open and was not at all good.

Very early the following day I retraced my steps, riding the mountain down in the crisp, clear air of a Himalayan morning. For an hour I sped downhill, delighting in the headlong progress and the air streaming past me; seeing no one except an occasional young shepherd herding his sheep. As the slope lessened and my speed decreased I became more aware of the great beauty of the terrain with its strange eroded rock columns and great fields of flowers, and bird song rising in a chorus all around. This scenery changed abruptly as I turned east into the Kangra Valley. A great wall of ice-fringed rock towered into the sky on the left, while the lower Shivalik Hills to the south were hidden by dense forests. A shallow boulder-strewn river flowed gently along by the side of the road, having lost its former wild speed on reaching the valley floor.

I stopped to picnic on chapattis which I purchased from a wayside halt supplemented with walnuts, jam and oranges which I had brought from Jammu. By now I had realized that it was necessary to carry quite a lot of food with me, in case of emergencies. Although the sub-continent is simply littered with places to eat and seldom is there more than a few miles between wayside cafés, the problem is that these hovels serve a very limited menu, altogether unsuitable for stomachs not brought up from infancy to coping with quantities of chilli. There is also the serious health risk endemic in such insanitary, fly-infested places. A small cooking stove would have solved the problem, had the fuel for it been obtainable. As it was, I compromised by eating only omelettes or boiled eggs since they could be cooked while I waited, and the same applied to chapattis and tea. Fruit and nuts were safe since I could peel or shell them. It was not an ideal diet though on which to cycle long distances in mountainous country.

The Kangra Valley grew wider the further east I went and villages and small towns became more frequent—squalid places these, in stark contrast to their idyllic settings. Dead dogs and the bloated corpses of rats littered their muddy streets. It was in one such place that I experienced a particularly nasty incident, which could have ended the journey right there. It happened around mid-afternoon when the day had become hot and sultry. I had had no intention of stopping, but a man had stepped out of his little café as I passed and waved a bottle of soft drink at me. I stopped, but before I had even got off the bicycle a crowd of men and youths closed in around me. No one said anything, they just stood there slowly chewing betel nut and occasionally spitting the red juices onto the dusty ground in front of me. One fat youth had pressed himself up against the front of the bicycle and was rubbing at his crotch while he leered into my face. The bottle had been opened in the meantime and was being tossed from hand to hand around the circle, until one of them thrust it suddenly at me, as though he meant to strike me with it. At the same moment, someone got hold of the back of the bicycle and twisted it over; down I went into the filth, breaking my sunglasses and grazing my leg—though I was unaware of this at the time. Up to that moment I had been virtually paralysed by fear, but as I hit the ground I became so incensed with rage, I could have done murder. I could hear them laughing and jeering above me and I hated them all. But somehow in the second or so it took to pick myself and the bicycle up, the rage evaporated and I knew that I had to do something decisive to end this ugly scene before it became a tragic one. Then it was as though everything was happening in a dream—I could see their open jeering mouths, the betel-stained teeth giving the appearance of blood dripping. It's like a medieval bear-baiting, I thought, or a cock fight and then I remembered a painting of the Spanish civil war; where people had been shooting and being shot—their mouths, too, had been open; but I couldn't remember who was the painter and this worried me because I could not concentrate. It was through this curious, dream-like state that I heard my own voice, icy calm and authoritative—as though I was addressing a class of fractious eight-year-olds. 'I am going,' said the voice, 'to fetch a policeman'. Even in my disconnected state I remember thinking, 'That's torn it', for it seemed a most feeble and inappropriate threat under the circumstances. It worked, though; the awful men fell back and I wheeled the bicycle resolutely through the space they left, trying not to hurry, or to show the fear which now, perversely, came flooding back. In retrospect, I think this was the most dangerous moment of the whole encounter, for had I rushed or shown the least sign of fear then, I think they would have been on me like a pack of dogs and there might have been another unsolved case of a missing Western woman. As it was, I waited until I was well clear before leaping on the bicycle and pedalling off as fast as my shaking legs would allow—the babel of sound pursuing me showed that the temporary lull was over.

I was terribly shaken by this incident, frightened and angry by turn. Gradually, though, the sheer effort of turning the pedals round calmed me down and the grandeur of the Kangra Valley asserted its soothing influence. All the rest of the day I kept worrying about it, trying to understand why they had attacked me. In the end I came to the conclusion that either I had been a catalyst for their floating aggression, as happens at football matches; or else through some previous experiences, they had developed a hatred for Westerners—a sort of reversed 'Paki bashing'. Fortunately I reached the night's rest house without any further alarms, and although it was a fairly gruesome place, the staff were friendly, which was far more important just then.

The next day was very hard as I was travelling against the grain of several ranges of hills, so that the road kept climbing and descending without really getting anywhere very fast. To make matters worse, I had another attack of 'the runs'. This is a serious inconvenience at any time, especially when cycling, but when cycling on the sub-continent it is little short of disastrous. There is simply nowhere to go! Indians squat anywhere, all over the place, but just let a Westerner even think about it and someone will appear, to stand and gaze. They have no inhibitions, so why should anyone else? She is going to squat, how interesting, let's whistle up a friend or two to share the fun. It isn't that they are perverted or mean to be nasty, they are just short of interest in their lives and lack the imagination to understand how other people feel. For anyone in a similar predicament, I offer the following discovery. Underneath the roads, particularly hill roads, there are culverts for draining off the rain water. Get into one of these and you will be all right, because they are too small for anyone else to try and squash in with you. It is probably better not to linger there, though, in case someone brighter than the average will realize that they can nip across to the other side and observe you from there.

I came eventually, after many stops, to the rest house at

Jodinarnagar. Remembering the cure for Delhi Belly, I asked the kind old chowkidar if he could get me some bananas and yoghurt. He looked mystified and brought me a pencil and paper for me to write the request. Later I saw him giving the paper to a younger man to read; both of them were scratching their heads over it. Back they both came to tell me they didn't know what yoghurt was, so it was my turn to scratch my head and think of a way of explaining. 'Milk,' I said, the young man got that as he knew a little English, then I had to think of a way of putting across the idea of sour—just like playing charades. They guessed it very quickly: 'Ah milk curd, we know it.' In a short while the chowkidar was proudly bearing a tray into the room and on it was a dear little silver teapot. 'Curd,' he announced with the dignity of an English butler. It was, too, a thin bitter yoghurt, which was surprisingly good when I had managed to get it out of the teapot. I slept after that and when I awoke at about 5.30 the following morning, I felt quite better and ravenously hungry.

The early mornings were always the best part of the day in India, before the traffic started and before the heat became oppressive. This morning I was particularly glad of the early start because I had a very steep climb ahead of me up a single-track road. In an hour I had gone from 3,000 to 7,000 feet. There was a thick mist at this height and pathetic little children of nine or 10 years were staggering along the road bent double under loads of firewood; they were shivering with cold and had no shoes, and each of them seemed to be afflicted with dreadful coughs. My lungs were also straining and I wasn't sure that I could get much further without breakfast, having had so little to eat the previous day. Just then I had to get off the cycle anyway to let a lorry come through and I found that I was squashed up against a wayside halt with a pile of eggs on a shelf in front of me. In no time a fire was lit and my breakfast was bubbling away on top of it. The next 2,000 feet went much better, and after that there were 16 miles of exhilarating downhill riding. This was not without its perils, being still a single-track road with very few passing places. There were great holes in the surface, too, and all sorts of domestic animals were using it as well as lorries. To add to the excitement, thunder had begun to roll around the surrounding peaks, and rain clouds were beginning to gather. Very soon, though, I was down to 2,500 feet at the crossroad town of Mandi, in bright sunshine, the temperature up in the 80s. This was a good place to have arrived at in time for lunch, because there was a tourist café here, serving the sort of food I wouldn't normally think of as luxurious, such as sausage, egg and chips. Here it was as good as a feast, and to sit and eat it at a plastic-topped dining table, seemed the very height of luxury.

The first uphill stretch out of Mandi was in the process of construction. Armies of small people with Mongoloid features were toiling away with wheelbarrows, shovels and hammers. Among them were quite young children and even babies. Some of these were carried on the backs of young women, while others lay in baskets under large black umbrellas, with an adult person squatting beside them chipping away at a pile of stones. I was so intrigued with this scene that I asked an Indian who seemed to be in charge who these people were. He told me that they were Nepalis who came here in family groups to maintain the mountain routes. They earned the equivalent of 45 pence a day—men and women, the children earning a little less, depending upon their size. All along the road were the rude tents which housed them—just woven rush matting hung on poles. There seemed nothing pathetic about these people. They looked sturdier and better nourished than many Indians I had seen; a smiling, unhurried race. What did seem odd was that as poor a country as India, with so many people starving to death each year, should import foreign labour to maintain the roads.

After about nine miles of hot, dusty riding along the unsurfaced stretch the road entered a steep, narrow valley, down which a river thundered its way. Thunder crashed overhead and great sheets of lightning leapt about the sky. Towers of swirling grey clouds had built themselves up, out of nothing, in a matter of moments. It was immensely impressive and not a little frightening. I hoped that a person on a bicycle would not prove to be a good lightning conductor. Rain came in sudden sharp showers and as quickly stopped again. In seconds I was as wet as it was possible to be; it didn't seem worth putting on my waterproof, besides the heat was still oppressive in spite of the showers. Suddenly the temperature dropped and what fell now was not rain but hail the size of marbles. As I cowered down under the bombardment it grew heavier, and I realized that the size of the hail was increasing all the time. There was no time to root about in the panniers for my waterproof, it wouldn't be a lot of use anyway; what was needed was shelter and fast. There was a shack within about 50 yards and as I struggled up to it, two men were in the process of building themselves into it by boarding up the open side with planks. They pulled me and the bicycle inside without ceremony and finished the boarding up. When I had recovered enough to take stock, I found I was streaming with blood from innumerable cuts. I had been extremely fortunate to have found shelter, as people and animals were frequently killed by these freak hail storms—the size of the hail reaching anything up to the dimensions of a tennis ball. The storm lasted about 20 minutes, during which time the two men made tea, and heated water for me to wash my wounds.

About two miles further on I came upon a long line of stationary vehicles. Once I had struggled to the front of it I found a huge landslip blocking the road. On top of it were more of the Nepali road-workers, beavering away to clear it, two to a shovel. They tie a rope close to the blade and one pulls while the other pushes, which doubles the number of the employed if nothing else. Willing hands helped haul the bicycle over the mountain of rubble and as I cycled on past the waiting vehicles on the other side I could see that many people were casting envious glances at my superior mode of transport.

I had the road to myself once again because of that landslip and because of several others further up. This was just as well, because the valley had narrowed further into a truly spectacular gorge, with the river plunging down in great cataracts and waterfalls. Occasional temples were built into the steep banks of the flatter sections. It was lovely to be able to cycle slowly along enjoying it all without having to watch out for other traffic.

I finished the day at a wretched rest house in a squalid little town at the foot of the Kulu Valley. Any shelter was welcome, though, in a night of continuous storm. The Kulu Valley is known as The Valley of The Gods, and from the way the thunder and lightning were being tossed around, this seemed singularly appropriate. When I awoke after a disturbed and hungry night, I found the rain was still bucketing down, though the aerial theatricals were over. Water was pouring into my room. The other bed was quite saturated and there were deep enough puddles on the floor to provide me with a sizeable paddling pool. Whatever the weather was like outside, it was high time to move.

Before I could do so, I received a visitor. It was the young electrician from the next door room who had come to the rest house the previous day to repair the lights. Unable to do anything with the antiquated system, he had been benighted there and was now seeking distraction. 'You come with me,' he ordered peremptorily. 'Take tea,' he added. I didn't much care for his tone, but tea sounded very welcome, so I agreed to accompany him to a café. It wasn't really a good idea, because he was one of those Indians whose conversation tends to be bellicosely patriotic. He started in straight away with, 'Why you come India?' Not content with my answer, he snapped his question out again, 'But why you come India?' This time he didn't even wait for a reply, but changed tack abruptly. 'India very poor country. Britain very rich country.' I agreed since it was obviously expected of me. 'Indian peoples very illiterate, very simple, very good peoples.' I could think of quite a few I had met who were none of these things, but thought it simpler to nod agreement. I was therefore much taken aback by his next sally, 'Why for you not like Indian peoples? Indian peoples mirrors of nature!' He paused for a while to enjoy this thought and then started to tell me how foolish I was to contemplate cycling off in the rain. 'Better you stay with me, have food, talk. I tell you about India. You will enjoy very

much.' But on that score I had no compunction about dis-
agreeing.

I set off in shorts and cagoule, with plastic bags tied over my
shoes—a good outfit for rainy weather, with nothing to dry
out on arrival. The rain was all-pervading, and the nearby
river, now in full spate, overflowed its banks; but there was
nothing like the depth of water on the roads that there had been
in the Pakistani floods. It was very cold and my hands grew
quite numb and swollen. Surprisingly, my bare legs felt no
discomfort, probably because they were moving round too
fast. An hour later the back tyre punctured, but as it was only
the third puncture in over 2,000 miles, I couldn't seriously
complain, especially as it happened just outside a suitable place
for breakfast. The villagers were delighted to have such a
novel entertainment and offered me the shelter of a covered
verandah to effect repairs. This was a mixed blessing since
most of the male villagers crowded onto the verandah with
me, the better to watch and keep dry. So what with the lack of
space and my stiff swollen fingers, I took an age over it.

By mid-afternoon the cloud base began to rise and disperse
itself with the rapidity with which it had gathered 24 hours
earlier. As I entered the town of Kulu, the sun was shining and
steam was pouring off every surface. My spirits rose with it.
They rose even further after I had put away a, for once, quite
adequate meal, organized by a charming tourist officer. He
also arranged for me to stay at the Nagar Castle Rest House,
'Very number one, special rest house,' he assured me. 'Only
maybe you not able for it,' he added mysteriously. I thought
he might be tactfully indicating that it was beyond my means,
since it was so special, and I only a poor bicyclist. But after
searching for the right words, he explained, 'Very much high
road, maybe you not come there.' I was not worried on that
score, after all the hills I had already ridden, so I assured him
that I was 'Able for very high road' and pedalled off with a chit
for the chowkidar.

Three hours later I thought perhaps the tourist officer had
been right. A narrow muddy track of quite unbelievable
steepness seemed to be going on for ever. Somewhere high

above me, hidden in cloud, was Nagar Castle, but I had little hope of reaching it, for I was completely out of energy. The hard riding coupled with the inadequate food of the past few days had at last taken their toll. I stood there, bathed in perspiration, definitely not able to go a foot further. Four ragged little urchins sidled up and stood watching me, Tibetan boys from the refugee camp I had ridden past at the foot of the slope. One of them took off his cap and held it to show me what it contained. 'Magic mushroom,' he said. 'You buy?' I knew that 'magic mushrooms' were a powerful psychedelic drug, for the travellers at Ringo's had warned me about them, saying how easy it is to mistake them for ordinary mushrooms—with drastic consequences. The boys, though, once I had convinced them that I didn't want their fungi, were a godsend. They were only too eager to earn a little money by helping me push the bicycle up to the castle. I was not really able to take in very much of my surroundings by the time we reached it, being by then in an advanced stage of exhaustion. Just vague impressions of a fortress-like place, with walls of immense thickness; perched over dizzy heights. I was led to a huge dimly-lit room and went straight to bed.

13

Down the centre of the valley flowed a river the colour of jade, tumbling in places over white rocks. Trees lined the banks, newly clad in delicate spring leaf. The upper slopes were clothed in dark green pine forests and above them the white peaks towered. The lower slopes were a patchwork of tiny fields and terraces. Brown-skinned people in brightly coloured clothes, large gold rings in ears and noses, were working there, some of them guiding primitive ploughs, pulled by oxen, others carrying large wicker baskets on their backs, the shape of cornucopias.

From the verandah of Nagar Castle I could look down on this scene as the rulers of the valley had done 600 years earlier. A medieval village clustered around the base of the castle; steep, winding alleyways, with wooden houses almost touching above them. Hindu shrines and temples were dotted about in the few level places. In the one sizeable level place adjacent to the castle the local men played an interminable game of tossing coins. I watched this game for a long time before I decided that its rules were too complicated for me to work out.

A quite enchanting place in which to rest up for a while and regain some lost weight, it was made even more enjoyable by having the company of Adam. I met him as soon as I emerged from my room onto the verandah, after sleeping right round the clock. A lanky boy with a shaven head, huddled shivering in a corner, watching the dawn turning the western slopes pink.

'Hallo,' he said. 'Saw you come in on your bike last night. Can I have a look at it?'

Having pronounced it a 'smashing bike' we were friends at once and he invited me to his room for a cup of tea. Seeing that he was only about 12, I expected to find some adult person around, but no, he was entirely alone and set about making tea in a competent manner. Over the next few days I learnt his story. An English boy whose parents had separated when he was about six, he had stayed in England with his mother, while his father had gone wandering around India. He had, he said, been very unhappy at home and at school and had not got on with his mother's new partner. His father had come back to visit him—having in the meantime discovered religion in an Indian Ashram, a type of settlement for studying practical Hindu philosophy. Seeing Adam so unhappy he had brought him to India to live with him in the Ashram. Now Adam had discovered religion, too—hence the shaven head. They didn't live in the Ashram any more because their conversion was completed, he told me. It had been an exercise in getting rid of all aggression and since both he and his father were not aggressive people to start with, they had taken less time about it than most. His father had a new girl friend, whom Adam quite liked and together the three of them travelled about, between Holland and India, making a living by buying and selling things—ethnic jewellery, mostly. Sometimes, as now, the other two went off somewhere, leaving Adam to his own devices. He approved of this, because it fostered his independence and Adam had dreams of being his own man as soon as possible. Then, he thought, he might live the life of an initiate of Siva, travelling the forests with a saddhu, with trident and begging bowl, smoking hashish and having religious experiences.

But for the few days I was there, he came around with me and like any 12-year-old, he took great delight in airing his knowledge of the language and local customs. He showed me how to make puja—Hindu prayers at the local temples, the priests all treating him with perfect seriousness. He was well known in the little tea shops too, ordering 'special chai'—an improvement on normal tea, with an authority born of custom. In the evenings, which got very cold once the sun had set, we sat in his room, which was warmer than mine, since it had a fire. Here he cooked vegetables, stews and rice, which were greatly superior to the food served by the chowkidar. I grew very fond of Adam and worried about his lack of education—he didn't even have the rudiments of reading. For all his Hindi phrases, it was clear that he was not able to carry on a conversation in that language and mix with Indian boys of his own age. It seemed to me that he was isolated in the narrow culture of the perpetual world travellers, and would grow up belonging nowhere, unless he did indeed become a follower of Siva.

My next objective was to explore the head of the Kulu Valley. Accordingly I took my leave of Adam and Nagar Castle and cycled the lovely hilly back road to Manali. More of a track than a road, this way avoids most of the children who have learnt to beg from the tourists. By mid-season this valley becomes a highway for coachloads of visitors, many of them rich Europeans who delight in flinging handfuls of coins to the appealing little mites with their big grins and out-stretched hands. This unthinking generosity has serious consequences, worrying both to the authorities and to the parents of the children. The few rupees, so easily got, represent a great deal of wealth to these simple, hard-working people. The children begin to regard begging as a way of life and turn their backs on their parents' life style. India already has more than enough beggars and once children become professional, they are no longer appealing little mites, but importunate whining nuisances from whom it is extremely difficult to extricate oneself.

Most of the people I passed on the road were friendly and waved and smiled at me. I admired the free aspect and upright carriage of the old women, as they strode along, often with huge loads on their backs, carried in the distinctive, conical baskets. When I stopped to photograph them, they posed proudly, not attempting to hide their faces, as women so often had in other places. The villages I passed through were attractive, with timber-built houses a little like Swiss chalets, each with a deep verandah on which looms were set up. When

I stopped to admire the brightly coloured cloth which was being woven, someone always beckoned me up to take a closer look, but no one tried to sell me anything. Or rather no one in the villages tried. Somewhere between them, small boys invariably appeared, proffering hallucinogenic mushrooms.

When I reached Manali, after the leisurely and delightful ride, I saw that I had arrived at a tourist Mecca, for hotels and eating places lined the main street and it was all much cleaner and more luxurious than the usual town in these parts. Since the tourist season was still delayed by the recent spell of bad weather, I felt reasonably confident of having the place to myself. I had the attention of all the local hotel touts to myself, too, since they had no one else to work on. They descended on me in a delighted horde and realizing that the best means of defence was to accept the services of one of them, I quickly chose the most vociferous.

'Me agent for very best Manali place. You not like, I take you other place. All very good, very clean. You see, you like.'

Then seeing the opposition fading away, he got down to business:

'What you like, ha? Town noisy place, I think you like better outside town. I take you very good, clean place. Not too much money. You like.'

Plainly he was a professional who could assess his client's requirements in a twinkling. We wandered off into the northern fringes of the town. Here were scattered many new buildings, all recently built or in the process of being finished, and bearing rustic signs in English—like 'Singing Winds' or 'High Places'. I chose one out of the three I was offered, they all seemed to be owned by the same local syndicate and there was little to choose between them, since they were all clean, cheap, and enjoyed marvellous views of the great peaks at the head of the valley. I carried up the bicycle and settled in.

Along the verandah from my room, which was on the corner and so enjoyed views in two directions, was a young German woman, the only other tourist in Manali. We got talking when her small daughter had come toddling along the verandah to inspect the new arrival. She had recently arrived from Dharamsala where she had been 'sitting at the feet of the Dalai Lama'. Her life was in a mess, she told me, and the Dalai Lama offered the only solution for her, only now there were further complications and she had had to come away to think things out. She told me that Dharamsala was full of young people from the West, who saw the Dalai Lama as their spiritual leader. I was intrigued, visualizing a host of hippies sitting meditating among the eternal snows. She said it wasn't really like that, though, and that besides, the hippie movement was now over, with the few remaining ones being hard-line junkies. The kind of people who came to Dharamsala now didn't belong to any group, they came on their own, just to be near the Dalai Lama. It was being near him that brought spiritual peace, she said, you couldn't explain it. Later that evening, she was dining in the same restaurant as I had chosen. With her and the child was a handsome young Indian man. The child played happily with her food but the other two just sat, gazing sadly at one another. I thought that he must have been one of the 'complications'.

Within a short distance of Manali were some of the most beautiful villages I saw in the Himalayas. The houses were two-storeyed, built mainly of wood and each having an intricately carved balcony around the upper floor. Great stone slabs covered the roofs which were low-pitched with deeply projecting eaves. The streets were also paved with great slabs of rock and deeply sunken, so that each house stood on a raised platform, supported by stone walls and planted with almond trees. The combination of the delicate, pink blossom against the stone and the weathered wood—the whole scene set against the panorama of the snow-covered mountains—was a pure delight.

I cycled happily between these villages for days, soaking up the spring sunshine and eating good food. At first glance it appeared that nothing had changed here for centuries; the people still following an age-old style of husbandry, with age-old implements. In many of the villages Western families had moved in; only one or two as yet, but it seemed clear that more would follow. I wondered what effect their very different life-style would have upon the indigenous population. Would they gradually be displaced and their homes become the holiday cottages of wealthy city-dwellers, as had happened in many beautiful areas of Britain? One could only hope not.

In other places in the valley there were many Tibetan refugees, eking out a subsistence on poor land and living in makeshift shacks of such inadequacy that I could not imagine how they had survived the winter in them. Throughout the Himalayas these sad Tibetan camps stand as a reproach to a gross, inhuman action. For India they are yet another insurmountable problem in a seemingly hopeless war against poverty.

On my last day I cycled up the valley as far as I could go towards the Rohtang Pass. Had I been a month later on my travels, and the season not so delayed, I should have been coming down this way from Ladakh. That road, though, climbs to over 14,000 feet and I doubted that it would become passable at all this year. The higher I climbed, the rougher the terrain grew and the Tibetan camps became more frequent. Then I was above the terminal moraine and in snowfields, with just a ribbon of road winding steeply between high banks of cleared snow. It was like cycling up a cresta run, but as there was no luggage on the bike it didn't feel too arduous. Parties of Tibetan women were busy with shovels and wheelbarrows keeping the road clear. They were bundled up in layers of clothes and shawls while I was finding it extremely hot in shorts and a thin shirt. The sun shone brilliantly out of a fiercely blue sky and the snow-dazzle would have been blinding without dark glasses. The Tibetan women had been issued with bright orange goggles which contrasted very oddly with their long black skirts. Apart from these women, I had seen no one and no vehicle since the last Tibetan camp, hours before. As I turned another of the interminable bends, the road ended abruptly, at a 20-foot high wall of solid snow. Quite a large party of Tibetan women were having a tea break here, resting on the backs of their shovels, or sitting in the wheelbarrows. Seeing me, some of them jumped to their feet and started throwing snowballs in my direction—whether to discourage me from going on, or just in general friendliness, I couldn't tell. We were at about 9,500 feet at this point, where the altitude begins to have a euphoric effect, so perhaps they were just feeling very happy, as I was.

I took some photographs before starting down and as I was putting the camera away, it fell and started off down the road, gathering momentum fast. It kept well ahead of me for 2,000 feet, since I had to go cautiously because of the thick layer of ice on the road, while it was far better shaped for a toboggan run, with no sharp edges or projections to halt its progress. When I did catch up with it, it seemed little the worse for its wild career, and continued to function perfectly for the remainder of the journey.

It was not easy to leave the Kulu Valley and only the thought of busloads of visitors about to descend upon it finally got me going. I kept stopping to take a last look back and each view seemed lovelier than the one before. Only the little boys hawking their mushrooms and calling 'Hippie, hippie' in their loud raucous voices finally got me cycling with determination. At Kulu I stopped to stock up with food in preparation for the remote valleys ahead.

In a few hours I had cycled a distance which had taken three days, going up. I was back now at the head of the gorge where I had experienced the freak weather. It looked less dramatic in bland sunshine and from the amount of traffic on the road I guessed that all the avalanche debris had been cleared. Not that the traffic was any inconvenience to me, since at this point I crossed the river to a much smaller road, which, after losing more precious height, began a long, steep climb to the Jalori Pass. At least, I hoped it did. With my inadequate local map, I could never be quite sure of any road and I was often glad that I carried a compass to check my general direction. There was an additional uncertainty about the pass. At over 10,000 feet, it might very well not be open since the snow line was still at about 7,500 feet. If I couldn't get over it, it would mean a detour of several hundred miles. I reminded myself that to travel at all, one has to be an optimist.

I pressed on through the hot day in an entirely different landscape of bare brown rock and deep, brown rivers. When I stopped for a picnic lunch, I chose a quiet spot overlooking a temple at the river's edge. It seemed far from any habitation and yet before I had even begun to eat, a small girl with a hare lip had come and sat herself down a short distance away, fixing me with an unblinking gaze. A young couple had also popped up out of nowhere and were busy poking about in the opened panniers. I felt decidedly harassed. The little girl was not too difficult to dislodge, I just pressed a small coin into her hand and turned her around and she trotted off happily enough. The other two were another matter. The young man kept making signs to me, as though smoking through cupped hands. Later, I learnt that this meant he was either offering me hashish or requesting some. At the time I hadn't the remotest idea of what he was after and was more intent on stopping the young woman from rifling through my possessions. In the end it was simpler to ride off and find a more peaceful place.

During the rest of the day's ride I saw no one. The few villages that there were in that infertile valley were tiny places clinging to the higher slopes of the mountains. Precipitous paths led up to them, often skirting sheer cliff faces. Goats grazing the thin brush of the eroded lower slopes, dislodged stones and dust onto the road. Eddies of wind, funnelling down the gullies, lifted more dust, so that I was soon covered with a layer of it and felt I must have swallowed several kilos more.

I was not sorry to reach Banjar and find that the rest house existed. It was a splendidly sited place and quite a struggle to climb up to. The chowkidar seemed surly but led me round to the back of the building and pointed to a row of what looked like cow stalls. I think they had in fact been built as accommodation for horses, but now they were noisome little cells, each containing a bed liberally strewn with dead beetles and other debris. Few of them had more than the rudiments of a door, and they looked as though no one had used them in a long while. Still it was shelter and I paid up cheerfully when the chowkidar thrust out his palm. He went off to his quarters at the end of the garden where he was immediately engaged in conversation by an old woman who had been spying on us with great interest. They sounded as if they were having a most bitter quarrel, but as many conversations in India are conducted in loud, hectoring tones, I wasn't alarmed. I was more interested in discovering which of the little cells was the least awful and in finding somewhere to wash. In my search, I came to the front of the building. Here was a covered verandah with several decent bedrooms leading off it, all unoccupied. While I was standing there wondering why I couldn't have one of these rooms, the chowkidar and the old woman appeared. The chowkidar was all set to forestall any request: 'V.I.P. rooms,' he snapped, spreading out his arms in front of one of the bedroom doors, and shaking his head vigorously. Stung by what I took to be an odious assessment of my worth, I drew myself up and said firmly, 'I am V.I.P.' To my surprise, the old lady appeared to be siding with me, smiling and nodding agreement. The chowkidar's defences collapsed; in next to no time I was installed in the nicest room with a tray of tea and a bucket of hot water for washing. I decided I would always try to establish V.I.P. status in future, since it procured such benefits, chowkidars being clearly unused to catering for travel-stained females on bicycles.

Before I left the following morning, I tried to find out from the chowkidar if the Jalori Pass was open. His English, though, was even less than my few words of Hindi and he was not good at mime either. So the only information I could glean was that the road was of monumental steepness. This was certainly the case as I found immediately and was glad that I had forced myself to eat the unappetizing rest house food, so as to have the necessary strength to tackle the initial slopes. I hated starting off the day on steep gradients before my muscles had had time to warm up on a flatter stretch. The road surface was covered with mud and gravel, too, which made the riding even more difficult. I crept on upwards, making slow progress and having to stop frequently to clear the impacted mud from between the wheels and mudguards. After a couple of hours of this, I arrived at a village where a bus stood with lots of people standing by it. I stopped at the nearby shack for a glass of tea and to enquire about the Pass. Soon the question was being considered by everyone present, and after about 10 minutes of heated discussion, a spokesman came forward to tell me the general conclusion.

'We think it is not open,' he said. 'But maybe you can come there with bike.'

This sounded encouraging, but he went on: 'We think you not come there on your own, but maybe if you have two strong men to help, then you come over.'

I asked him where I could find such men.

'Here,' he replied. 'Very good men, they porters for you, bring you safe over' and two young men were thrust forward. I asked what their services would cost and a sum of about five pounds was mentioned. This was equivalent to several days' wages for each of them, but it didn't occur to me to bargain, which was a mistake, as I realized later in the day.

We set off immediately, the young men wheeling the bicycle and all the other young men and boys of the village accompanying us, for the first half mile. They set a cracking pace which it was all I could do to keep up with. Every so often we had to stop to clear the mud off the wheels which annoyed one of the porters very much. He seemed to be the leader of the two and spoke a little English. 'Fast, fast,' he kept urging me, as I scraped away the mud with a twig. 'Very far, fast, fast.' Eventually they decided that it would be quicker and easier to carry the bicycle. Accordingly I took the panniers off and we made a sling for them; so each porter had a load of about 30 pounds, very little by portering standards, though more awkward to carry than a rucksack. After this, they decided that we should leave the road and take short cuts, going vertically upwards through impressive forests of pines whose roots projected outwards, making a sort of natural ladder. We went up at such a pace I thought my heart would burst with the effort. Every few hundred feet we all dropped to the ground and lay gasping for breath. It was a silly way to tackle such slopes, as I well knew; a steadier pace would have achieved equal progress with far less effort. Besides, I resented rushing through such beautiful scenery with no time to enjoy it, but I was unable to put this idea over to the porters, who were growing surlier as the climb proceeded.

Crossing and recrossing the line of the road, we came eventually to where there were no more shortcuts, for the road had out-topped all the surrounding country. Here the porters staged the first of their sit-downs.

'Not go further,' said the spokesman.

'I'm not going back,' I said. 'Not after all that effort to get here.'

'Rest house here, you stay here, maybe get through when road clear, tomorrow maybe.' I pointed out that I could have got this far unaided by keeping to the road. I had hired them to carry the bicycle through the snow at the top of the pass and explained that if we didn't do this I wasn't going to pay them.

'We not your servants,' said the surly porter angrily. 'We go back. You pay now.'

Seeing there was no shifting them through argument, I loaded the panniers back onto the bicycle and started to push it up the road. Immediately they sprang to their feet and followed. After a little while, they silently resumed their loads and we went on in silence for a short way until we came to a band of Tibetan road-workers cheerfully shovelling at a wall of snow. As far as I could judge, it was less than a mile to the summit and the gradient looked very gentle. To my surprise, the porters made no demur about proceeding, by steps, to the top of the 20 feet of snow covering the road—probably because of the watching Tibetans. But as soon as they were out of sight, they staged another sit-down.

'Not go on. We cold.'

The snow had melted on the surface and we were occasionally sinking up to our knees in it, but the sun was blazing down out of a clear sky. Whatever else it was, it certainly wasn't cold. I pointed out that I was clad in shorts and short-sleeved shirt, and that I was perspiring quite freely.

'Foot cold,' they said, pointing accusingly at the thin edge of tennis socks protruding above the tops of my cycling shoes. They pulled up their trouser legs to show that they had no socks. I can't say that their discomfort exactly wrung my heart. By this time I realized that all their stops and complaints were designed to extract more money and I was determined not to give in to this, for I feared if I did so, they would go on demanding more and more. I had lots of plastic bags with me for just such use. Plastic bags worn inside boots keep the feet warm and dry when walking through snow or soggy ground and many mountaineers and porters use this method. I demonstrated their use to these two, wishing that I had thought of it earlier as my socks were already soaked. The porters rejected my offer with contempt so to save time I lent them my spare two pairs of socks, which they accepted and into which they somehow squashed their considerably larger feet. After this they tried various ploys, the main one being the considerable danger of the journey. This was nonsense, since all we had to do was to keep to the crest of the ridge, beneath which the road must run. Besides it was clear from the numbers of footprints which way the route went; there were even occasionally sweetpapers on the snow. Nor were there any slopes above us to avalanche. In fact it was like being on top of the world and so beautiful with the surrounding peaks blue as sapphires and the immense pine forests stretching out below us that even the grumbling porters were silenced for a short while by the grandeur of it all.

At the summit, which was 10,200 feet, stood a simple temple to Kali, consort of Shiva, and two little boys of about seven and nine were manning a tea house in a sort of cave beneath it. They had walked up from a village on the other side, a distance of about nine miles, and I think we were their only customers that day.

The porters' last threat had been to turn back at the summit and leave me to make my own way down. This would have been extremely difficult, since there was just as much snow on this side and the slope was considerably steeper. However, because of the little boys watching, they set off with no argument at all and ran down the slope at a tremendous lick, with me plunging and falling in pursuit. In a very short time the surface of the road began to appear in patches through the snow. Once again the porters sat. I decided that this had better be for the last time, since I was heartily sick of them and their grumbling.

'Very dangerous road back,' moaned the English-speaking one. 'We not come village this night.'

This was more plain nonsense, for we had taken five hours to get this far; going back, unladen and mainly downhill, they would do it in about two or at most three hours. I paid them the price we had agreed and they promptly threw the money on the ground, but retrieved it almost immediately when it threatened to blow away. They were not at all keen to give me back my socks, but I really needed these as I would not be able to obtain others in those remote regions. I gave them the plastic bags instead, which would serve them much better, since the socks were wringing wet.

They stood there in silence, watching me struggling down through the remaining snow, which grew stickier with every step. About half an hour of alternately carrying the cycle or just dragging it and I was below the snowline. It was lovely to be alone to enjoy my surroundings at last. All around were rhododendrons, 60 feet high, ablaze with scarlet blossom. The road was too eroded and broken to ride on, so I walked, delighting in the scents of pine resin and wet leaf mould. Suddenly I remembered that it was Easter Day; back home everyone would be celebrating it in some way. In spite of the porters, I would not have changed places with anybody. Never had I spent an Easter Day in such glorious surroundings.

14

There was no sign of any habitation as I walked down the upper reaches of the valley when suddenly, slipping through the trees in ones and twos, came a band of ragged little boys. They ran straight up to me with no shyness and no pushing, smiling sweetly as if to welcome me. The bicycle was patted and stroked gently as though it was a horse and then they walked gravely alongside, holding on to me or to parts of the bicycle as I continued down the mountain. As we walked they called to companions I couldn't see, until they too came running through the trees to join the others. In a short time we had become quite a procession. I could quite understand the temptation to scatter·largesse in these circumstances; they were such delightful children, who were looking for nothing more than to enjoy the novelty of walking down the road with a foreign lady and her bicycle. I wanted to reward them for the sheer pleasure their company gave me. I resisted, having seen what this sort of giving had done to the children of Kulu. Gradually the procession dwindled away, until just one little fellow remained. He had pride of place, holding on to a handlebar and was not going to relinquish it easily. 'Rest house?' I queried. He said something in Hindi and pointed ahead. We walked on a little further and then I had the idea of lifting him onto the saddle. Never have I seen a child look so proud and so apprehensive at the same time. I hoped that some of his friends were observing him, since it was clearly his big moment. I think he was relieved as well as sorry when we finally came to the rest house—such pleasures are not without a certain strain. Before he left me, he made a charming little Indian salaam.

I turned the corner into the driveway, thinking with pleasure of the children and wondering if the chowkidar would be around when I was suddenly assailed by a flood of English voices. Unable to believe my ears, I looked ahead and saw on the little green lawn what appeared to be a great crowd of unmistakably English people drinking tea and chatting. I couldn't quite take it in. Apart from young Adam, I hadn't seen an English person in weeks and that wild, remote spot was the last place I would have expected to come across such a scene. I felt so confused and shy I rather wanted to turn tail and run. In all fairness, it was almost as much of a shock for them. They had hardly expected to see a lone English woman with a bicycle emerge from the snows. When we had all recovered, we introduced ourselves. They were an English party on an expensive and beautifully organized Himalayan walking holiday, with mules and scores of porters. They shouldn't really have been in this place at all, but snow had delayed them and now they were waiting for their mules to catch up.

Since the party had taken over the small, two-bedroomed rest house, I was invited to muck in with them. I was only too pleased. Having got over my initial shock, I was finding it most enjoyable not to have to go through the usual evening hassle with a reluctant chowkidar.

The jingle of bells interrupted the conversation and a string of mules accompanied by smiling porters swept onto the tiny lawn. The party greeted them with loud cheers and surged forward to collect their luggage. I wondered what the hurry was, and soon discovered that it was in order to get at their supplies of whisky. I'd almost forgotten the pleasure of a pre-dinner drink. While we drank and chatted the porters were busy erecting the tents and cooking dinner. They had it all organized and ready in the time it took the rest of us to put away only a very modest amount of alcohol. This was probably just as well, since I had eaten my last meal 14 hours previously and was right out of practice at drinking, anyway. The food was delicious—at least I thought it was. The rest of the party, fresh from the effete West, found it less to their liking and many of them were very worried about the lack of hygiene in the kitchen. I'd been thinking how incredibly clean everything was. My standards had taken a tumble, or else I'd become more acclimatized to life in Asia. Either way, it gave me a warm glow, making me feel quite the seasoned traveller.

Like a child on a Sunday school outing, I savoured every detail of this unexpected treat. After-dinner coffee; chocolate; sleeping in a tent; a cheerful porter waking me up with a mug of hot tea in the morning and a proper breakfast afterwards. Perhaps most of all, I enjoyed the sheer delight of conversing fluently.

I was given a very noisy send-off which was picked up and echoed by the local children, so that I descended the valley to resounding cheers. I needed all my attention for the deplorable track, though, for it descended very steeply with a surface of sand and boulders. Tremendous drops down to a gorge on the right were totally unprotected. It was extremely dangerous riding and every time I braked, the sand made the back wheel skid alarmingly towards the precipices. Just the terrain for a puncture, I thought, and no sooner thought it, but it happened. Punctures are not really very much trouble; the worst thing about them is getting your hands filthy repairing them. I set about this one quite happily, until I discovered that both my tubes of rubber solution had solidified and were unusable. Consternation! Where on earth would I find rubber solution in this remote area where there just weren't any bicycles? I had one spare inner tube which would do for this repair, but if I punctured again, I would be in considerable difficulties. At a rough estimate, I had about 400 miles of very rugged country to traverse before reaching Dehra Dun, the first town where I could hope to find a bicycle shop. Resolving to ride with the utmost caution, I continued downwards until, from a bracing 4,000 feet, I reached the lowest and hottest place in those parts, at 2,500 feet.

There was a village here where I had not planned to stop but an enormously fat woman saw me ride up and came waddling over, after struggling up from the wickerwork chaise she had been reclining upon. She laid a restraining hand upon my arm and beckoned for me to follow her. I was led to a small café, where the woman indicated I should sit down at a table. She vanished into the rear of the building and emerged shortly with a plate piled high with rice, vegetables and dal. I could see nothing for it but to eat. The woman meanwhile set herself down at the entrance to repel any curious villagers. When I'd finished she made signs that I should pay her and I held out a palmful of small change. From this she selected a few coins, to the value of about 12 pence, and then waddled back up the street to her chaise. With travellers so thin on the ground perhaps this was the only way of getting custom.

From here the road began another ascent of monumental steepness but at least it had a surface, so there was less danger for the inner tubes. For hours I wound around the hairpins, grinding away in my lowest gear and feeling more and more dispirited and tired. I couldn't think why this was, until I looked at my watch and discovered that I'd been cycling for about six hours without a stop. I'd badly underestimated the distance, and there seemed no possibility now of reaching the rest house I had planned on for the night. So at the next village I enquired if there was a nearer one. Apparently there was and several of the local males accompanied me to show me the way. At first, the chowkidar would not hear of my staying for he said every room was full with visiting doctors. The local males were very much on my side, though, and after much fierce argument, I was told that I could spend the night on the sofa in the dining room. When the doctors returned, they insisted on doubling up, so that I could have a bedroom— much to the chowkidar's fury, it seemed.

The doctors were a jolly bunch of men and women who were travelling around some of the remoter villages on a health care project. It was just 'a drop in the ocean', they said. They could achieve very little in the time they were there but they enjoyed the break from hospital routine. For the vast majority of Himalayan people, medical care was just not available, and considering India's problems, the doctors could not see that changing in their lifetime. Many people in the cities were in an even worse plight, they said. At least the air was good here.

For the next few days I wandered the valleys and hills of this superb region ascending and descending many thousands of feet every day, sometimes through forests of tall pine trees which stretched for many miles and sometimes through wildernesses of deep gorges and rushing rivers. I walked as often as I rode because of the parlous state of the tracks and roads. Often it was necessary to ford swollen rivers where they crossed the track. This was a laborious business of unloading the panniers and wading through the boulders with them, then returning to make the crossing again with the bicycle. None of this made for very fast progress, but I didn't mind because I had no wish to hurry through such glorious scenery. There were wild flowers everywhere in great profusion, and always the shimmering peaks formed a backdrop to everything I saw.

In the remotest of the villages I passed through, I had the distinct impression of being the only white woman they had ever seen—sunburnt to a dark mahogany though I was by now. They stared at me with profound disbelief, as though doubting the evidence of their own eyes. Most disconcerting, but not intimidating since I never felt that they were hostile.

The only people I saw between villages were little bands of Nepali road-workers. Like me, they appeared to be in no hurry, but seemed always to be resting in the sunshine or playing with their babies. If I came upon them by some obstruction, like a broken bridge, or a landslip, they would always give me a helping hand across. They seemed to consider it quite an honour to wheel the bicycle, a change, I suppose, from their wheelbarrows. Sometimes, if they were brewing tea, they would offer me some. It took some getting used to, because they flavoured it with butter and salt; but I welcomed the opportunity of sitting with them for a while. They seemed to be so contented with their lot, always smiling and friendly. Although they happily shared anything I offered, such as bananas or raisins, they never begged, and they didn't stare or become excessively inquisitive like the Indian villagers.

Every evening I came upon a rest house where I had expected to find it. Each one was very like the others; a simple place which provided a bed and the same barely edible food. But each was set down in such a superb situation that if I went to bed hungry, at least I had my fill of some of the finest scenery in the world. Only two of these rest houses stood out in any way. One was in quite a large village and rather more stylishly appointed than the average. I had been shown into a spacious apartment where I had discovered the delightful surprise of a shower that actually worked instead of the normal bucket and jug arrangement. I'd just started to strip off, in preparation for this treat, when the chowkidar had suddenly reappeared—Indians never knock, but just arrive like genies.

'Memsahib, come quick,' he said excitedly.

Hastily rebuttoning my shirt, I asked him what the trouble was.

'No trouble, Memsahib, Deputy Engineer want to see you.'

I thought the deputy engineer could wait until I had washed and changed, but the chowkidar disagreed, with much vigorous head-shaking.

'Later you wash. Deputy Engineer very V.I.P. man. He say you come now.'

So very conscious of my travel-stained, baggy shorts and shirt and of the day's accumulation of sweat and grime, I followed the chowkidar to meet this august personage. Further along the verandah he threw open a door, salaamed deeply and motioned for me to enter. At first sight, I thought I had come upon a drunken orgy. The room was very dimly lit because all the blinds had been lowered. Men sprawled about the floor in relaxed attitudes, clutching glasses and giggling. Centre stage, enthroned like a pasha on the double bed, reclined what could only be the Deputy Engineer himself. He too was clutching a glass, waving it around in a rather vague gesture of welcome and hiccoughing gently.

'How you are English lady?' he enquired politely amidst the general giggles and his own hiccoughs, which he controlled with some dignity. 'We are drinking rum. You English like very much to drink rum, I am thinking. You will be so kind and have drink with Indian mens.'

This clearly was an order. A chair was pushed up close to the bed for me to sit on and I was handed a very large glass of dark brown liquid. It wasn't like anything I'd tasted before. Perhaps they made it themselves. I treated it with extreme caution.

Indians have a curious attitude to alcohol; it isn't forbidden as it is in Pakistan, but neither is it readily available. They seem to regard drinking it as an illicit pleasure—rather like small boys smoking. Perhaps having an English woman present added to the occasion, or perhaps they were just being kind. I unfortunately was not really in the mood to share the fun. It wasn't really my idea of bliss on a hot sunny afternoon to sit behind drawn blinds with a roomful of giggling men and submit to a barrage of uninhibited questioning.

'What is your age?' 'How much cost your bicycle?' 'What you earn in England?' 'What your husband earn in England?'

There was no way I could escape. I didn't dare swallow the tumbler of rum for fear of the consequences. Also, as the Deputy Engineer had absolute power over who stayed at the rest house, I couldn't risk offending him. So I just sat, sipping occasionally at the rum, and nodding agreement to such dubious ideas as 'India and Britain are the only two democracies in the world, isn't it?' and 'No one has such good government as America.'

I was rescued after two hours of this by the Deputy Engineer's wife who had come to take her inebriated husband home. I had not seen the last of him though. Several hours later, he returned with his wife and six daughters. 'I have brought family to see famous English bicycle,' he announced as they all marched in without ceremony. Fortunately, I had had my shower some time before and was fully dressed. 'Famous' English bicycle was in separate pieces in the bathroom, undergoing treatment. Undeterred, they all trooped in there to view the various bits, pick them up, comment on the weight and so on. Then mercifully they left and I was able to gather up all the scattered bits and pieces and reassemble them.

The following day started with a bracing 10 miles up a steep mountain—Himachal Pradesh's last fling before it became Uttar Pradesh. The next 20 miles were all downhill but on surfaces of sand and boulders where I couldn't really let rip. Besides, I was seriously concerned now over the state of my tyres. One was completely bald, as was the spare. The remaining one, which I had put on the back wheel (which wore out the faster), was not much better. After a while I didn't have to remind myself to exercise caution, because the road stopped being a road and became a dried-up river bed instead. Now it was a question of being lucky if I could walk pushing the bicycle; very often it had to be carried. This state of affairs lasted most of the day, with only a very rare stretch where I could ride. It was on one of these that the disaster I feared struck. I punctured.

A heavily laden bicycle cannot even be wheeled along without destroying the tyre and damaging the wheel. Since I couldn't mend the puncture, having not yet managed to find fresh rubber solution, I was well and truly stuck. Had I been in a less remote spot, a lift might have been available, but I hadn't seen any kind of vehicle all day. Then I remembered a curious story I had read of a missionary in Sind. He had been in a similar plight and had managed to ride home after stuffing his tyre full of banana skins. I couldn't find banana skins, but perhaps grass or something similar might work as well? There wasn't any grass either where I was just then, but by sacrificing one of my shirts, all my underwear and spare socks; I was able to pad out the tyre sufficiently to walk it along without damaging it further.

There was by now no question of being able to reach the proposed stopping place that night but my map showed a forest rest house to be no great distance away. Even so, it was six o'clock before I reached it, shattered with exhaustion and quite badly dehydrated, having found no village and no water since early morning. The rest house was locked and there was no one about; nothing for it but to go on in the hope of finding the chowkidar somewhere about. A mile down the track I came to a couple of shacks, one of which was a tea house. The usual contingent of local men were lounging about outside, drinking tea and looking for diversions. As I appeared—a number one diversion—they called excitedly to those men inside and they all trooped over to have a good stare, and to poke and prod the bicycle.

'Rest house?' I began. The posse nodded vigorously in unison, and pointed back uphill to where it was. 'No chowkidar,' was my next conversational gambit. This met with blank uncomprehension until I had repeated it several times and then light dawned on the assembled faces. 'Ah yes,' said one ancient, who had been scratching a hole in the handlebar padding to see what it was made of. 'Chowkidar is here inside.' After a few moments, a youth was dragged out by several of the men. At a glance you could tell that he was not the sort of chowkidar who welcomed travellers. He gave me one disgusted sneer and returned inside. The other men stopped prodding the bicycle and rushed in after him. Soon fierce argument was in progress, but I could see through the window that the young chowkidar was quite impervious to it and was busy staring into space, trying to rise above it all. The other men began to run out of steam, so I went in to add my arguments. I told him that I had to stay there, I couldn't ride on with a flat tyre and that anyway I had every right to stay at the rest house. I was a V.I.P. English Memsahib, I added, remembering how well this appellation had worked in other rest houses. It didn't cut any ice with this youth, however, he just continued gazing into space in the most irritating manner. I don't know if he understood any English anyway, because the old man seemed to be doing a vigorous translation. In the end, I gave up and walked off, thinking what a good thing it would be if all chowkidars could be better instructed in what their function was supposed to be.

The road made a wide loop just there to cross a river bed, so in about half an hour I was just opposite the tea shack, on the further side of the river. The whole posse was outside waving vigorously for me to return, and I guessed the men had managed to persuade the chowkidar to relent. With nightfall pretty close, this was no time for false pride, and I hastily retraced my steps. I wanted to have some tea and something to eat before going back up the road to the rest house, but the English-speaking ancient, who had taken up my cause, said that we must hurry after the chowkidar who had already started up the hill.

When we arrived I was shown to a very small room with just a plank bed and a table in it. The chowkidar, still very surly, gestured for me to follow him to a small kitchen, where he filled a little metal pot with water from a bucket and handed it to me. He fastened the kitchen door behind him with a large padlock and stalked off back down the track without speaking a word. The old man stayed a moment to tell me about a bus which was leaving early in the morning and then he too departed. I hastily dropped some sterilizing tablets into the dirty water in the pot and while I waited for the required 30 minutes to elapse, I set out to see what facilities the place offered. It took very little time to discover that there were no facilities: no lights, no lavatory, nowhere to wash, and worst of all, no water. I had been finding that with the expenditure of so much energy in temperatures of 80° or more, my body needed about a gallon to a gallon and a half of fluid a day. There was about half a pint of water in the pot that the chowkidar had given me and I wondered how I would manage until he returned to cook the evening meal. I returned to my room, drank the foul-tasting water in the pot and promptly fell into an exhausted sleep.

I woke up a couple of hours later feeling really ill and tormented with thirst. No one was around, so it seemed that the chowkidar would not be returning to cook a meal after all. I did not think that I could survive the night without something to drink and wondered what on earth I could do. My earlier search had revealed nothing; the only water in the place appeared to be the half bucketful in the locked kitchen. I felt about in my luggage for the stub of candle I had and lit it while I pondered the problem. The time had come, I decided, for desperate measures. Taking the candle, I went to inspect the padlock. There was a pickaxe lying conveniently near the door; with it I prised open the lock. There was all sorts of debris floating in the water and I was quite shaken by my own action in breaking into the place, not to mention my fear that the chowkidar might return at any moment and catch me at my burglary. But for all that, it was all I could do to stop myself falling upon the water and draining it to the dregs. Telling myself to be sensible, I returned to my room and fetched my water bottles, filled them and added sterilizing tablets. Then I closed the door and hung the padlock back in its position. I pressed the arm down and to my surprise it clicked shut. I hadn't broken it after all.

Back in my room, I waited impatiently for the time that the tablets took to work and then told myself to drink slowly. The sheer nastiness of the taste prevented me from gulping it down, which was just as well. Almost immediately I felt a little better and after half an hour I was able to eat the last few raisins I had with me. Still feeling far from well, I decided to take a sleeping tablet in the hope that a long uninterrupted sleep would effect a cure.

Just before I dropped off, I had the impression that I could hear a radio whining away, and Indian male voices giggling, close at hand. Secure however in the knowledge that the window and door were bolted, I passed into oblivion. The next impression was eight hours later, and it was of loud snores, close at hand. By the pale light filtering through the shutters, I could just make out the time on my watch; it was a little after five. Apart from feeling very sticky and dirty, and hearing these strange snores—in my head as I thought—I was quite recovered. I dressed and went out to see the dawn. As soon as I opened the door, the source of the snores was revealed. Within inches of my door, two charpoys were placed close together and three young males, one of them the chowkidar, were lying there in close proximity, clad only in their underpants. I must have disturbed them in opening the door, for there were embarrassed giggles and a cover was hastily pulled up to cover all three heads. While I walked down to the end of the compound, they fled one after another into the main building. I couldn't think why they had chosen to sleep right outside my door, unless they had been protecting me from possible marauders, or more likely perhaps, stopping me from escaping with rest house property. It would have to remain yet another unexplained mystery of Indian travel.

As soon as they were dressed the young men made signs for me to accompany them back to the tea shack. I left a sum of money in my room to compensate for the water I had taken and hoped the chowkidar would realize what it was for.

In spite of the early hour, most of the local contingent were around to watch the bus come in. It only came once a week and thus had novelty value. There wasn't even time for a glass of tea before it hove into view, so it was just as well that I had been woken by the boys' snores, or I would have missed it, and goodness knows how I would then have got the poor afflicted bicycle to where I could find some rubber solution. Willing hands helped haul the bicycle to the top of the bus where there was a little rail to stop luggage falling off. There were several men sitting up there, so I thought I would sit there, too, the better to protect the bicycle; since Indians are so casual about other people's possessions—though I suppose after the previous night's escapade with the water, I too had become rather casual about the rights of property and couldn't with justice complain about this attitude in other people.

My decision to ride on the top provided added interest and amusement for the onlookers and continued to do so through-out the journey. I think this was because only the poorer peasants normally sat up there, or possibly it was the place allotted to the outcastes. But after my previous experiences of crowded buses in Pakistan, with people smoking, spitting and coughing everywhere, and jostling for the all too limited space, I found it infinitely preferable to be in the fresh air. It was exciting, too, as the bus careered around the hairpin bends, and low branches swept close over our heads, threaten-ing to dislodge us.

The bus stopped frequently to take on new passengers and let others off. Men scrambled up and down the fixed ladders to the roof, dragging sacks of produce with them, and it was not at all easy to keep the bicycle from being damaged, particularly the wheels. They were a really friendly crowd, though, much more considerate than the average, and when we had reorganized ourselves after each stop, squashing up to make room for the newcomers and finding something to sit on and to hang on to, we all settled down quite amicably. The conductor was the real menace. He was a large man with the unenviable task of collecting fares from the latest arrivals while the bus was moving. That he didn't find this too easy was evident from the despairing expression on his face as he launched himself forward from the top of the ladder onto the flat roof, landing on anyone or anything that happened to be there. He was not a popular man, it seemed, for no one was prepared to help him by passing the fares back to him; so he had perforce to crawl all over the roof, clutching at anything and anyone for support as the bus swayed and bumped over the appalling surfaces.

I had reckoned that it was about 70 miles to Dehra Dun, but the land was so broken up by ravines and deep gorges that the road had often to wind around the hills for many miles in order to make a single mile of progress in the right direction. Although I was following the line of the Himalayas, it was necessary to descend almost to sea level in order to make for Nepal. There is no road as yet which runs east–west at a higher altitude, and the first point of entry into Nepal was some 700 miles further to the south-east. Most of those miles would be through the burning plains of Uttar Pradesh. Already, as the bus wound its way downwards through the foothills, the air was growing perceptibly hotter and dustier. I thought with growing nostalgia of the cool upland valleys I had left.

All day the bus ground on towards Dehra Dun and the headwaters of the Ganges, the temperature increasing with every mile. By four o'clock we were winding down through the Shivalik Hills—the lowest range of the Himalayas—and Dehra Dun was just below us. After two days without a wash and with my stomach seemingly stuck to my backbone through under-use, I was looking forward to the comfort of a good hotel.

15

It was the high season for marriage in Northern India. I discovered this almost as soon as the bus reached Dehra Dun and the bicycle and myself had been set down, conveniently outside the tourist office.

'The very best hotel, please,' I requested of the pleasant man inside, feeling that only the very best would do after the hardships and tribulations of the past two days. He recommended one just across the road. It was full. Back at the tourist office, the helpful man assured me there was 'No problem'. He would phone around the other good hotels—'Plenty very good hotels in Dehra Dun.' There certainly seemed to be a large number. He telephoned at least 20. They were all full.

'No problem,' he said sending out a boy to fetch tea. 'Maybe not so good hotel not full.' He telephoned some more. I was very impressed by his perseverance, but it was all to no avail.

'I am very, very sorry,' he said. 'I think all hotels full. Nothing for it, you must have somewhere for sleep. There is only lodge left. I take you. Come.'

Leaving the bicycle to be guarded by the boy, he took me across the road and up a long, steep flight of stairs, squashed between shop fronts. I followed in some trepidation, since he had made the place sound so dire. When we reached the top, I found we were on a flat, paved roof, with two rows of concrete cabins facing each other. They looked rather like bathing huts on an English beach. One was available and I was shown into it. It was no worse than the rooms in Ringo's flop house at Delhi. There was a bed with mattress, a table and a bench, and a half-wall, behind which was a hole in the floor—flushable, and a cold water tap set low down, so as to be in reach of the left hand while in a squatting position. A bucket and an electric fan completed the furnishings. The whole place was pretty grubby by Western standards, but not by Indian ones, and after the last night's accommodation I could almost persuade myself that it went some way to supplying the luxury I craved. The proprietor was very helpful and arranged for someone to carry the bicycle up and supply a bucket of hot water. He also told me why all the hotels were full. This was a particularly auspicious time for weddings, he said, and Indian people liked to marry in a holy place, where the waters of the Ganges flowed down from the Himalayas. Since the wedding parties could number anything up to 100, towns in the area like Dehra Dun, Haridwar and Rishikesh did a roaring trade in the marriage season.

Perhaps it is necessary to have been without the means of washing for two days in hot dusty conditions, to appreciate the sheer delight of a bucketful of hot water. After washing myself, I dealt with my clothes, including those which had done such sterling work inside the tyre. These were really none the worse for the experience. I rigged a clothes-line out of the luggage straps and left the lot to dry while I went out to have a look at the town.

It seemed a very bustling place after the quiet of the hills, full of streets of open-fronted shops, with noisy traffic bullying its way through with an excessive use of horns. Everywhere, in the busy streets, and the quieter ones, there were men peeing into gutters or against walls and the smell of urine was pretty powerful. But what really repelled me was the number of rats which were running in and out of shops and restaurants with seeming impunity. I had read that one fifth of India's produce is devoured annually by rats and from the numbers of them in Dehra Dun, I could quite believe it. Still they didn't repel me enough to stop me buying all sorts of edible goodies, though I made sure that everything I bought could be peeled, shelled or washed. I also found some rubber solution and returned to the lodge to effect repairs. It was so hot in my concrete cabin that although I had been out for only an hour, the washing had already dried. The fan helped things somewhat, but the electricity failed every half hour or so and by the time I had finished with the bicycle I was soaked with perspiration and ready for another bucket shower.

That evening I had promised myself the best meal that Dehra Dun could provide and accordingly made my way to a smart restaurant recommended by my friend in the tourist office. Here I tucked into a huge chicken biryani with all sorts of appetizing accompaniments and lots and lots of fresh lemon juice to drink. It was quite a while since I had had a decent meal and two days since I had had anything except fruit and nuts. This abstinence had not had the same effect as the lack of washing water. I was defeated before I was halfway through and when I tried to squeeze down just a little more the sight of large brown cockroaches scuttling across the floor finished my appetite altogether.

Walking back through the dark streets to my lodge, I had to exercise extreme care to avoid treading on the many bodies bedded down for the night on the pavements. It was still very hot and remained so all night, making sleep difficult. The fan stopping and starting with the erratic electricity didn't help, either. I thought I had seen enough of Dehra Dun and would move on in the morning.

I didn't get my first glimpse of the Ganges until I reached the sacred city of Haridwar. It was a most impressive river, over three-quarters of a mile wide and lined with bathing ghats where pilgrims were praying, immersed up to their shoulders in the water. It looked cool and inviting, but not being a Hindu, I didn't think I could join them. Instead I went and slaked my thirst with lime juice and soda. The town was full of brightly robed priests, many of them being driven around in bicycle rickshaws. One huge, fat saddhu in voluminous yellow robes, his hair tied in a topknot and holding a tall trident, looked for all the world like Neptune sitting in state. There were wild-haired ascetics too with painted faces striding along with begging bowl and walking staff.

I went to the tourist office to see if they had a more up-to-date map of the area than the one I had purchased in

Delhi, and to enquire about the position of rest houses in the locality. There was a real male chauvinist in charge, who refused to have any dealings with the despised sex. He would only address me through a young man from New Zealand who happened to be in the office at the same time. It was a very bizarre exchange which achieved nothing useful in the way of information or maps. Before he left, he said to the young man, 'Tell her she must not ride bicycle on back road to Raninagar. There is forest full with wild animals on the way.'

I wanted to reply that after some of my experiences with the males of the sub-continent, wild animals no longer held any terrors for me. This thought amused Bob, the New Zea-lander, but we both decided that it wasn't quite the thing to say to the tourist officer, useless though he was. So instead we went off to have a cup of tea and exchange views about India.

I crossed the wide Ganges, which now looked even more beautiful and inviting in the excessive heat of the day, and soon came to the forests, where I had been warned to expect wild animals, but not a whisker or a tail showed itself. If there was anything as exciting as a tiger lurking there, I thought he would probably keep well clear of predatory man. What I did find, which was of much more immediate interest, was a rest house where none had been marked on the map. It was a rather superior place with a lovely garden, though difficult to get into, because the chowkidar had gone off for the day somewhere, taking the key with him. The mali who tended the garden was a resourceful fellow, though, who having organized some tea for me, went off to seek assistance. Soon he returned with a young man from a neighbouring forestry camp who managed somehow to get the door open. I was invited to visit the camp after I had bathed and rested, to see something of the work there and to take dinner with the young man and his newly married wife.

Unfortunately, it was almost nightfall when he came to collect me, so I saw almost nothing of the camp and the work there, but I did spend a most enjoyable evening with the young couple. He, Arju, was in charge of the camp and had spent four years at university and a further three years of practical study to prepare for his work, though it was difficult to credit this from his appearance, since he looked no more than 21. His marriage, of course, had been an arranged one. His wife looked a mere child, though Arju said she was 17. She had had very little education and spoke no English, so Arju did all the talking while she quietly and gracefully moved around their tiny two-roomed hut, preparing the evening meal. From the way his eyes followed her movements and the way that she smiled shyly over her shoulder at him, it seemed clear that they were happy with one another. Tending the forest, as Arju called his profession, was as much a part of his religion as a means of livelihood. He tried to practise what is finest in Hinduism—a love of all living things, Ahimsa, which calls for total vegetarianism, a refusal to wantonly hurt or damage anything, even a fly, and a willingness to see the Absolute in everything and everyone. He was a very impressive young man in his gentle and entirely unassuming manner.

Later, as he walked me back to the rest house, I saw a quite enchanting display. The air was full of little, dancing lights, like tiny stars just overhead; or Christmas tree lights playing hide and seek about their branches. To my great delight, I realized I was seeing fireflies for the very first time. During the night, a noisy electrical storm broke overhead, with the thunder crashing around so continuously that I could not sleep, so I stood at the window to watch the great sheets of lightning rending the darkness; and through it all, the fireflies danced.

I left the following morning in a torrential deluge but within a few miles I had passed out of the rainy belt, which must have been confined to the forest area, and was in a dry dusty zone, with sugarcane fields all around. Soon sugar refineries began to make the air horrid with their stench and villages of unrelieved squalor began to appear. I didn't care to stop at any of these, either for breakfast or lunch, because of the hordes of staring males of all ages that pressed about me when I tentatively put foot to ground. Some parts of Uttar Pradesh are said to be amongst the most backward and depressed in India. Certainly, this area seemed worse than anything I had yet seen.

There were a lot of distressing and disfiguring ailments among the children, too: running sores, harelips, facial growths, and most looked malnourished and miserably clad. Quite young boys plied the desperately hard rickshaw trade, and everywhere children of all ages could be seen staggering under burdens far too heavy for them. The sheer extent of India's poverty seemed overwhelming here, and it made a depressing day's ride.

Moradabad is a brass manufacturing town and not a lovely place, but it has one quite reasonable hotel—the only one, said a man who had courteously stopped to direct me to it. I was very glad to find it, because the heat of the afternoon had become rather more than I could cope with. I was now down practically to sea level, with the temperatures up in the 90s and increasing daily. Until I reached Nepal and began to ascend again, I should need to make very early starts and try to reach the end of each day's journey before midday. With this in mind I attempted to have an early night, but it was not to be. The hotel had a resident reporter who decided that my arrival was a scoop, which he could write up for the national newspapers. Accordingly I was interviewed at exhausting length and finally got to bed at midnight. I didn't sleep well anyway, because it was so hot and the fan kept stopping and starting with the electricity cuts. When I did drop off, biting insects soon had me conscious again.

In spite of feeling totally unrested, it was a relief to set off on the bicycle in the comparative freshness of early morning. Once past the environs of the town, with its open stinking sewers, dreadful shanty camps and clouds of flies, it was a pleasant landscape of open fields and roads lined with jacaranda trees where the scents were of ripening grain, fruit and blossom. Harvest was in progress and it was possible to imagine that time had stood still for centuries and that bullock carts were the only form of wheeled transport, trundling over the wide, unhurried land. That was until about eight o'clock when the less lovely lorries made their appearance, shattering the illusion and adding their nauseous effluvia to the increasing heat.

By 11 a.m. I was in the town of Bareilly, enjoying an early lunch and listening to the views of an Indian officer at a neighbouring table. He was savage in condemnation of the conditions in his country. It was in a state of moral decline, he said. The police were a ludicrous mob who had turned their guns on their own government and were held in ridicule and contempt by everyone, no longer able to maintain the semblance of civil control. The army had to do everything and yet it had no fair say in the country's policies. The only hope for India, he maintained, was to have a military coup and then they could settle the Pakistan threat on their western borders before going on to bring discipline and order to their troubled country. The journalist of the previous night's interview had expressed similar views, though he had not hoped for a military coup as a solution to India's problems.

I made my first mistake of the day at Bareilly: I didn't stay there. It was no more appealing a town than Moradabad had been and it smelt as bad, so as I did not yet feel unduly tired, I thought I would push on to the next rest house, which was marked on the map as being only 20 miles away. If it wasn't there, another was marked eight miles further on. The countryside was so infinitely more pleasant than the towns, I felt it was worth the effort. The 20 miles didn't go too badly, though subsequently I found the temperature had risen to 98° that afternoon. Only when I reached the place where the first rest house should have been, and wasn't, and never had been, did I realize how close to the limits of my strength I was. It seemed an impossibly long eight miles to the next place, and all parts of my body were complaining, but I made it and where the rest house should have been was a police station. I did not think I could possibly manage the 15 miles to the next town, so I asked the policeman at the gate if he knew of any rest house in the area.

That was my second mistake of the day: I should not have looked for help from a police station. Before I knew it, I was inside the gate and had become the afternoon's entertainment for about 30 undisciplined, bored men in various states of slovenly undress. I was given a cup of tea and then sat there in a cloud of flies while they fiddled about with my bicycle, laughing fatuously when I asked them to leave it alone. I began to understand the army officer's frustrations with such a law-keeping force; it did seem ludicrous to assume that such men could command any sort of respect. When their equally undisciplined children arrived on the scene, to add their quota of tourist-baiting, I decided their offers of help could go hang, I had had enough. I cycled off with the horde giggling and calling 'Halt, halt!' behind me.

Before I had gone half a mile, my energies recharged by anger, I was flagged down by a higher-ranking policeman on a motorbicycle. He said he was the superintendent and demanded to know why I had left so precipitately when ordered to wait. Indignation making me bold, I told him that I had had more than enough of his men's rudeness and stupidity and didn't see why they should order an English woman about anyway since I had done nothing amiss. He changed his tone then, apologizing for his men and saying that they were only ignorant, uneducated types. I must forget all about them and remember only him, since he was quite different and knew how to behave towards a lady. He then flagged down a lorry and commanded the driver to take me and the bicycle the 15 miles to Shajahanpur. I couldn't refuse the lift, indeed I was really glad to have it, but it was embarrassing to be thrust on the hapless driver by a superintendent of police. There were other passengers in the cab. One of them, a young man in his early 20s, tried to get me to adopt him; the only way out of 'this awful country', he said, was to be adopted by an English or American family. This was not the first time I had received this particular request, nor was it to be the last. These young men all saw England as abounding in wealth and opportunities. If only they could get there, they thought, their problems and frustrations would cease. It was useless to try to persuade them that the England of their dreams just didn't exist.

The third mistake of the day was in coming within a mile of Shajahanpur. The lorry had dropped me at the outskirts and I had cycled into the centre to look for an hotel. No sooner had I put foot to ground, than I was surrounded by a crowd of youths. A mob would be a more apt description, for their behaviour had the sort of mindless group aggression of a crowd of bully boys looking for trouble. They jeered and jostled, cannoning into me from all sides. It was a really frightening situation, from which I could see no way of extricating myself. Fortunately, a young man, somewhat older than most of the youths, had seen my plight and had pushed his way through the crowd to my side. He told me to follow him closely and somehow, with threats and shoves, he managed to clear a way through. As soon as we had an open path he seized a bicycle and yelled for me to ride as fast as I could after him. I needed no encouragement to do so; I could easily have outpaced him, so frightened was I of the mob. They were now in hot pursuit, mostly on foot, though some had bicycles and one lot were in a sort of van. This vehicle managed to come alongside in a narrow street and hands reached out and tried to grab my arm. Somehow I managed to keep my balance and carry on as the van dropped back, halted by some obstruction. We raced on, turning innumerable corners, until the sound of pursuit died away behind us. We stopped then to recover our breath and my rescuer asked me where I wanted to go. He said he did not dare leave me, as the mob would be prowling about looking for me. I asked him why they were behaving like that. He shrugged his shoulders and said he did not know, but he thought perhaps they had nothing better to do, there were a lot of 'bad, violent men' in those parts.

There were four hotels in the town, none of them particularly inviting and all of them full. Twice during our tour of them, the mob had caught up with us and resumed the chase. We were both thoroughly exhausted and it was difficult to think what to do next. It occurred to me then that it was a Sunday, so I asked the young man if there was a Christian church in the town. There was, and hoping that there would be someone there who could help, we set off again. Once more the mob sighted us and were soon in full pursuit, baying like a pack of hounds. As we raced through the church gates and up the path, they were closing on us, making enough noise to compete with the hymn-singing pouring out through the open windows and doors. Several worshippers, hearing all the din, came out, just as we reached the doors and collapsed breathless on the steps. They advanced purposefully on the bullies who immediately turned tail and fled. They then turned to us for an explanation of the unseemly way their Sabbath service had been disturbed. I was quite incapable of speech, shaking with reaction now that the danger was past. My young rescuer did all the explaining, while I just stood there staring at the ground, trying hard not to cry. I didn't even manage to thank the young man properly, for he went away before I had recovered my equilibrium.

Two of the congregation were teachers at a nearby Technical Institute run by an American Methodist Mission. They said there was a guest house there and offered to escort me to it. I was only too glad to accept and to cycle away from Shajahanpur with these two dependable men to protect me. As we rode along the quiet country lanes, they talked about their work at the Nave Institute, which provided training for youths of 16 to 18. One of the main needs for youngsters in this area of high unemployment, they said, was to be trained in skills which they could take back to their villages. Carpentry, tailoring, and light mechanical and electrical engineering were the main subjects offered. Discipline was strict, otherwise the boys, fresh from their villages, quickly became infected by the negative attitudes of the town youths, many of whom were unemployed. There had been a general drift to the town from the country over the past few decades as the population had grown. This trend, they felt, had to be reversed, since there was much unemployment in the towns.

Dot and Hank Garwick, who ran the College, utilized the excess rooms in their large, old-fashioned bungalow for guests who, like me, found themselves in the locality with nowhere to go. I think they never ran out of rooms, since few people find much to draw them to that part of India. They were a warm-hearted couple and their home was a good place to relax in and lick my wounds.

Looking back now at this part of the journey, I sometimes

wonder why I did not give in to circumstances and put the bicycle on a train to the Nepalese border. At the time though, it never occurred to me to do so, even when the going was really tough, or I'd been badly frightened. This was certainly not for reasons of economy—the journey thus far having cost a fraction of what I had anticipated; nor did I think I must cycle every foot of the way or lose face. It was far more because I felt this less attractive region was an intrinsic part of the journey, somewhere it was important to see, even if I should not want to repeat the experience—as C. S. Lewis put it, in his Narnia books, it was taking the adventure as it was sent. The compensation for the hardship was the number of friends I made in the most unlikely places.

I spent the next day with the Garwicks, mainly lying in the shade or under a fan, for the temperature rose dramatically after about eight o'clock and was up to the 100° mark by midday. It could reach 120° or even 130° at its worst, I was told, and then the only way to survive was to wrap oneself in wet sheets and stay under a fan. I was glad that I had only about four days' journeying left before I started the climb out of these hot plains, since I couldn't see how I could wrap myself in wet sheets on a bicycle.

At 5 a.m. the next morning, I was on my way again. The Garwicks had very gallantly risen early to see that I had breakfast and to provide me with all sorts of sustaining things to eat en route. In two days, if all went well, I should reach the town of Gonda, where I was to stay with friends of theirs who ran a mission school. For today I had to rely on a rest house, marked on my inaccurate map. No one at the college knew if it existed, so I could only hope.

The apricot dawn, full of low-flying white egrets, quickly faded, giving way to a pale, hot sky that seemed to be pressing down with increasing persistence on the flat dusty fields. The road bordered by closely planted leafy trees was a ribbon of shade in the burning landscape. One tree, the peepul, had such a dense canopy it felt actually cold beneath it. Hardly anything moved anywhere, just an occasional lumbering buffalo or oxen cart, its driver, clad in dhoti and singlet, seemingly asleep, swaying gently on his perch. By 10 o'clock the sun had climbed above the tallest trees and the road was no longer shaded. The heat was so great the land appeared insubstantial, shimmering as though under water. Even with a handkerchief tied around my forehead beneath my hat brim, it was impossible to stop the sweat running into my eyes. If the rest house had not appeared just then, I would have been obliged to stop and seek shade, since any movement at all, let alone cycling, had become too great an effort.

The chowkidar of this rest house was one of the suspicious sort, though not unkind. He allowed me the use of a washroom and a shady verandah, but not of a bedroom, that would have to wait until the district engineer called by later in the day. This information was relayed to me by a young man the chowkidar had rooted out from somewhere. A student, I think he was, and quite objectionably opinionated. He sat himself down on the verandah beside me and talked at me for an hour, until totally exasperated, I told him to go away. Once he had gone, a little group of children who had been hovering nearby in the garden, plucked up courage and came over to have a closer look at me. They were nice children who didn't know any English, so we could only smile at each other, which suited me very well after the exhausting young man.

Just as it was getting dark, the children returned with two women who were obviously their mothers. By smiles and beckoning, it was made clear that they wished me to accompany them. I was led to a modest little house on the edge of the rest house compound and entertained to tea and popadoms. By this time, I knew about two dozen words of Hindi. One of the women had about the same amount of English, so we couldn't engage freely in conversation. Nevertheless, smiles, nods and a little mime served almost as well. It was one of the nicest tea parties I have ever attended. The women were at great pains to express their approval of my cycling—at least, that was the impression I received. I hope I got it right, because earlier, the annoying young student had been most disapproving of my activities; he seemed to disapprove of everything to do with Western women, especially the ridiculous waste of money spent in educating them. I gathered from him that only boys in this region went to school—which he thought was an admirable way of keeping women in their proper place.

After an hour and a half of mime and tea-drinking, the district engineer arrived. He was the husband of one of my hostesses and as charming and helpful as most of the engineers I met at the various rest houses. He instructed the chowkidar to let me have a bedroom and to prepare dinner for me. Dinner never arrived, but thanks to Dot Garwick's sandwiches, I didn't starve.

In the morning I ate my last orange and a packet of Protein-snax and set off at 4.45, in the hope of reaching my night stop at Gonda before 11. Things went wrong straight away; there were no roads. According to my map, there should have been quite a choice, but all I found were a few dirt tracks that meandered around the sunbaked fields, going nowhere in particular. By 8.30 I was dizzy from the heat, for there was no shade at all. I kept going, keeping in roughly the right direction with the aid of the compass, but finding it a fearful effort. By 10.30 I reached the tiny town of Fatephur, less than halfway to Gonda, and I knew that I could cycle no further that day. I would have to find some sort of transport for myself and the bicycle, since I didn't think there was anywhere else to stay. Seeing me standing undecidedly by the road, a driver of a car stopped and asked if he could help. After explaining my difficulty, the driver said he would make enquiries for me. Soon it seemed as if everyone in Fatephur had involved themselves in the proceedings, advice and counter-advice flying backwards and forwards. But everyone was amazingly kind and considerate and seemed to deem it an honour that I had cycled to their town. I was taken into the shade and a chair and very welcome cool drinks were brought. While they argued over the problem, I was content just to sit there and drink.

The sheer quantity of liquid I seemed to need in Northern India never ceased to amaze me. Before I had started, I had been warned to make sure that I drank at least a gallon a day. I was getting through twice that much and yet frequently felt dangerously dehydrated. I think it was all lost in perspiration, as I seldom needed a lavatory. A lot of the liquid had to be tea, or fizzy sweet drinks, as on this occasion, since water could never be drunk untreated. The amount of sugar in all these drinks probably served as much needed calories.

The result of all the deliberations was that there was nowhere nearer than Gonda to stay and to get to Gonda—about 40 miles away—was not too difficult. It would mean taking a branch line two stops to Barwal Junction and then changing to the broad gauge railway. A college P.T. instructor said that he would accompany me to the junction and help me with the bicycle. Actually most of the men came along to the station to bid me goodbye and to help hoist the bicycle into the luggage van, which was about four feet up from the platform. I was amazed by the kindness I received in this place, especially remembering the awful time at Shajahanpur. I supposed I had just been fortunate at Fatephur in being befriended by the more responsible townsfolk. Possibly though, it is as many Indians maintained, and there are towns there which are predominantly 'bad, evil places'.

At the junction, the P.T. instructor sought out an ex-student of his—a fat, jolly individual who looked as though he couldn't possibly have ever engaged in anything as strenuous as P.T. He was told to look after me and put me on the train to Gonda. Without all this assistance, I do not think I should have been able to make the journey. The station itself was difficult enough, being crowded with people taking advantage of the shade, prone bodies covering most of the platforms. The train to Gonda, due in two hours, was an express which did not stop long enough for the loading of goods. So although I could travel on it, the bicycle could not. My helper was wonderful. Somehow he had all the station officials, from the station master to the boy who swept what platform wasn't covered with bodies, determined to accomplish the impossible. They kept coming up to tell me not to worry, everything would be done to get me on the train. 'Maybe we must bribe,' said my helper, instructing me on how many rupees to have available.

We filled in the waiting time by drinking endless cups of tea. The tea came ready mixed in teapots with lovely small conical clay cups. These cups were destroyed immediately after they had been used, not in the interests of hygiene, but to avoid the possibility of caste pollution.

When the train came, all was confusion, with people jumping down from the carriage roofs and others trying to scramble up. The second-class carriages were filled to bursting point, with bodies and belongings tumbling out of the windows. I didn't know where I was going to go; it depended on the whim of the guard. An official seized the bicycle and rushed down to the brake van with it. Moments later, another official raced it up to the other end. The station master was holding a fierce discussion meanwhile with a travelling railway dignitary in the first class. The upshot of all this was that the bicycle was loaded into a first-class carriage and carefully propped between two lavatories—one European type, the other Indian. After giving hurried but heartfelt thanks to all my kind helpers, I was ushered into a compartment with the railway dignitary, an elderly gentleman, clad coolly in a white singlet and dhoti with his sacred Hindu thread proclaiming him a high caste Brahmin. The carriage was furnished with a bed on either side and after I had paid my fare, my travelling companion kindly loaned me his air cushion to use as a pillow. I lay down and fell immediately into a profound sleep.

At Gonda, I found I was something of a celebrity, on account of the interview which I had given in Moradabad. Several daily newspapers carried the article, headed 'Cycling With A Difference'. 'The stakes were high and so were the spirits,' began the high-flown prose, and went on to describe me as an 'exuberant lady, in with a purpose'. Exuberant was not an adjective I would have considered appropriate to how I felt at this time, though it suited the style of the article, which gushed on for several columns with a fine disregard for accuracy or grammar. Nonetheless, the 600 children who attended the mission school I stayed at for the next two nights, gained great cachet from it and I had to stay on in order to exhibit the bicycle and give an impromptu lecture on the journey. At the end of the address I asked if there were any questions. There was just one: Could they please have a go on the bicycle?

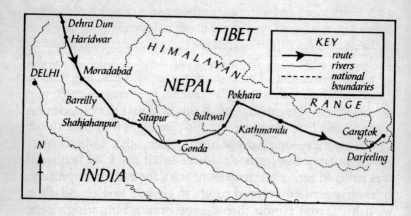

Dehra Dun to Sikkim

16

The Nepalese border was a day's ride from Gonda and I would have easily made it in four hours or so under normal conditions. By now, though, it seemed fairly clear that I was suffering from something more than just exhaustion and the heat. Even cycling along a flat, shaded road had become a grim struggle against waves of nausea and dizziness. I had severe cramps in my stomach, too, which at times had me doubled up in agony, unable to continue. I began to doubt that I would ever reach Nepal.

At about 10.30, I came to the railway station of Barhni, where I had been told that retiring rooms, on the same principle as rest houses, were available. But when I enquired, I found this was not so, and that retiring rooms were only available at Naugarh, 25 miles further on. Perhaps I looked as ill as I felt when I made these enquiries, for the kindly station master immediately invited me into his office and placed a chair for me under the fan. I stayed there through the worst heat of the day, being fussed over and plied with innumerable cups of tea. The station master wanted to make a bed on the floor for me to spend the night, but I thought I had imposed enough on his kindness, and after taking a shower in the waiting room—by the simple expedient of removing a plug of sugarcane from where a tap would normally be, I struggled on towards Naugarh.

Whether Naugarh would have appeared less squalid if I had not been feeling so ill, I can't say. I certainly wouldn't advise anyone to spend a night there, as the only accommodation does seem to be the station retiring rooms. The one I was given was black with ancient grime and the electricity had failed—which meant no fan—in a temperature the equivalent of a moderate oven. There was no water either in the attached washroom, although that had not deterred previous occupants from using the lavatory. As there was no door to this washroom, a terrible stench filled the place. The station seemed to be used as an outdoor dormitory, with nearly every inch of platform space covered with prone bodies. The needs of all these people were served by the single lavatory in the waiting room, also without water.

Still, just to be able to lie down in private was a luxury, and since I was already ill, I reasoned, without much logic, that I was unlikely to catch anything else. Having run through my checklist of the various ailments I might have contracted, I settled for amoebiasis, also known as amoebic dysentery. The symptoms seemed to fit—acute stomach pains, brought on particularly by exertion and heat; nausea, dizziness, etc. I was lucky, I thought, considering the present circumstances, that amoebiasis wasn't always accompanied by diarrhoea. None of the antibiotics I carried would be much help with this particular bug, so there was nothing I could do except press on and get to higher altitudes as soon as possible. If it didn't get better then, I could go to the Mission Hospital at Pokhara, some 200 miles over the mountains.

All through the journey I had been looking forward to reaching Nepal, and not only because it contained the majority of the highest peaks in the Himalayas. The accounts I had read of it made it seem one of the most fascinating countries in Asia, a fabled Shangri-La isolated from the rest of the world until 30 years ago when it had suddenly flung open its doors to the Western world.

It was the thought of being so close to this Shangri-La that drove my protesting body on its way the following morning; that, and the relief of getting away from the noisome station. So eager was I to cover the distance, I didn't notice the Police Post from which one obtained one's exit stamp, and a police car was sent after me to bring me back. I had great difficulties then in establishing that I was a harmless traveller and was interrogated for quite a long time by a stern official, whose only English seemed to be 'For why you not stop, huh?' He repeated this phrase each time I said anything, such as 'I didn't see the Police Post' or 'I'm very sorry, I didn't know the Police Post was hidden behind a brick wall.' Only after I had run out of permutations on the theme did he relent and stamp my passport.

I cycled back into the sandy scrub of no-man's land, keeping a sharp lookout for the Nepali Police Post, as I did not wish to be interrogated twice in one day. Mile after mile I rode without spotting it, and soon the road surface became so broken that it required all my attention, and I didn't notice the little house set back from the road, which was the border control, and had to be whistled after to come back. The Nepalese were perfectly affable and even worked the handle of their garden pump for me, so that I could wash the dust off my hands and face. After the border, the road gave out altogether and I had six miles of sand to struggle through until I came to Lumbini.

It was a pity that I was not feeling well enough to appreciate being in this uniquely holy spot, the birthplace of the Lord Buddha. Even the great pillar erected 2000 years ago by the great King Asoka, when he came here to pay homage, seemed of less importance than obtaining local currency with which to buy something to drink. I sat in the slight shade cast by the Asoka Pillar, wondering how on earth I would find the necessary strength to continue, when two youths of about 19 came up and asked politely if they could be of assistance. Transport up into the mountains was what was clearly needed, and the boys thought this would be no problem. In next to no time they had found a lorry carrying a load of sand whose driver was prepared to take me, for a modest fee. Somehow the cycle and I were installed on top of the sand and I think I must have fainted at that point, for I knew no more until I became aware that the engine note had changed and we were grinding up slopes in a low gear. Soon I was able to sit up and take notice.

The mountains rose abruptly from the level plains, first the

Shivaliks and then the Mahabarats. These were the same ranges I had ridden over two weeks ago in Himachal Pradesh and since then, they had been a faint outline on the northern horizon. I had been following a course parallel to them as they swung down south-eastwards. Here, 200 miles nearer the equator, they looked very different, with sub-tropical vegetation clothing their slopes instead of forests of pine and cedar. The people looked different, too, or rather they looked like the Nepali road-workers I had met in India, smaller than most Indians and with mongoloid features.

Near some villages, wheat bundles were spread out over the road, so that the wheels of the passing traffic would thresh out the grain; a wasteful, inefficient method of harvesting, but one I was to see everywhere in Nepal. Everyone seemed very friendly, waving and smiling as the lorry passed, and I thought I would enjoy Nepal very much, once my health had recovered. Already I was feeling much better at the higher altitude and by the time the lorry dropped me off, I felt able to think of cycling again.

For the last few miles I had been joined on top of the sand by a young teenage boy who had climbed out of the cab in order to show me an ugly suppurating wound on his bare foot. I cleaned it for him and put some antiseptic ointment and a dressing on it, explaining by mime and through the little English he knew that he needed to keep it covered and out of the sand until it healed. Before I left, I saw why he had shrugged at my advice. He and another boy were employed to unload the lorry as fast as possible. They worked in a frenzy of activity, shovelling and kicking the sand through the narrow tailgate, while the driver exhorted them to greater efforts.

There were five very steep miles to Tansen, where I planned to stay for the night at the Hotel Siddartha. Children, who could run uphill for short distances faster than I could cycle, pursued me the whole way, crying 'Paisa, Paisa'. It was hardly possible to stop on such steep slopes to give them the money they were demanding, even should I have wished to do so, which I did not. When they saw that they were not going to get anything, they gave vent to their frustration by throwing stones at me. This Shangri-La was clearly going to have its drawbacks and its dangers. I wished that the travellers who had scattered their largesse without thought for the consequences could have been here now to shield me from the flying missiles. As it was, I raced up the inclines at a speed not at all suited to my fragile condition and arrived at Tansen feeling harassed and rather wretched.

The Hotel Siddartha was a tall building and clean for those parts. Most of the first floor was taken up by a long room, which was the dining room and bar, where all sorts of domestic chores were taking place, like washing children and peeling vegetables. The other floors were a warren of little dark cells, except for the top floor, and here there were two comfortable rooms, with washing facilities and fans. I liked it very much and would have stayed longer than one night, had I not needed to hurry on to the hospital at Pokhara.

Tansen, perched on the top of the Mahabarat Range, had the most stunning views I have ever seen from a town; and from a little hillock, just outside, I could see right across the Midland Valleys to where the Himalayas reared up their awesome bulk, peak after peak. I sat on the hillock, identifying them all with the aid of the guide book I had with me. It was not possible to linger very long because of the importunate small boys who had followed me up from the town. So I returned to the hotel and made do with the view from the interesting dining room instead.

In the morning, I found that the long rest and higher altitude had restored me considerably, and I was ready to start the day with something approaching my accustomed energy. This feeling was helped by the fact that I began the ride with a wonderful downhill swoop, which went on and on until I crossed the Kali Gandaki River, having lost about 3,000 feet of height. The weather was wonderful, delightfully cool after the heat of the plains.

At first I almost changed the unfavourable views I had formed about the local children. Every village I rode through, out they all came, calling 'Bye, bye', smiling delightfully and waving to me. I smiled and waved back, thinking how charming and unspoiled they were. It wasn't until I came to my first uphill stretch and was going considerably slower, that I began to notice that the eager little hands were held up in the universal begging pose, and the word 'paisa' began to separate itself from all the other words. The dear little things were demanding money. When they saw they weren't going to get any, they adopted various ploys; one was to call me rude names, but since I hadn't picked up any Nepali as yet, this hardly mattered. Another ploy was to snatch at the bicycle or anything on it; but quite the nastiest was to run alongside and quick as a flash, to thrust a large stone into the spokes of the front wheel. Quite small children of six or seven did this, but the older ones were even more intimidating. Going slowly up a long steep incline, I was pursued by two, whom I took to be in their early teens. They caught up with me before I reached the summit, loping along, one on each side. Then one reached out to grab the handlebars, while the other drew back his fist and said 'You give me money'. I had no choice but to stop, at which both of them closed in. Only by waving my penknife threateningly at them, could I get them to back off and leave me alone.

Shortly after this incident, I met a fellow cyclist, the first and only other cycling traveller of the whole journey. There is a great sense of camaraderie amongst people who have been fortunate enough to discover this delightful form of transport. We like meeting one another and exchanging experiences; discussing the road ahead and hazards to avoid and so forth. This meeting was made even more welcome because of bicyclists being so thin on the ground in these parts. He was a young man from Austria who had cycled here three years ago and said he found the country very much changed for the worse. All these villages bordering the road, he said, had sprung up overnight, after the road had been built. The people who lived there had left their remote villages in the hope of better opportunities; cut off from their roots and their traditional ways of life, they quickly became demoralized. He didn't think he would ever come back to Nepal again, mainly because of the menace of the young children who he considered were well on the way to becoming out and out highway robbers. I thought this, too, and even as we sat talking in the small outdoor tearoom, we were constantly plagued by little monsters, baiting us and attempting to steal things from the bicycles. I asked him what happened if one gave them money. (My guide book, which was written by a Nepalese, particularly asked readers not to give anything, as it made beggars of the children.) The Austrian said he had one day as a last resort given some small coins which had been flung back at him, because it wasn't enough! As we sat there trying to talk and guard our possessions at the same time, a schoolboy would pass and noticing how we were being tormented by the small children, would attempt to drive them off. Although they returned within seconds, it was encouraging to see what a change in attitude a little education could achieve. The real problem of Nepal is that education, like so many other services, is still only available for the minority.

When I was not being bothered by small boys, I was enjoying the ride very much, for the scenery was superb and very varied, with all sorts of interesting flowers, birds and butterflies around that I had never seen before. Then, quite suddenly, the sky darkened and it poured with rain. Expecting it to stop just as suddenly, I didn't bother to put my waterproof on and was soaked in seconds. It was heavy rain which fell in lumps that hurt on impact. Less than twenty-four hours after being tormented by heat, I was suffering from cold.

The sky stayed overcast, and when I reached Pokhara, several hours and several mountains later, it was almost dark and did not look a particularly attractive place. My friends at Ringo's in Delhi had told me to go straight to the lakeside to find a room at one of the many lodges there. These cheap accommodation places have proliferated like mushrooms and there are now dozens of them, all vying with each other for the foreign custom. They have exotic names like 'Lodge of the Shining Light', 'Krishna Lodge', even 'Jesus Christ Lodge'. Fairly basic amenities are offered, as listed on the card I was given at one of them.

Hotel Sanju and Lodge

1. We can sarve with Asian and Astrelian Meal
2. We can sarve by Pottors (porters for trekking)
3. You can enjoy with Himalan Hills—Front Side to Lamjung Himal and Backside to Manaslu Himal
4. We have toilet.
   Single Bed Room Rs. 5 Double Bed Room Rs. 10 Common Bed Rs. 4

I wanted something a little better than this, but not the other extreme, of unashamed luxury at 25 dollars a night. While I was considering the alternatives, and at the same time trying to fend off some Tibetans who were eager to purchase the bicycle, I was hailed by an elderly English couple, who thought that I needed support. 'Don't you sell it to them,' they called. 'They'll have the shirt off your back if you let them.' This couple bore me off to their hotel and like the seasoned travellers they were, they had found somewhere which was modestly priced but comfortable. Later I shared a table with them for several meals and grew very fond of them. They had lived and worked in India for many years and had quite looked forward to their retirement in England. The actuality had proved very different to the dream. Living on a fixed income, their lives became a daily grind of trying to make ends meet, which was achieved only by the constant exercise of the most stringent economies. Tiring of this grey existence and of English winters, they had come back to the sub-continent. When I met them they had been touring around for six months, using local transport and spending far less money than living in England cost them. They had no intention of ever returning: when they were tired of wandering, they said, they would find a nice little house in Rajasthan and settle there.

When I awoke the following morning and glanced casually out of the window, a stone's throw away, seemingly, towered the giant peaks of Macchapuchare and Annapurna. In the foreground, the unflawed surface of green lake water mirrored their images. It was almost too much to take in, especially with the dawn shining in a pink glow on the snow and ice of the awesome upper slopes. Because the previous day had been so overcast, these mountains had been invisible as I approached; seeing them so suddenly revealed had enormous impact. Perhaps that is why the scene imprinted itself so indelibly on my mind, so that now I have only to close my eyes to see the vast symmetry of Macchapuchare, glowing in a pink dawn.

Soon after breakfast I cycled off to The Shining Hospital, named by the local people because of the sun shining so dazzlingly on its tin roof. It had been built 20 years before by the United Missions to serve the needs of the population for many miles around. I had been a little worried about calling on its services, as the medical needs of Nepal are very great and doctors very few, one to 100,000 of the population at the last count and those living mainly in the Kathmandu Valley. However, I was assured that the modest fee they charged foreigners helped with the mission's costs. In any case, the terrible complaints contracted by Westerners, in what is reckoned to be the dirtiest country in Asia, make some sort of medical care for them imperative, tourism being by far Nepal's largest money-provider.

The English doctor whom I saw was in little doubt that I was suffering from amoebiasis and thought that I had probably had it for some weeks. Being so fit had stopped it getting a real hold and enabled me to keep going for so long. He said it was a nasty condition which could leave one very weak and depressed. The treatment was a course of tablets and lots of rest, and I was advised to begin this at once, rather than waiting for the results from the laboratory. I needed no urging to do so, for when I was weighed I found I had lost about 20 pounds of my normal nine stones.

Had I been able to choose a spot in which to be ill, I'm sure I couldn't have done better than Pokhara. The ten days I spent there, taking my pills and resting as ordered, convinced me that I had indeed discovered the true and original Shangri-La. After the first day or two, I didn't even feel ill any more and was able to eat hugely and begin to regain my lost weight. Each morning I began the day with a swim in the warm, green lake. Five o'clock was best for this, as then the peaks were always clear and unclouded and I could float there on my back watching the sky around them change from a dove-grey to a glory of apricot-pink. Later in the day they were often obscured by cloud, for the rainy season was fast approaching.

The choice of this early hour for a swim had practical considerations, too, for I could never take a bath in my hotel quarters, as the water would only come out of the outside overflow and not through the taps. It was the chatter of the local women filling their water jars at this overflow, which was just outside my window, that woke me so early each morning. Sometimes I wondered if it had not been fixed that way on purpose, for their convenience.

Much of the day I spent sitting at the open-air café in the hotel courtyard which was on the main thoroughfare and well placed for viewing the mountains and for observing what was going on around the lake. There was always a wealth of interesting happenings, the most startling of which occurred among the freakier of the Europeans. Magic mushrooms were the 'in kick' and these were pedalled quite openly by dear old Nepalese ladies, sitting with their baskets at the lakeside. The young people who indulged in this drug were liable at any time to break into quite bizarre behaviour. I just missed the full scene of a young man who stripped off all his clothes in the main square, dancing and singing grand opera. I only saw him being led off, still singing, by the local policeman, while the old ladies were hiding their faces and having the vapours, on account of being so modest and not used to seeing nakedness. Another young man got himself into severe trouble when under the influence of the mushrooms, for he fell to attacking everyone who was riding a bicycle, including the local police-man who had been sent for to arrest him. A less aggressive spectacle was afforded by a German man who had come to the conclusion that his large white dog was misnamed, being really a god. He made a tour of all the lakeside cafés, begging everyone to recognize the animal's divinity. 'God not Dog, God not Dog,' he intoned, tears coursing down his cheeks, while everyone looked away in embarrassment: no one ever seems to know what to do in such situations.

The resident Europeans were very worried by all this, and wanted the police to clamp down on the sale of the drug, as they considered the Nepalese already had far too low an opinion of Westerners and were coming to despise them more and more. This was only true of the older Nepalese, I thought; the younger ones, the boys that is, seemed keener on copying their habits and throwing off their own customs. This could be seen in their adopting Western dress and joining in the naked bathing, which went on everywhere, in spite of the notices forbidding it. Water is a divine element in Hindu and Buddhist faiths; one is supposed to treat it with respect. Many of the local boys had also learnt to smoke hashish, but I never saw any of them freaking out on magic mushrooms.

The majority of the Westerners were perfectly normal people, who were either passing through on their world travels, or had come there in order to go trekking through the high Himalayan valleys. So there was never a shortage of interesting company with whom to talk and share meals. I particularly enjoyed hearing about the people and places which the returning trekkers had visited. The idea of doing something similar appealed very much. Certainly the only way to get to really high altitudes would be on foot, as there were no roads which went anything like as high as I had already been in India and Kashmir.

In some ways Pokhara was like a skiing resort at the height of the season, the permanent residents submerged by the visitors and making a livelihood from them. The family who ran the café where I spent so much of my convalescence was typical. They had left their village home with their baby son the previous year and hired the small, run-down shack in my hotel courtyard. A partition had been built to provide a room for their customers when it rained, leaving the remainder for the kitchen and the family's living quarters, a space about 10-foot square. It was best not to penetrate into this back area if you were at all squeamish about hygiene; being on antibiotics, I wasn't too worried. By working hard from early morning to late at night, leaving the baby to rear itself most of the time, they were achieving a better standard of living than they could ever hope for in their village, at least in economic terms. They were both intelligent and quick to adapt, learning to cook all the strange sorts of food which Western youth seems to like—banana fritters, eggs and bacon, brownies, buffburgers—the menu was endless.

While I was there, their young nephew, a boy of 10, was brought down from their village to live with them and learn the trade. He was one of the happiest and most willing little boys I have ever met and everyone loved him. In only a few days he had learnt to pronounce all the words on the menu and trotted to and fro with the orders, beaming with delight. When he wasn't waiting at table or lending a hand in the kitchen, he was playing nursemaid to his little cousin. This young scallywag was a sturdy, independent two-year-old, a great trial to his parents because of his persistent habit of removing all his clothes. Perhaps he already had ambitions to join the freaky set.

Tibetans were another distinct group in Pokhara's varied scene. There was a large refugee camp for them further up the valley where they turned out quantities of ethnic jewellery and woven belts. These they hawked around the lakeside, offering to barter them for anything Western. A tatty old pair of denim jeans or a worn-out sleeping bag could be exchanged for something quite exquisite. My bicycle attracted them like flies and I was never able to go around on it without scores of them gathering to make offers for it. If trade was slack, some of the younger Tibetans would come and sit themselves at café tables and press the diners to buy their necklaces and bangles. I bought several pieces in this way until the other travellers asked me not to; they said I spoilt the trade by not bargaining hard enough. Some of them paid for their travels by picking up these things cheaply and selling them at a profit when they returned home, so after that I let these experts do my buying for me.

Not everything was idyllic in this lovely place, however, and certain things grew increasingly hard to bear after a while. For one thing there were rats in large numbers. Often I would hear them scuttling across the roof at night and on two occasions I found items of my clothing badly gnawed by them. Dirt too, in the form of piles of rotting garbage and open sewers, was everywhere about. Worst of all was the constant noisy throat-clearing and spitting that all the native people indulged in, as they had done in India and Pakistan. Unless people have been subjected to this constant spitting, I think it would be difficult to appreciate how obsessed one can become about it, especially in a part of the world rife with tuberculosis. Any two Westerners, discussing the sub-continent in my hearing, always named spitting as the single most trying aspect of life there, and one had only to hear the noise of a throat being cleared to see everyone around flinching and taking preventive action.

Until a few days before I left, there had been a total electricity failure. This was a blessing in many ways, for candlelight disguised the squalor around the cafés; but as the candles flickered and often blew out in the evening breezes, it was difficult to avoid eating the foreign bodies which appeared in the food from time to time. I didn't realize how fortunate I had been until the electricity was restored. Then the peace was shattered; from every café and lodge, loud pop music blared out over the lake all day and far into the night. This, as it happened, coincided with a change in the balance of the freaks to trekkers. As the weather grew warmer and the monsoon period approached, the trekking season began to draw to a close and the lodges lowered their already modest charges. The freaky set took over; magic mushroom incidents in-creased and the smell of pot was all-pervading. The time had come, I decided, for me to leave Pokhara and complete the journey to Kathmandu.

17

No one can take the wrong road to Kathmandu, for a statue of King Prithvi Narayan Shah stands at the crossroads, pointing to the route that he took when he set out from here, 200 years ago, to conquer that rich city and so create the kingdom of Nepal. Until that time, there had just been scores of little princedoms, separated from one another by the excessively rough nature of the terrain.

Nepal had then entered a period which could be likened to Europe in medieval times, with a great flowering of the arts, but a short and brutish life for the majority of the people. While the rest of the sub-continent was being colonized— mainly by Britain—Nepal remained independent, since there were few pickings there worth the effort needed to exploit them.

The Shah dynasty has continued in uninterrupted succession until the present day, but after 1846 they had served merely as puppet rulers; for in that year there had been an extraordinary take-over, when the chief minister had killed off all his opponents in a terrible 'night of the long knives', and established the effective ruling dynasty known as the Ranas. They couldn't get rid of the king, since in their particular form of religion—a unique mixture of Hinduism and Buddhism— the king was a minor deity. Each new royal heir was removed from his parents soon after birth and brought up to be as dissolute and ineffectual as possible; so as to be available for state functions, but to cause no trouble to the usurpers. Total nepotism ensued. The Rana family ran everything and kept the rest of the people in a state of serfdom. Very few visitors were allowed into the country, and then only with severely limited freedom of movement.

Then towards the middle of this century, the reigning puppet king, Tribuvan Shah, proved to be more enterprising than his forebears. Rumour has it that instead of indulging in the dissolute pleasures prescribed for him by the Ranas, he had been secretly reading for years such works as Adam Smith's *The Wealth of Nations* and Thomas Paine's *The Rights of Man*. These had fired him (as they had fired so many Englishmen of the 18th century) to do something for his poor, downtrodden subjects. Taking advantage of a state visit to the newly independent India, he had sought help from that country in staging a coup to liberate Nepal from the Ranas.

Since that time Nepal has been an open country, and people have flocked to visit it, particularly the hippies of the '60s. The shock of this sudden contact with the West on a people living an essentially primitive life-style was bound to have grave consequences. No people can step straight out of feudalism into the technological age without suffering profound culture shock and a disorientation of traditional values.

As I cycled along the rather gloomy ravines which led towards Kathmandu, I reflected on this history. I was glad I had had so much time to read up on it while convalescing in Pokhara, for it helped very much in understanding the attitudes in the country. The begging, the aggressive children, the veiled dislike; all this was hardly surprising, given the circumstances.

Several of my new acquaintances were also leaving Pokhara that day, but they were going on the express bus which had been scheduled to leave an hour after my departure. It got to Kathmandu in one day, whereas I would have to stay half way, at Mugling. I kept expecting it to pass me, since I was not going particularly fast, because it was very hot and I was still supposed to be taking it easy. But even express buses in Nepal are not really speedy. Not until I had done about 55 miles, including three stops for tea, did it catch me up, belching out clouds of exhaust and with all my friends waving and cheering out of the windows. I caught it up again at Mugling which was the half-way staging post, where all the buses halted to cool down and where the passengers were fed and watered.

After my friends had left to continue their journey, I felt a little depressed at being left alone at Mugling, for it really was a most dreary place. It existed solely as a service point for transport and consisted of about 20 fly-infested, noisome hovels, all sporting grandiose signs, claiming that they were hotels. As there was nothing to choose between them, I booked into the one where I had drunk tea. Upstairs there were three tiny spaces divided from each other by wood partitions, full of gaps and knot-holes. Someone's meagre possessions were taken out of one of these spaces and it was mine for 40 pence. It had a plank bed with a thin cotton quilt by way of a mattress and the window space was covered over by the 'hotel' sign outside. Clearly there were no washing facilities, or any other facilities either, but then at that price, what could one expect?

The patron told me of a good bathing spot by the river, which he said was 10 minutes' walk away and seldom visited by anyone. Since Mugling offered no diversions other than a constant stream of noisy traffic, I thought I would go to this place with my books and washing and spend the rest of the day there. I had first to cross the wide, swiftly flowing river by a rope bridge, which swayed and bounced with every step. After this, a precipitous path led to a stream tumbling down from the hills, which formed a deep pool before entering the river below. I stripped off and lay there soaking until I felt cool again. I was just washing out my clothes which had been soaking in the pool with me, when I heard voices approaching. Hastily I grabbed my dripping shirt and held it over my wet front. Three young men hove into view. I yelled at them to go away while I dressed. They didn't understand and continued to approach, making gestures that they wanted to wash their hair. Conscious of my exposed back, I yelled louder at them to go away, and obligingly they moved off so that I was able to scramble into my shorts and clean shirt. No sooner was I vaguely decent again, than the path below turned into a thoroughfare, with cows, goats, goatherds, cowherds, small boys and women coming to get water and to wash clothes; so much for the patron's information!

Later I wondered if the other information which he pressed upon me during the evening meal was equally inaccurate. He was a young man, one of the minority of educated Nepalis, and politically aware. He painted a picture of Nepal which equalled anything in Third World countries for corruption, chicanery, misappropriated funds, foreign aid finding its way into Swiss banks and dissenting students thrown into gaol and never being seen again. I was to hear such stories many times—but I had no means of assessing their truth.

The next day's ride was longer and more exacting, being a series of steep ups and downs, though mainly ups, especially the last part, where a large mountain guarded the entrance to the Kathmandu Valley. I struggled up this, making very heavy weather of it, for I reached it at the hottest part of the day and was not yet fully recovered from the amoeba. Much of the way, sheaves of wheat spread over the road to be threshed by the traffic had added to the difficulties, and then when I came to the top of the last slope, I had to walk the first downhill miles because the road was under repair.

After that stretch, things improved and I sailed down to Kathmandu in fine style, trying to take in the fact that I had made it. In a little under four months, I had cycled about 4,000 miles, much of it through difficult mountain terrain and here I was in Kathmandu. I felt a little twinge of disappointment that there were no flags to greet me.

First things first, sightseeing could wait. What I most wanted was to find my mail and catch up on news from home. I hadn't had any letters since Lahore, three months previously. So instead of plunging into the wonders of Durbar Square which I had dreamed about for so long, I made my way straight to Yeti Travels, which housed the American Express Office, and was soon in possession of a large pile of letters and a much-needed new tyre. Clutching these treasures I then set off to find the hotel to which I'd been recommended. This was Dwarika's, a lovely place, set in beautiful gardens on the outskirts of the town, with priceless old woodcarvings built into the fabric. It was outside my price range but I felt I should celebrate my safe arrival in style and move on to something more modest the following day. The management, however, were rather intrigued by my arriving on a bicycle and when I had told them something of my journey, they kindly offered me free accommodation for a few days.

I was shown to a room of the sort I had not seen since leaving England, with elegant furniture, carpets and a bed spread with clean white sheets and pillows. No fewer than seven light fittings were dotted about and six of them worked! My bathroom had a real bath in it, plumbing which functioned as it was supposed to and didn't smell, and a sit-down lavatory with a seat. Such luxury seemed altogether too much. But it was the sheer, sparkling cleanliness of everything which was really overwhelming; what with all the excitement of reading my letters, the kindness of the management and still being a little weak from the amoeba, I found myself in tears.

The present-day traveller is about 30 years too late for Kathmandu. Medieval cities with their narrow paved streets do not combine well with wheeled traffic, not even bicycle rickshaws. Constantly blaring horns and tinkling bells have the hapless pedestrians pinned against walls most of the time, rather than gazing at the crumbling splendours of temples, shrines and the hundreds of other fascinating things which make up this unique city. Only the sacred cows and bulls which wander freely about everywhere, eating the piles of rotting garbage, are treated with consideration. These animals may walk with impunity anywhere they like. Should they choose to have a rest in the centre of the street, then the traffic will go carefully around them, or come to a halt altogether. On the larger roads, bordering the ancient city, there are circular grassed traffic islands, where there is always a cow or a bull lying down, quietly ruminating. Once, in a narrow alleyway leading off the main square, where vegetable stalls were pressed so closely together that it was difficult to pass between, a cow had lain down and died. Before the cart had come to remove it, the body was covered with flowers, placed there by devout people.

Early morning or after dark was the best time for sight-seeing. Accustomed as I was now to rising at 4.30, I loved to wander the streets, watching the city waking up. There were no other Westerners about at this hour, only Nepalese making their early devotions at the small shrines; ringing the large swinging bells outside, before they entered to place their offerings at the feet of the god. Durbar Square, where the old Royal Palace and most of the outstanding temples were, could only really be seen in its entirety at this early hour. Later it became clogged with traffic and stalls selling everything imaginable, from vegetables to prayer wheels. Once, my early morning wandering was further enlivened by the sight of a young elephant, quite unattended, running at a furious pace through the streets. No one pursued it. Only at this time too, could one be free from the attentions of all the men and boys who made their living from the tourists. The rest of the day, every yard of the way was beset by cries of:

'Change dollar!'

'You want buy—drugs . . . flute . . . nice bracelet . . . my sister . . .?'

From the shop doorways, men would implore you to enter: 'Only look, no need buy, only look.'

Nearly everyone was friendly and good-natured, though; it was only the occasional youth who would upset young female tourists by making obscene suggestions while they were viewing the erotic carvings on the temple struts. Small boys too, whose lives were entirely spent on the streets among the touts and the illegal money-changers, sometimes got out of hand and started to abuse people with the foul language they could have learnt only from Westerners.

The bicycle continued to be admired, and unless I was visiting an outlying temple or another town in the valley, I left it behind because I grew tired of constantly being pestered to sell it. When I did take it around, I was also approached by people who wanted to tell me about Nepal's social and political evils, as the patron at Mugling had. This was because I had been invited to contribute a piece to the English language newspaper soon after my arrival, and people who had read the article recognized me from the description of the bicycle. Thinking that I was a journalist, they hoped I would publicize what they told me. So several times I found myself taken into secluded places, with a man on the lookout outside, while they poured out their troubles. There was of course nothing I could do, except to listen sympathetically.

Freak Street was the area I chose to move to after my few days of luxury. It was the antithesis of Dwarika's, and if it had once had another name, that had long been forgotten. Leading straight out of Durbar Square, hippies had made it their own in the '60s and now all the old Nepali houses there had become lodges. Neither cleanliness nor comfort were to be found there, and the rats made their presence noisily apparent. But it did have tremendous atmosphere, was delightfully central and cost next to nothing. Every lodge in Freak Street and the other medieval streets around, contained restaurants. There was no national cuisine which was not represented—Austrian, Swiss, Indian, Tibetan, French, Nepali, Chinese, American, Health Food, to name just a few. There was even one street, called Pig Alley, which specialized in pie shops. Everywhere one went to sample these delicacies, travellers from all parts of the world were regaling each other with accounts of the various ailments they had contracted in Nepal. Nearly everyone had, like me, contracted amoebiasis or guardia and the sinister yellow eyes of those suffering from hepatitis had me rushing off to the mission hospital, to top up my gamma globulin. All these illnesses are directly caused by dirt and I think I must agree with the people who claim that Kathmandu, for all its fascination, has to be one of the filthiest cities in the world.

At night, though, Kathmandu was magical. Fantastically tiered pagoda roofs, tall columns, topped by gilded figures, were outlined against a star-filled sky with moonlight shining on the snows beyond. The dimly lit streets hid their piles of rubbish and crumbling facades, revealing instead the lamp-lit temples. Religious music, played on primitive instruments, continued far into the night with people informally and singly going in to make their devotions. Then the illusion of being in another century was overwhelming.

I could happily have spent my remaining four weeks in the Kathmandu Valley, for there was more than enough to interest me in Kathmandu itself, and its surrounding monasteries and temples, as well as two other medieval cities nearby to explore. But at the head of the valley, the great range of the Himalayas stood as a perpetual lure and no city, not even Kathmandu, could compete for long with such a rival. It was already late in the season and most of the trekking had ended until after the monsoons, which were due very shortly, but I felt it would be unthinkable to have come so far and not make an attempt to see something of the high, remote areas of Nepal. I took the problem to the Sherpa Co-operative, run by Mike Cheney, an Englishman who had lived most of his life in these parts and had helped with the organization of many of the successful assaults on the great peaks. He thought it would be possible to make a fast trip up to the glaciers below the Langtang Peak, if I was accompanied by a Sherpa to carry the pack. Last year the B.B.C. had made a film of Freya Stark doing the same journey and Mike had organized the expedition, including the pony to carry Freya Stark. An enormous number of porters had been necessary, not just for the equipment; the way was so precipitous in places that the pony had to be carried, too.

Most of the Sherpas had by now returned to their villages but a few younger ones were left. These youngsters grew ever more reluctant to leave the delights of Kathmandu and return home to help with the harvest, I was told. Two of them were selected for my trip. Karma, a 19-year-old, was to serve as guide at a wage of about one pound twenty a day, and Chandra who was a little younger was to be porter and earn just under a pound. In order to travel fast, we wouldn't camp, but would sleep and eat in the villages through which we would pass.

We set off the following day and after a short bus ride, started up the steep path towards the distant glaciers of the massive Langtang Himal, beyond which lies Tibet. For the next 15 days, I would be in a world where the only wheels were prayer wheels, turned by hand or by the waters of small streams, and porters provided the only means of moving goods. In no way could this be called a remote area, though, at least not until one was at about 13,000 feet. There were villages every few miles and the rough track was a highway for the trafficking of all types of commodities. People used the track constantly, the great loads on their backs supported from a band about their foreheads. All the steep slopes around the villages were terraced into small fields and planted with a variety of crops which changed, with the increasing altitude, from semi-tropical on the lower slopes, to subsistence pastures for yaks at the extreme level of habitation, at about 14,000 feet.

Each day followed a similar pattern. We would leave our night's lodging at about seven after tea and a light snack, and walk until 10.30 or so, when we would stop at a village for the main meal of the day—always rice, vegetables and dal. Then we would continue for about another three hours, until we reached the village selected for that night's stop where we would have another meal and retire to our beds as darkness fell. We always tried to find a place en route where we could wash ourselves and our clothes before ending the day's march.

Having the two boys to carry the gear made walking very pleasant. For them it was a sort of holiday, too, since their loads were normally three or four times heavier and they didn't have to cook or make camp as they did on other expeditions. Karma had a smattering of English, but Chandra had none. They seemed very fond of each other and chattered away all day at the tops of their voices. I usually went on ahead so as to enjoy a little quiet and to see the many birds which flew off at the sound of the boys' voices. There was always something of interest to see, so they constantly caught up, looking puzzled that I should find things commonplace to them so fascinating. One day I had been watching the curious way wheat was being harvested by stripping off the heads between two sticks—leaving the stalks standing. It was as well they caught me up then, because as I was about to take a photograph of an old woman sitting in front of a great heap of wheat heads she suddenly sprang up to attack me. The boys fended her off, but couldn't explain what I had done to offend her. Normally the people liked being photographed, though most of them expected a reward for the service.

The villages were various in character, those lower down being thatched and mud-plastered with ochre-coloured walls while those higher up were predominantly stone and roofed with large heavy slabs. The higher we went the dirtier and more Buddhist the villages became, with prayer flags on tall poles fluttering in the wind to bear the prayers to heaven as the flags are slowly worn away. Conditions were very primitive with plagues of flies everywhere. Great care was needed to stay healthy and I exercised stringent control over sterilizing the plate, cup and cutlery I carried, and also in adding iodine to all the water I drank. Nevertheless, I was glad that we were staying with the people in their own homes and not camping, because in spite of the discomfort, it was fascinating to glimpse into the lives of these hillfolk.

Many trekkers had previously walked this route and the local people were now used to Westerners. It seemed to me that our presence among them had done little to enhance their lives. True, the few who kept lodges welcomed the small increase in earnings, but for the majority it simply made them aware of the vast disparity of wealth between themselves and the developed world. Once we were three days' march from the start of the track, there was almost no outside aid available: no schools, no doctors, not even a health visitor; and yet the government of Nepal extracted money from every foreigner who visited the area. In each village, children and adults would approach me for cigarettes and chocolate, but mainly for medicine. I was shown a variety of conditions which could have been dealt with for a very modest outlay. Painful eye complaints were prevalent, mainly caused by smoke from cooking fires or exposure to the blinding light reflected off the high snows. Scalds, burns and cuts were common among the babies and children; aggravated by the insanitary conditions, these had often turned septic. My slender supplies of anti-septics were soon exhausted, for I found it impossible to refuse the little crowd who gathered around so trustingly in each village we visited.

One morning, when I had for once been sleeping alone in a sort of loft over a cow stall, I awoke to find an old man sitting quietly beside my mattress. How long he had been there I didn't know, but it transpired that he had heard of the good effects of my eye drops from people I had treated earlier and had travelled for several days in the hope of meeting up with me, for his own eyes were badly affected. Alas, by that time, my stocks were exhausted. What made the lack of medical care even more annoying was that some aid or other had been supplied to build a hospital high in the valley. Although the building had been completed some time before, it contained neither personnel nor any drugs or equipment.

A pretty little girl of three or four with a mop of curly, matted hair was brought to me one day by an older brother. She was hopping along on one foot, the other having an ugly infected sore place on the big toe. I had nothing left except the iodine with which I sterilized the drinking water, so while she held her foot up trustingly for me, I applied a few drops to the place and waited for the reaction. It wasn't long in coming. I thought her howls would bring the rest of the villagers rushing to her rescue, but the older boy held on to her and smiled to reassure me, so perhaps other trekkers had used iodine before. I tried to compensate for the betrayal by making the child a bandage with a strip of clean handkerchief and this was so successful that all the other children began to look for sore places, so that they could have a bandage, too.

One evening I was invited to visit a religious ceremony at a tiny village a little off the beaten track. As Karma spoke so little English and there was no one else there who spoke more, it was difficult to make out what was going on. I gathered that it was a ritual spirit-burning for the headman who had died and been cremated some weeks previously. The intention was to make sure that the spirit departed to heaven and didn't remain to haunt the village. A small roofed platform had been built on tall poles in a central clearing and in it had been placed objects of religious significance and offerings of food. Around it, in slow motion, danced a circle of chanting people; first the women, then the men. On the verandah of the dead man's house sat a Lama, intoning from an enormous book, while musicians beat gongs with their curved sticks. In front of the priest was a seated effigy of the dead man dressed in his best clothes. Locally brewed beer, called *chang*, was flowing freely and everyone seemed happy and enjoying the occasion. People approached me for cigarettes and pushed mugs of *chang* at me. Small children sipped from the adults' beer while the smallest of them squatted down to defecate wherever they felt like it. They would then be slapped by the bigger children, who quickly kicked dust over the offending mess.

The bigger children, by which I mean the seven- to 12-year-olds, seemed often to be the most responsible members of their families, the girls especially, taking on the rearing of the smaller children and many of the household duties. On this occasion they seemed the only rather disapproving section of the otherwise contented gathering. I was drawn into the circle of swaying, chanting women but could not seem to pick up the rhythm which looked deceptively simple. All the women wore heavy, circular, gold earrings three to four inches across and nose rings, too. Most of the men had a single hooped golden ring in one lobe. All the women wore long skirts while the men wore short tunics and loin cloths or shorts. Occasionally a bright woollen balaclava replaced the traditional Nepali cap and showed that the proud owner had been a porter on a climbing expedition. The ceremony gave no signs of ending when I left several hours later and I thought it would probably continue until all the *chang* was finished.

Rounding the corner of the track one day, I came upon a distressing scene. Two young women were playing with a little bird which was rather like a bluetit. One of them had it fastened to her dress with a length of twine the other end of which was tied to one of the bird's legs. They were making the poor thing flutter to the limit of the line, then hauling it back again. Before I had time to stop myself, I had darted forward to rescue the bird, and consequently had to get Karma to negotiate a price for it. Too late I realized that my thoughtless action would probably result in more of these tiny creatures being caught and offered for sale to passing trekkers. Later I saw many small children supplied with these living playthings on a string. The birds fortunately did not survive long, but their pathetic corpses would still be dragged behind the toddlers long after they were dead. Although the children had no toys as such, I found it a curious anomaly that in a Buddhist area with its respect for all forms of life, such a cruel practice was not only tolerated, but actually encouraged by the adults.

The higher we climbed the more intoxicating grew the air and the more beautiful the views. One lovely mountain which dominated the skyline to the north was Ganesh Himal, called after the elephant-headed son of Shiva. The Himalayas are traditionally the home of the gods, particularly of Shiva, whose holy lake, Gossainkunda, we detoured to see. It lies at the head of a lonely valley at 14,000 feet. Here Shiva is supposed to lie sleeping off his excesses and the waving weed fronds in the water are taken to be his long wild hair. Later in the year thousands of Hindu pilgrims spend an all-night vigil here. I found it a rather forbidding spot, though the view from the top of the pass, 1,200 feet above the lake and marked by hundreds of prayer flags and religious cairns, was quite spectacular.

A few thousand feet lower down this side valley were ancient forests with trees almost as tall as the giant redwoods of California. Many of these trees had fallen and lay where they fell, mouldering away. Few people came here and as a result the place was teeming with flora and fauna of the widest variety, including great cushions of orchids and rhododendrons of all colours, blooming so late in the year because of the high altitude.

We met up with Karma's father and cousins in this valley. They were guiding an English couple and we all spent the night at the only lodge there, with the English couple in a tent and all the porters in a wood shed—sleeping in a heap for warmth and comfort, like puppies. I shared a floor in the lodge with a young man from Lancashire who was a professed Buddhist. At some time in the night I was awoken by my companion shouting and throwing things across the room. By the light of his torch I saw the back end of a dog disappearing through the open door. In the morning when I looked for my watch which I had left on the floor beside me, it wasn't there. It was found eventually, where the dog had dropped it before rushing out. Half the strap had been eaten. I was horrified to think of how starved the poor brute must have been, but relieved that he hadn't swallowed the whole watch.

Back in the main Langtang Valley the scenery changed dramatically once the 13,000-foot mark was passed. It was a cold treeless landscape of stone and tough, wind-swept grass. The people who lived above this height had a grim struggle for existence, with a growing season so short that it seemed hardly possible to produce a crop. Nevertheless there were Tibetans in their tiny rock-strewn fields, ploughing the ground with the help of yaks. As we passed, they would lean over their low rough walls and offer to sell me items of jewellery. Children with runny noses and hacking coughs would run up with a baby almost as big as themselves tied to their backs, signalling that they were offering me the child to photograph—for suitable payment. Karma distributed cigarettes to all the children (against instructions) and they were soon puffing away with great gusto. Everyone in the Himalayas seemed to smoke if they got the chance and my two helpers were already badly affected by the habit, smoking as much as a couple of packets a day. This was a pity since Karma had ambitions to be a 'tiger' and carry on the big international climbs.

Much of the path at the higher altitudes was divided down the middle by a shoulder-high wall covered with Mani stones. These are flat stones inscribed with the sacred Buddhist text and there are hundreds of thousands of them in these walls, which stretch for miles. They must have taken centuries to construct, and that they had been built at all in such a remote and inhospitable terrain, where survival itself seems a miracle, was evidence of the deeply religious beliefs of the people of these parts.

When we reached the lodge at Langtang village, we had first to enter a kind of courtyard which was filled with old yak bones and other refuse all covered with flies. Outside the low shack, which was roofed with torn rush matting and appropriately labelled Yak Hotel, three figures and a baby lay in an unlovely heap on the ground. Karma tried to rouse the woman in the group with repeated cries. Eventually she stirred, half sat up, looked round at us, groaned, and subsided back into the heap. A man, her husband I assumed, appeared, and rushed at her with shouts and kicks. Reluctantly, she got to her feet and stumbled into the shack, rearranging her clothes as she went. The two men in the heap and the baby moaned and groaned and wriggled into new positions. 'Black people,' said Karma contemptuously. 'They don't wash.' One glance inside the shack was enough to convince me that it would be the height of folly to stay in such a place. The conditions in most of the lodges had been tolerable if one forgot about Western ideas of cleanliness, but this was squalid by any standard. The only thing to do was to climb up to the end of the trail as quickly as possible, take a brief look at the scene and then retrace our steps to the previous night's lodging.

Sixteen thousand feet was the limit of the trek. After that the final third of the mountain is an awesome series of glaciers and snow-covered rock faces, accessible only to the very best mountaineers. As we gazed up into the swirling clouds which swept across the cliffs we saw figures descending. It was a Japanese expedition which had just successfully tackled the peak, after four weeks of effort. Burnt almost black, but looking fit and triumphant, they strode off at a great pace, back towards the fleshpots of Kathmandu. I too was heading back with a deep sense of triumph and achievement. I had not stood upon the summit of a 24,000-foot peak, to gaze northwards into Tibet, but I had reached a height 3,000 feet above any peak in Europe, and I had seen something of the wonders of the world's high places.

18

Darjeeling was once a pearl in the necklace of British Raj hill stations: bungalows, churches, schools and clubs once graced the steeply terraced hillside that faces the vast bulk of Kanchenjunga across the valley. They are still there, these relics of the colonial past, but for the most part, they moulder away under rusty tin roofs. Here and there the ghost of a villa, with a touch of the Scottish Baronial about it, is a poignant reminder, not of past glories but of a cosy middle-class life, with rambler roses over the porch and servants who knew their place.

I was staying at The Planter's Club, which was managed by a tough old colonial lady who seemed to be able to cope with the changing times by largely ignoring them. The building itself had a commanding position on one of the higher terraces and reminded me of an English cricket pavilion, except that it was two-storeyed. It was built of wood and was slowly rotting away, with gaps appearing at the base where mice could go in and out. The long windows had many of the panes painted over, perhaps to economize on curtaining.

Never had I seen such convoluted plumbing. It seemed a miracle that it worked at all, but wonderfully hot water was always available—as long as no one else tried to run their tap at the same time. Actually the heat of the water did have drawbacks, as at some period the inside of the bath had been painted and as one lay there, revelling in the heat, large streamers of paint like pale seaweed detached themselves and adhered clammily to one's body.

The manager had persuaded an Australian girl to share her room with me, as there was no other available, the club being considered a prestigious place to stay and therefore full of rich, middle-class Indians visiting their children at their British-type boarding schools. These Indians seemed far more English than the English and were hanging on to a way of life and a scale of values long since redundant in Britain.

Life at The Planter's revolved around the dining room with its three square meals a day. These could be good, indifferent or frightful—like off-fish followed by off-pork followed by the sort of suet pudding that is lethal to anyone over school age. The crockery was old and monogrammed. Much of it was chipped and the glaze cracked and discoloured. Perhaps this was why the ageing staff missed the ingrained dirt, especially on the jugs and teapots. There was a lot of blackened, plated silver about, too, though often the silver salt cellar—minus spoon—would be flanked by a cracked, pink plastic pepper pot. Sometimes, instead of a sideplate, one would be given a saucer.

Three very ancient waiters presided over the dining room, each clad in a uniform of dark trousers, frayed white tunic and a woollen hat. The waiter who served at our table had no teeth, real or false, and no hair either, as we soon discovered, for he removed his hat frequently to mop his brow. He had a nice sense of distinction between dinner and luncheon: for the former he wore boots and moved about at a funereal pace, while at luncheon he appeared without shoes or socks and often broke into a shambling trot if he was falling behind the other two waiters.

My companion and I felt that we were not entirely approved of by the waiters: perhaps we were not grave enough, or did not employ the correct redundancies of speech as did the Indian guests. Maybe it was our attitude to the food that was all wrong for we never saw the Indians refusing anything even if it was off-pork or off-fish.

As soon as my permit came through, I left Darjeeling and set out for Sikkim. India is not very keen it seems on having too many people pouring into what it considers sensitive areas and Sikkim is one such place. To get permission to stay longer than a week is very difficult and they are not really happy about individuals wandering around alone, but prefer organized walking parties which can be guided along a specified route. With so little time, I should not be able to see much. It was a really close look at Kanchenjunga that I most wanted; for that, Perman Yangste on the west side of the country would be the nearest spot I could hope to reach. There was also a famous Buddhist monastery near the capital city, Gangtok, that I was keen to visit, so I made Gangtok my first objective. Several times on the way, what I took to be plain-clothes policemen demanded to see my permit.

Gangtok was not an exciting town, though I liked the people. They were rather like the Nepalese, though their cultural ties with Tibet were stronger and their religion was closer to Tibetan Buddhism. I spent a day there wandering through the grounds of the old royal palace while I waited for the tourist office to organize my visit to Runtek Monastery. At the top of the ridge was an area called the Deer Park which was supposed to be where Buddha had preached his famous sermon. It was a sad little place with a miniature zoo. A Himalayan bear was housed in a cage too small for it even to stand up in and some beautiful creatures called leopard cats were languishing in hot pens where there was nowhere they could curl up out of the sun. Some Indian tourists were beating at the bars of the cages, driving the animals into a frenzy of rage and frustration; particularly some poor macaque monkeys, who were hurling their bodies against the bars in a vain attempt to get at their tormentors. I left the place quickly in case I should be tempted to say or do something rash.

Later I was captured by some young Sikkimese children who were eager to practise their English. They bore me off in triumph to where their teacher was sitting in an orchid sanctuary, and I was invited to share their picnic of bread and curried potatoes. They were having an outing from their school which was run by the Ba'hais, a faith I knew very little of, but which the children did their best to explain. It sounded a lot saner than what had been expounded by the American Baptists in Pakistan. Afterwards I visited their school and was amazed at the poverty they lived and worked in.

Arriving at last at the monastery compound, I was greeted by a monk who pointed out a notice written in English. This instructed me to proceed to the Purifying Room where a monk would instruct me in the purifying procedure. I did this and in a small room full of images and butter lamps I was handed a glass of water and given to understand that I must rinse my mouth out with it. This created something of a problem, spiritually pure it might be, but physically safe it almost certainly wasn't. One bout of the dreaded amoeba was quite enough, so I declined the water, holding my stomach and groaning to attempt to show the reason for my refusal. After some discussion with other monks, it was decided that I could be purified outwardly instead and I was made to bow my head while the purifier threw a generous amount of the water over me, followed by a couple of handfuls of coloured rice. I presented him with a money offering and it was then considered safe for me to pass the terrifying painted demons who guarded the door into the Puja or prayer hall.

The Puja hall occupied most of the ground floor. The walls were covered with huge bright pictures of Buddhas, demons, monsters and allegorical animals. From the high ceiling were suspended long, many-coloured silken banners. At one end there was a kind of altar covered with hundreds of butter lamps and a shrine-like construction also hung with silk and decorated with skulls, flowers and many ritual objects. Most of the floor space was filled with wide, carpet-covered benches where the monks sat cross-legged. There were over 100 of them, ranging in age from little boys of five to very old men. They were all dressed alike in sleeveless silky yellow shirts and long maroon skirts, with maroon shawls around their shoulders. Just one was dressed differently and I supposed him to be the Chief Lama. He was in golden satin robes and sat in an open space in front of the altar. Around his waist was an apron embroidered with a terrifying demon and on his head was an enormous hat, shaped like a coolie's, but made of rich silk and having a long spike rising from the centre hung about with various items, including a skull. At his feet lay a wax effigy and a three-sided dagger, and in his hand he held a long black scarf, as did a few other monks who were sitting on elevated seats at the other end of the hall.

Five rows of monks had musical instruments. Most of these were gong-like drums which were suspended above their heads and were beaten with curved sticks in a slow rhythm, to which the monks chanted. The chanting would go on for about five minutes and then would come an interval in which the other musicians let rip, with no particular pattern, on gongs, bells, giant drums and 12-foot long horns. While this cacophony of sound was thundering through the hall, the monks with the black scarfs would flick them backwards and forwards and make complicated gestures with their hands. The Chief Lama did this too, and made passes with the three-sided dagger over the wax effigy.

It was obviously some ceremony of exorcism and tremendously exciting to watch, but as there was no one there to ask, I couldn't find out what anything signified. This type of Tantric Buddhism is very obscure and is practised now in only a few places. I felt very fortunate to have been able to observe some of its rituals.

The tourist office at Gangtok had told me that I would find a very comfortable hotel at Perman Yangtse, but when I arrived there just before dark, the staff must have been having a day off, for there was no one around and the place was dark and deserted. It was some way from any civilization and I wondered what I should do. Fortunately I spotted a couple of men nearby and they spoke English. When I had explained about the hotel and they had confirmed that it did not appear to be functioning, they suggested that they should take me to 'The Captain'. 'Everyone goes to the Captain, he always knows what to do.'

That was how I came to be spending the night on a building site in the anything but comfortable sleeping quarters of a dozen Sikkimese men. It was also the beginning of one of the most rewarding encounters of my whole trip.

All I learnt the first night, while I shared the men's meal before being shown to a plank bed which the most committed ascetic would not have considered a treat, was that a school was being built and that it was considered a very important work, to which many people were contributing their spare time and money. The Captain, who seemed a man of boundless energy and charisma, was in charge of the work. It was from other people that I heard the Captain's story. He had been in the Sikkimese army at the time the country had been annexed by India. Like many Sikkimese, his had been a dissenting voice to the take-over and with other dissidents he had been imprisoned in India. His prospects looked very bleak and it was said that he experienced some sort of religious revelation while in gaol, and began to offer up Buddhist prayers and to persuade his companions to do likewise. Cynics would say that the military coup which brought the Indian Government down soon afterwards, would have happened anyway. The Captain, released by the Junta, came back to Sikkim determined to do something about preserving the religious and cultural values of his country, before they could be entirely swallowed up. A Buddhist school seemed to him the obvious choice; a school which taught English and Tibetan as the second and third languages, not Hindi as would all the government ones. This site had been chosen because Perman Yangste—The Monastery of The Sublime Lotus—has a very special significance for Sikkimese.

The next morning I was taken around the building site. It was an ambitious project since it was to be a boarding school, covering the whole age range from five upwards. Scores of men and women volunteers were employed on all aspects of it. When a major task like laying a concrete floor was being undertaken, then the children were released from their studies in order to help. Money was constantly running out though, and the labour force had often to be deployed to something which could earn some ready cash.

I spent a long while trotting around after the Captain, climbing the scaffolding and being proudly shown all that was going on. Then he took me up to the monastery to show me the school as it existed at present. It was like nothing I had ever seen. The 140 children were housed and fed in dilapidated buildings whose original purpose had been to accommodate meditating monks. They had their lessons in any scrap of cover that could be found, moving to a new spot if the builders needed the space. In spite of such difficulties, the children were evidently profiting from their lessons and even the smallest already knew a respectable amount of English.

The principal of the school, Sonam Denjongpa, had gained a scholarship to Brown University in America and had married an American student, Maria, there. The rest of the staff came from traditional Sikkimese backgrounds. Maria, especially, welcomed a fellow Westerner, and when it was learnt that I had spent some years in England teaching primary school, I was invited to stay as long as possible, to share ideas and offer advice. Their enthusiasm and devotion were so infectious, I wished I had a longer time to spare, but I was able to stay only two nights before my permit expired.

A little room was found for me in the building where the youngest children slept and the first morning I was awoken at 4.30 a.m. by mini scholars chanting 'Hello Tourist, hello Tourist' through the glassless panes of my window. Having told them sternly that this was not a suitable form of address for a female visitor of mature years—though why I should have thought this quite escapes me now—one little charmer with a dazzling smile executed a perfect salaam and said 'Good morning, Memsahib,' thus disarming me totally.

I had almost forgotten that I had come here to gaze at Kanchenjunga, though to view its massive south face from the monastery ridge I had only to raise my eyes to see it appearing and disappearing through the swirling clouds of mist. For the most part I was too busy taking classes and observing all that was going on. Watching small competent eight-year-olds washing their own clothes and planting gardens when they were not busy with their lessons, I enjoyed every minute of my time there, lack of comfort and basic amenities notwithstanding. If I hadn't had a husband back home who was expecting me to return shortly, I would have been tempted to take up the offer of a permanent post. As it was, I only got away just in time, for the monsoons started the day I left and pursued me back to Kathmandu, flooding roads and carrying away bridges.

Epilogue

I had arrived in Delhi Airport at seven o'clock in the evening after the hour's flight from Kathmandu. At first I sat in the no-man's land reserved for transit passengers, perfectly relaxed for it had been a wonderful flight from Nepal, the aeroplane flying almost parallel to the Himalayan Range, with each peak visible and gilded by the rays of the setting sun.

Slowly my euphoria wore off as more and more of my fellow passengers were claimed by their airlines and led off to the luxury of the departure lounge. At least, I thought, anywhere must be more comfortable than this transit place where the only refreshment kiosk had closed before I had arrived. The only other diversion available was the ladies' washroom, but here all the floor space was occupied by the women sweepers, who were sleeping in there. They had sprung to their feet the first time I had gone in, and flicked a cloth at the wash basin, before advancing on me with a smile and an outstretched palm. My last few coins, Nepali rupees, had been received without much enthusiasm, and on subsequent visits they had not been prepared to shift enough to allow me to enter.

No one claimed me. From time to time I managed to catch some uniformed person passing through and ask him if I could be processed and escape from this limbo, but each time I was told to wait, there was 'No Problem'.

Still, I had no real cause for complaint and was suffering from nothing more than boredom—at least for the first seven hours. With only one hour left to take-off, I did think something should begin to happen. Each time I opened the door to the outside world and tried to attract somebody's attention, an official would frown and rush up to close it again.

With only half an hour left I began to get seriously worried; after all it wasn't quite like catching a bus, with another due in a few minutes. I hadn't been processed yet and the bicycle had still to be loaded. Greatly daring, I wheeled the bicycle through to the departure lounge.

'What you do here?' barked a uniformed attendant.

'I'm looking for my aeroplane,' I said firmly and showed him my ticket.

'Flight has been called. Why you not come? Maybe too late now. I see.'

Biting back anything I might have been tempted to say, I followed closely on his heels in case he got away, and very soon he stopped by a desk that had my flight number written up above it. Behind the desk I could see the aeroplane on the tarmac—my aeroplane—with the last passengers boarding her and the luggage doors being closed.

'Too late for bicycle, madam, very sorry,' said the new official, taking my ticket. 'We send it later.'

Five months ago I might have accepted this, but not now. The bicycle and I had travelled a long hard road together and together we were going home. I wasn't prepared to leave it, maybe to be lost forever on the sub-continent.

Bowing to *force majeure*, the official gave a shrug of resignation and ordered a baggage-handler to take the bicycle to the plane. No one came forward. Instead the whole row of them just stood there arguing about whose job it was. So I took it myself and wheeled it across the tarmac to the waiting aeroplane.

'I'm very sorry,' I said to the man who came forward to take it from me.

'That's all right, love,' he said. 'Always chaos at Delhi. Nice bike, I'll look after it, don't you worry.'

London
November 14 1983.

Technical and Other Details

The bicycle was designed and built by Ernie Young of Young's Cycles of Lewisham. It cleverly gets over the difficult problem, often experienced by female riders, of combining a long enough wheel base to give stability with a short enough top tube to be comfortable. Its vital statistics are as follows:

Grandini frame—Reynolds 531 double-butted tubing throughout.
Seat tube 21″
Top tube 20½″
Chainstays 17½″
Seat Angle 72 degrees
Head Angle 73 degrees
Bottom bracket to fork 23″
Trail 2⅛″
Brazed on carrier fittings front and rear
Campagnolo forged ends
Highly ornate lug work, to give the rider a sense of pride.

The Wheel—26″ Weinman alloy rims. Campagnolo Record small flange hubs. Spokes 14 gauge, rustless, crossing three.

Tyres—Michelin Speeds, because I find these are the best available for 26″ wheels, but they are not really very adequate for serious touring.

Transmission—Campagnolo Brevit Bottom Bracket. Stronglight cranks. Regina Oro five-speed block. Sedis chain. Duopar titanium rear changer. Campagnolo front changer.

Gears—Large Chain Ring 47	Inner Chain Ring 30
Cogs: 17 – 72	46
19 – 64	41
22 – 56	35
25 – 49	31
30 – 41	26

Saddle—Avocet Anatomical W 2.

Brakes—Campagnolo Grand Sport with Scott Malthauser brake blocks.

Stem—Cinelli with G.B. Randonneur handlebars, covered in Grab-Ons foam padding.

General Equipment

I discussed my wardrobe in Chapter 2; the only addition I would make to this would be the inclusion of a swimming costume and a cycling cape—do not listen to people who tell you that it never rains in India and Pakistan outside the monsoon period.

Essential items—A slow-burning candle and waterproof matches. Safety pins—particularly useful for hanging drying washing on the panniers. Compass and maps—if you can get them. At least two water bottles. A good knife and your own cutlery, plate and cup. Sunglasses. A sleeping bag and a thin cotton bag for sleeping in hot weather. A voluminous skirt for propriety when answering calls of nature in a countryside which is never unpeopled.

Luggage—I find that the bicycle is most stable when all the luggage is carried in tapered pannier bags, about two-thirds in the rear panniers and one-third in the front ones. I like to have lots of outside pockets on my panniers so that things I need frequently are easy to get at. I value the small map-holder which is fastened to the bicycle stem, which allows me to check my route as I ride—I also find that if I study the route when I'm making heavy weather of a long steep climb, it takes my mind off the discomfort.

Tools for the bicycle: there seems to me no point in carrying useless equipment. The only exception I make to this rule is to carry a few spare spokes. I cannot as yet replace a broken spoke, but hope that I would meet someone who could, in case of need. Otherwise my tool kit is as follows:

A set of lightweight Mafac spanners—horrid to use but they fit every nut on the bicycle.
Allen keys of the appropriate sizes.
Miniature pliers.
Two lightweight tyre levers.
A chain link extractor.
A tiny wireless screwdriver—there are additional screwdrivers on my Swiss army penknife.
Puncture repair kit.
Spare cables.
Two spare inner tubes and a spare tyre.

Photography: I took an Olympus XA completely automatic 35mm camera and it functioned perfectly despite various disasters and falling down mountains. Nine of the 10 rolls of 25ASA Kodachrome came out perfectly. The last, and in some ways the most precious of them, Kodak somehow managed to lose. I still haven't forgiven them.

Health

Travelling in the sub-continent exposes one to innumerable health hazards, especially to the dirt-related diseases. I protected myself as far as I was able by obtaining inoculations before I departed. Typhoid, paratyphoid, cholera, tetanus, yellow fever are all fairly standard precautions. In addition, I was injected with Gamma Globulin, which is a not universally accepted protection against infectious hepatitis. It certainly worked in my case, but I was careful to get it topped up before the recommended period of immunity had expired.

The main problem in keeping free of enteric diseases such as bacillary dysentery and amoebiasis, is the difficulty of obtaining adequate amounts of clean liquid to drink. The amoebic cyst is likely to be present in all sorts of places which have been touched by hand, such as crockery, fruit, food, etc. Rigorously washing everything is not possible when travelling, so apart from prayer there is little one can do except to sterilize all drinking water and wash one's hands frequently with carbolic soap. For sterilizing water, there seems to be no completely satisfactory proprietary product which is easily portable— except iodine, and as this is a mild poison, it needs to be used with a certain amount of discretion. I used Sterotabs from Boots, and when I thought I was in a particularly hazardous area I used iodine.

Malaria is rife in the Himalayas and present throughout the sub-continent. There are various preparations which are efficacious for this, but as the mosquitoes quickly become resistant to them, a traveller is supposed to enquire of the local health officer as to which brand it is best to use. I didn't find any such information available and carried on taking the once-a-week variety which I had brought out with me.

Tuberculosis is also very prevalent and it is as well to have a test to see if one is immune.

I carried antibiotics for use in emergencies; fungicidal and anti-bacterial cream, against skin infections; antibiotic eye ointment, plasters, bandages and burn cream.

The most essential health care I considered was a good insurance policy which would enable me to be flown home should I become seriously ill. I never regretted the cost of this, since it removed such a weight of anxiety, particularly after visiting a typical local hospital.

Also in Unwin Paperbacks

BORN IN TIBET

Chögyam Trungpa

Born in Tibet tells the vivid story of the early life and escape from Tibet of an incarnate lama of high rank. It includes a fascinating account of the author's religious education and the way of life of Tibet before the Communist take-over. When the people rebelled against the Chinese Communists, Trungpa Tulku began a journey which led him eventually to India. His escape makes a story which is both exciting and moving, but throughout the book there is a thread of compassion, for Trungpa Tulku can bear no hatred for those who set out to destroy the Tibetan faith and way of life.

'A delight and an eye-opener to the real life of a Tibetan monk and the difficulties he endured in his flight from the destroying Chinese invaders'.

Middle Way

'Deeply moving document ... a sense of humour and great courage seeps through this experience'.

Science of Thought Review

THE TIGRIS EXPEDITION

Thor Heyerdahl

Thor Heyerdahl's *Tigris* adventure began in the Garden of Eden on the bank of a river that flows from Ararat, where Noah's legendary ark once came to rest. It took him and his companions from nine nations in search of sea routes which he was sure must have been used by the ancient Sumerians 5,000 years ago on vessels like his own. His voyage down the Tigris, through the Gulf and eventually the Indian Ocean led to many discoveries and included many hazards. Modern shipping, bandits, reefs, and politics dogged *The Tigris Expedition*. Finally with permission to land only in the tiny republic of Djibouti and unable to continue the voyage for political reasons, *Tigris* was ceremonially burnt in protest against the intervention of major powers in African disputes which resulted in death and misery for millions of local people.

'The descriptive writing is as always good – the storms at sea; the pirates who demand exorbitant sums to haul them off the mud flats; and the excitement of playing with the sea creatures'.

Daily Telegraph

'a fascinating story of enterprise, history and adventure ... backed by beautiful illustrations'.

Financial Times

John Ebdon

EBDON'S ODYSSEY

A chance encounter set John Ebdon on a single-handed expedition to the Cyclades. There he fell irretrievably in love with the country, the island people and their way of life.

This brilliant, often very funny, account of his adventures in the islands of Andros and Kos is concerned with people, primarily the men and women of two villages in the islands but also with fellow countrymen who blundered into his life there.

EBDON'S ILIAD

A return to Greece and to Kos in the Cyclades sets John Ebdon on a fresh round of adventures – funny, sad, ridiculous and poignant.

This book, like *Ebdon's Odyssey*, is about people: The Proper Young Woman and Knickers-to-Match, who invade his midnight accordion music or disturb his musings at the Taverna, and also the islanders Stephano, the irrepressible lecher, the long-suffering Klimi and the indomitable Mama Barbunia.

Also in Unwin Paperbacks

Born in Tibet	£2.95 ☐
The Tigris Expedition	£2.95 ☐
Ebdon's Odyssey	£2.50 ☐
Ebdon's Iliad	£2.50 ☐

All these books are available at your local bookshop or newsagent, or can be ordered direct by post. Just tick the titles you want and fill in the form below.

_____

Name ....

Address ....

....

....

Write to Unwin Cash Sales, PO Box 11, Falmouth, Cornwall TR10 9EN. Please enclose remittance to the value of the cover price plus:

UK: 55p for the first book plus 22p for the second book, thereafter 14p for each additional book ordered to a maximum charge of £1.75.

BFPO and EIRE: 55p for the first book plus 22p for the second book and 14p for the next 7 books and thereafter 8p per book.

OVERSEAS: £1.00 for the first book plus 25p per copy for each additional book.

Unwin Paperbacks reserve the right to show new retail prices on covers, which may differ from those previously advertised in the text or elsewhere. Postage rates are also subject to revision.